Sex IN Psychotherapy

Other Books by Lawrence E. Hedges

Hedges, L. E. (1983/20th Anniversary Edition 2003). *Listening perspectives in psychotherapy*. Northvale, NJ: Aronson.

Hedges, L. E. (1992). *Interpreting the countertransference*. Northvale, NJ: Aronson.

Hedges, L. E. (1994a). *In search of the lost mother of infancy*. Northvale, NJ: Aronson.

Hedges, L. E. (1994b). *Remembering, repeating, and working through childhood trauma: The psychodynamics of recovered memories, multiple personality, ritual abuse, incest, molest, and abduction*. Northvale, NJ: Aronson.

Hedges, L. E. (1994c). *Working the organizing experience: Transforming psychotic, schizoid, and autistic states*. Northvale, NJ: Aronson.

Hedges, L. E. (1997). *Strategic emotional involvement: Using countertransference experience in psychotherapy*. Northvale, NJ: Aronson.

Hedges, L. E. (2000a). *Terrifying transferences: Aftershocks of childhood trauma*. Northvale, NJ: Aronson.

Hedges, L. E. (2000b). *Facing the challenge of liability in psychotherapy: Practicing defensively*. Northvale, NJ: Aronson.

Hedges, L. E. (original manuscript). *Seven deadly fears: A journey into the mind-body connection in search of the fears that threaten your health, your emotional well-being and your relationships!*

Hedges, L. E, Hilton, R., Hilton, V. W., & Caudill, B. (1997). *Therapists at risk: Perils of the intimacy of the psychotherapy relationship*. Northvale, NJ: Aronson.

LAWRENCE E. HEDGES

Sex IN Psychotherapy

SEXUALITY, PASSION, LOVE, AND DESIRE
IN THE THERAPEUTIC ENCOUNTER

Routledge
Taylor & Francis Group
New York   London

Routledge
Taylor & Francis Group
270 Madison Avenue
New York, NY 10016

Routledge
Taylor & Francis Group
27 Church Road
Hove, East Sussex BN3 2FA

© 2011 by Taylor and Francis Group, LLC
Routledge is an imprint of Taylor & Francis Group, an Informa business

Printed in the United States of America on acid-free paper
10 9 8 7 6 5 4 3 2 1

International Standard Book Number: 978-0-415-87352-9 (Hardback)

Library of Congress Cataloging-in-Publication Data

Hedges, Lawrence E.
  Sex in psychotherapy : sexuality, passion, love, and desire in the therapeutic encounter / Lawrence E. Hedges.
       p. cm.
    Summary: "Sex in Psychotherapy takes a psychodynamic approach to understanding recent technological and theoretical shifts in the field of psychotherapy. Lawrence Hedges provides an expert overview and analysis of a wide variety of new perspectives on sex, sexuality, gender, and identity; new theories about sex's role in therapy; and new discoveries about the human brain and how it works. Therapists will value Hedges's unique insights into the role of sexuality in therapy, which are grounded in the author's studies of neurology, the history of sexuality, transference, resistance, and countertransference. Clinicians will also appreciate his provocative analyses of influential perspectives on sex, gender, and identity, and his lucid, concrete advice on the practice of therapeutic listening"-- Provided by publisher.
    Includes bibliographical references and index.
    ISBN 978-0-415-87352-9 (hardback : acid-free paper)
    1. Sex (Psychology) 2. Psychotherapy--Erotic aspects. 3. Sex--Psychological aspects. I. Title.

BF692.H43 2010
155.3--dc22
                                                                                          2010018537

Visit the Taylor & Francis Web site at
http://www.taylorandfrancis.com

and the Routledge Web site at
http://www.routledgementalhealth.com

Dedication

To Jaden Don Bell and Daniel Alexander Uribe

Contents

ACKNOWLEDGMENTS xi

INTRODUCTION: "BOY MEETS GIRL" xiii

        Historical and Cross-Cultural Considerations xv

        Brain and Neurological Considerations..xx

PART 1   PERSPECTIVES FOR CONSIDERING SEX, SEXUALITY, GENDER, AND GENDER IDENTITY

CHAPTER 1 SEX, SEXUALITY, GENDER, AND IDENTITY 3

        The Natural/Religious/Biological Perspective...................................... 3

        The Infant–Caregiver/Erotic Interaction Perspective....................... 6

        The Personal Identity Perspective 11

        The Perspective of Dissociation, Otherness, and

               Multiple Selves 14

        The Postmodern Social-Constructionist Perspective...................... 17

        The Race/Ethnicity/Sexuality Perspective....................................... 19

        The Perspective of Mimetics.. 22

        The Perspective of Trauma and Transgenerational Ghosts 24

        The Intersubjective Perspective 31

        The Relational/Thirdness Perspective 35

        My Relatedness Listening Perspectives Approach 37

PART 2   PUBLISHED ACCOUNTS OF SEX IN
         PSYCHOTHERAPY

CHAPTER 2   SEXUALIZED THERAPEUTIC ENCOUNTERS 45
            Some Relational Countertransference Issues 47
            Developmental Listening 52

CHAPTER 3   THE PERSONALITY IN ORGANIZATION:
            THE SEARCH FOR RELATEDNESS 55
            Précis: Listening to the Search for Relatedness—
                 The Organizing Experience 56
            Searles: Love in the Countertransference 57
            Ogden: Split-Off Homoerotic Brutalization 61
            Moss and Zeavin: Having a Man 64
            Buchanan: Ensnared by Eros 66

CHAPTER 4   SYMBIOSIS AND SEPARATION: MUTUALLY
            DEPENDENT RELATEDNESS 81
            Précis: Listening to Mutually Dependent (Symbiotic)
                 Experience 82
            Rosiello: Disavowed Love as the Erotic Countertransference 83
            Rosiello: Performance of Affect and Gender 87
            Orbach: A Countertransference Rape Fantasy 88
            Mitchell: The Horror of Surrendering 90
            Gorkin: Magical Cure by Copulation 92
            Gorkin: Sadistic Sexual Countertransference Fantasies 94
            Gorkin: Erotic Countertransference as a Clue to Gender
                 Identity Issues 95

CHAPTER 5   THE EMERGENT SELF: UNILATERALLY
            DEPENDENT RELATEDNESS 97
            Précis: Listening to Unilaterally Dependent (Self-Other)
                 Experience 98
            Lewes: Working Through Displays of Male Bravado 98
            Corbett: Countertransference Fear of Passivity—
                 "The Father Censure" 101
            Corbett: Case of Luke—Expanding Sexual Identities 103
            Coverdale: A Countertransference Reaction to
                 Budding Exhibitionism 105
            Mitchell: Maintaining an Open Clinical Position 108
            Wittkin-Sasso: The Analytic Use of Desire 111
            Hedges: Stephen, Sean, Pornography, and the Internet 113

CHAPTER 6   SELF AND OTHER CONSTANCY: INDEPENDENT
            RELATEDNESS 121
            Précis: Listening to the Independent Relatedness Experience 122
            Kernberg: Love in the Analytic Setting 123

McDougall: Homoerotic Stimulation in the
    Countertransference 126
Précis: The Listening Perspective Approach 130

PART 3   THREE EXTENDED CASE STUDIES
         ILLUSTRATING SEX AND SEXUALITY IN
         THE TRANSFERENCE, RESISTANCE,
         AND COUNTERTRANSFERENCE OF
         PSYCHOTHERAPY

CHAPTER 7   THREE EXTENDED CASE STUDIES 133
            Dora: Eros in the Transference 133
            Ted: Eros in the Resistance 139
            Charles: Eros in the Countertransference 150
            Conclusions 167

REFERENCES 171

ABOUT THE AUTHOR 179

ABOUT LAWRENCE HEDGES' OTHER BOOKS 181

INDEX 185

Acknowledgments

I owe the inspiration for this book to my very great friend and colleague Marty Klein, who as a couples therapist and sexologist has encouraged me every step of the way. Many dinner and late-night conversations with Marty have enabled me to take sex out of the psychotherapy closet and to encourage professionals to take a good hard look at how sex, gender, sexuality, and gender identification have an impact on both partners in the therapeutic encounter. With Marty's help, most of the material in this book has been presented to the Society for the Scientific Study of Sexuality and the Listening Perspectives Study Center.

Gerardo Avalos has skillfully managed this book to press. Gerardo Arechiga, Silvia Leyva, and Breta Hedges have painstakingly done the research and put many details in place.

As always, the background support for this book has been provided by Ray Calabrese and Breta Hedges. My work over the years has always been developed in collaboration with many psychotherapy colleagues, who participate in study groups with me and serve as a sounding board and a creative inspiration. Heartfelt thanks are given to the following:

Barbara Ammon
Linda Barnhurst
Judith Besteman
Paula Bush
Laura Caghan
John Carter
Amy Choi
Sandra Cohn Weiss
Jolyn Davidson
Robert Davison
Antoinette M. Eimers
Tim Gergen
Cheryl Graybill-Dale
Cindy Greenslade
Ann Goldman
Emily Gombos
Laura Haynes
Mauri-Lynn Heller
Jeanne Lichman

Laurie Lucas
Jane Mathews
Krysclie Mayer
Julie McAlpine
Marcy Middler
Karen Muna
Ruth Raskin
Jeff Schwieger
Audrey Seaton-Bacon
Barbara Smith
Charles Spicer
Nancy Taylor
James Tobin
Sarah Turner-Miller
Robert Van Sweden
Robert Whitcomb
Michele Woodward
Natalie Zucker

Introduction: "Boy Meets Girl"

Ages ago, the sun cast into orbit gaseous debris that, as it slowly cooled, turned into a molten mass with a hardened, rocky crust—the planet Earth with its *lithosphere*. Following planetary rotations, oxygen and hydrogen gases alternately condensed into water and ice and then evaporated into mist and clouds, followed by aqueous precipitation—the *hydrosphere*. DNA molecules began reproducing themselves in the mineral-rich oceans, thus giving rise to viruses and one-celled organisms—the *biosphere*. Cells divided and multiplied into conglomerates of cells until a division of labor was accomplished such that some organisms produced eggs and others produced sperm, allowing DNA materials to be mixed to produce genetic richness with survival value—the *libidosphere*. With the sexes defined, the pageant of the species slowly progressed through reptiles, mammals, and primates to produce the crowning flower of evolution: *Homo sapiens,* a species that *thinks*—the *noosphere*. And so, boys and girls, men and women are *naturally* attracted to one another so that they can be married and have babies to perpetuate the species. The end.

I hope to show in this book that most people on the planet today still cling to one version or another of this hopelessly naïve narrative, and that as psychotherapists it falls our lot to question every aspect of human sex, sexuality, gender, and gender identity brought into our consulting rooms to help people get beyond their own just-so sex stories.

More has been discovered in the last two decades about our sex, gender, and sexuality than has been known since the beginning of time. But, we have yet to unpack the rich implications of human sexuality that the technological era has made possible. This book surveys the many varied and fascinating perspectives we now have to aid us in our inquiries. Beyond that, this book seeks to blow sky high the many myths and just-so stories about sex, gender, romance, and desire created through the ages that limit us in countless ways.

We enter psychotherapy to explore aspects of our lives that are of interest and concern to us. For this reason, sex necessarily becomes important in psychotherapy. Every person in therapy has sex stories to tell, and every person in therapy is involved in living an ongoing sexual narrative with a past, a present, and a future that is full of fanciful myths and faulty assumptions. But, at the beginning of therapy, most of the stories resemble the just-so story at the beginning of this introduction in their simplicity and naïve logic. Only as the therapeutic engagement deepens do the ever-shifting complexities of sex, sexuality, gender, and gender identity begin to make their appearance.

There are many approaches to psychotherapy. The approach taken in this book can be classified as psychodynamic and relational. A task force of the Psychotherapy Division of the American Psychological Association has reported on the large body of empirical research findings that clearly establish that the *psychotherapeutic relationship itself* is the key variable in determining a favorable therapeutic outcome (Norcross, 2002). The ways in which sex necessarily enters the psychotherapeutic relationship are the topic of this book.

By way of introduction, I begin with a brief historical and cross-cultural survey of some of the diverse ways in which sex and sexuality have been regarded over time and in different cultural contexts. I then consider recent theories of brain and neurological functioning that have far-reaching implications for the ways we consider sex and sexuality in psychotherapy.

In Part 1 of the book, I define 10 perspectives that have emerged from the past few decades of technological and theoretical developments that hold revolutionary implications for psychotherapeutic approaches to sex and sexuality.

Part 2 of the book moves to consider reports from the psychotherapeutic literature of actual sexualized encounters that have occurred between therapists and clients, along with their implications for psychotherapy practice.

In Part 3, I present three extended case studies from my own practice that illustrate how sex appears in the transference, resistance, and countertransference of psychotherapy—leading to my conclusion that we need no longer be phobic about sex and sexuality as critical aspects of ethically guided relational psychotherapy.

Historical and Cross-Cultural Considerations

Sigmund Freud, in his *Three Essays on Sexuality* (1905/1975), observed that, while scientists have puzzled for decades on the nature of human sexuality, every person on the street corner knows exactly what sex is. His comment was intended to highlight the complex, elusive, and extremely personal, idiosyncratic, and yet subjective nature of sexual experience.

The contemporary refrain "I am what I am what I am" echoes Freud's observation that everyone holds firm subjective convictions about what the nature of his or her sexuality is—along with the somewhat defensive uneasy feeling that many others hold views at variance with one's own views—with one's own just-so sex stories, as it were.

Ludwig Wittgenstein, in his 1953 *Philosophical Investigations,* elucidated an array of different kinds of "language games," with complex but agreed-on procedures and rules that characterize all human interactions—including the complex grammars of sex and sexuality. In addressing any area of study, Wittgenstein was concerned that we not mistake the frame or culturally constructed lens through which we view and interpret things for the phenomena themselves, that is, that we not take for granted any preconstructed interpretations. Nowhere are these dangers greater than in our studies of human sexuality, with our many personal and cultural biases and preconceptions.

We discover on reading the penetrating scholarship of philosopher Michel Foucault (1978), in his three-volume study of the history of sexuality, that the concept of sexuality itself has appeared as late as the mid-19th century, when psychologizing about ourselves and others began. Foucault faulted us for projecting modern Western notions of sexuality onto other historical eras and cultural orientations. For example, what a grave error it is to misunderstand the mentoring relationship in ancient Greece between older free-born men and free-born prepubescent boys (the future leaders of the Greek city-states) as "homosexual"—for nothing could be further from the historically documented truth of the ancients' experience.

Foucault (1978), effectively translating both Greek and Latin texts for us, demonstrated that although the ancient mentoring relationship was emotionally (and, at times, physically) intimate, it was at all times conducted within the public eye, idealized the exclusion of sexual acts, and disdained any boys who retained the passive mentoring position beyond puberty. So, what was the early mentoring relationship all about?

Foucault's (1978) detailed and scholarly analysis of the structure of Greek, Roman, Middle Ages, Renaissance, and 19th-century European societies allows us to understand that it was only through the mentoring relationship among free-born (and later among aristocratic) men that subjectivity and intersubjectivity as cultural phenomena gradually emerged in Western civilization. When, for example, the virtues of love among men are extolled in Plato's *Symposium*, it is the *intimate intersubjective experience* that is primarily discussed, whereas physical love is explicitly disdained.

While the topics of subjectivity and intersubjectivity have interested philosophers for several centuries, it has only been in recent decades that the development and maintenance of subjectivity and intersubjectivity have been scrutinized in a wide range of multidisciplinary studies, including infant research, neurobiology, and relational psychotherapy.

The concept of sexuality as we know it today is distinctly modern and Western in origin. Sexual historian Christine Downing (1991, pp. 3–8) pointed out that the word *homosexuality* was first introduced by a German physician in 1869 and injected into English only in 1892. *Heterosexuality*, as its counterpart, first appears in the *Oxford English Dictionary* only in 1900. Even as late as 1928, definitions of *lesbian* appear only as "residents of an Aegean island"—with no sexual implication. *Sappho* refers only to a Greek poet whose sensual (not sexual) poetry was rediscovered in the mid-16th century. Sex historian J. Brown (1986) declared that it has only been with the 20th-century trend toward objectively labeling people as entities according to certain of their behaviors that *lesbian* has come to mean love between women (pp. 6–20). Other sexual identity-group labeling has arisen only in the past few decades.

In 19th-century medical studies, the term *sexual inversion* was applied as a psychological label for men with pervasive feminine tendencies and for women with pervasive masculine tendencies, but same-sex sexual activity was not implied by "inversion." By 1905, Freud could declare, "The pathological approach to the study of inversion has been displaced by the anthropological" (1905/1975, p. 139). Wrote Downing (1991):

> In earlier [i.e., pre-19th-century] periods sexual behaviors were classi-
> fied along different "fault lines," not on the basis of whether one's pre-
> ferred partners were members of the same or the opposite sex as oneself.
> For example, in the medieval world the most important distinction was
> between procreative and non-procreative practices. Anal or oral sex was
> condemned even within marriage, and regarded as more sinful than rape
> or incest because it was non-reproductive. Among the *ruling* Greeks ...
> significance was attached to whether one played the active or the pas-
> sive role; a free adult male might appropriately be sexually involved with
> both male and female partners, but it was essential that with both he
> be the penetrator. Among the Romans, the important dichotomy was
> that between givers and receivers "of seed," it was acceptable for an adult
> male *citizen* to be fellated or to penetrate a male or female but not to
> himself suck another's penis or to allow his anus to be entered. (p. 5)

Sex historians appear unanimous in the opinion that, *until quite modern times and still in most places in the world,* all of the behaviors we now associate with homosexualities and other strange or "queer" sexual groups and practices have been a common part of life, but that in various cultures and during different time periods, societies have ordered sexual behaviors according to different schemata. For example, sexual practices have historically varied *according to the prevailing concerns of each society*—concerns such as property ownership and inheritance rights; patriarchal domination needs; class and clan distributions of wealth; population losses and reproductive needs; surveillance practices in prisons, schools, the military, and the clergy; social distributions of power; warring and colonizing interests; and more recently, the international military and tourism sex industries, as well as an array of international civil rights and child protection demands.

Foucault (1978) suggested that essential to the 19th century shifts in distinction from sexual *activities* seen as "inverse," "queer," or "perverted" to the *psychological definitions* of "the invert," "the homosexual," and "the pervert" have been due to the (power-based) belief that these labels refer to *distinct subjective psychological positions* of identifiable groups of individuals. As such, the labeling psychologist and the pervert form an exhibitionistic-voyeuristic dyadic unit—the fascination with the motives, fantasies, and the hidden life of the Other, along with the confessions elicited from those Others, constituting both the sexual activity of the observing professional and the power position being sustained (i.e., heterosexual male domination).

Both Foucault (1978) and sexual historian Hocquenghem (1978; as cited in Downing, 1991) saw these newly emergent sexual identities as an artifact of 19th-century science and the formation of a bourgeois society invested in maintaining a heterosexual patriarchal order. This view is consistent with Engels's postulation of the association between private property and the valorization of the patriarchal society so that all expressions of sexuality that do not serve the capitalistic ends of perpetuating the family as a source of labor become socially repressed.

This historical perspective invites individuals from labeled sexual, cultural, or ethnic minority groups to scrutinize carefully how *identity labeling both distorts and shapes their development and their individual experience.* For example, in *The Second Sex* (1947/1952), Simone de Beauvoir demonstrated clearly how labeling women as objectified Other profoundly affects women themselves as they internalize the label along with its prejudicial implications, definitions, and identifications as secondary otherness. True, there may be "secondary gains" (rewards) for accepting such objectified social labels, but the overall consequence is that the individual is provided, often at considerable expense, a *self-definition* and a *group identity* that may well do considerable violence to an individual's personal sense of evolving freedom and subjectivity. For example,

> Because the prevailing view of sexuality makes polymorphous, unfocused sexuality terrifying to everyone, those who act in response to homosexual desire are ready to surrender to the "recuperative" interpretation that this constitutes their sexuality per se, are ready to accept a homosexual identity. Better this identity than none. They themselves fail to recognize what Hocquenghem takes to be the *truth* about homosexual desire: that it "represents an arbitrarily frozen frame in an unbroken and polyvocal flux (1978)." (Downing, 1991, p. 6)

Before leaving this brief historical perspective on sexuality, it is of interest to note that the modern tendency to *confess* sexual identities was seen by Foucault (1978) to be heir to centuries of the Catholic pastoral confessional practice first decreed by the Lateran Council of 1215. Foucault painstakingly traced the institution of the confessional from the beginning 1215 command that every Catholic engage in an annual confession of improprieties to the modern tendency to confess oneself (privately and publicly) in various ways on a continuous basis. From the "I looked, I touched, I violated" over the centuries and through numerous methodological revisions in confessional guide manuals, emerged the "Father, I have sinned"—and still later, "Father, I *am* a sinner." Thus, the shifts in the confessional from a variety of *transgressive activities* to the sense of a *sinning being* contribute significantly to a growing cultural definition of a *subjectively experienced unitary self known as confessed to another.* Public confessions of self, self-orientations, and self-justifications are a quite recent and growing cultural phenomenon, one no doubt attributable to the wide availability of various forms of public communication media.

Foucault (1978) saw in the eventually widespread practice of the confessional not only the growing Western tendency to define a clear sense of self, but also the gradual accrual of power by the church and the growth of a clergy of professional observers whose predominantly voyeuristic sexual activity hides behind the veil of the institution of the confessional. The self-confessional motif of psychotherapy thus inherits centuries of culturally conditioned readiness to accept group labeling and surveillance practices—be they gender, ethnic, racial, able-bodiedness, or sexual. According to Foucault, numerous other culturally defined power centers, especially those of government, politics, economics, prisons, schools, medicine, and psychology, have readily adopted the culturally condoned surveillance procedures: *self-confessional* and *other-labeling*.

In conclusion, what we have received from the 19th and 20th centuries is a pluralism of objectively defined and culturally marginalized sexualities that serve as a modern myth to define and structure who we are as individuals, how we think about ourselves, and how we behave sexually. Within this modern myth, then, whatever we see and reach out to touch with sexual curiosity, interest, and desire thus becomes a shaper of our sense of self and a key determinant of our subjectivity and our personal destiny. Our personal identities and subjectivities thus become defined and regulated by culturally determined processes of self-confession and other-labeling.

As psychotherapists, we run the risk of playing heir to the pastoral confessional and thereby colluding in the definitions of our clients' received beliefs about who they are sexually. We do clients no good service by simply accepting at face value whatever individually and group-constructed confessions—just-so stories—called "identities" and "orientations," that they bring to our consulting rooms. Taking into consideration the history of sexual practices and definitions, we would do well to be forever questioning ourselves and our clients about whatever may be their and our own sexual interests, curiosities, desires, identities, and engagements and how we have arrived at various self- and other-definitions—especially regarding our sexualities. Laura Caghan's work (2010) on transgender and gender-varied phenomena takes the lead in advocating a thoughtful, relational approach to working with each psychotherapy client's subjectively stated gender and sexuality positions.

Brain and Neurological Considerations

How scientists have come to learn about brain and neuron functioning is a fascinating story now being told by many neurological researchers.[1] What has unfolded over time are different ways of thinking about the massive fund of research data made available by recent technologies. It is now clear that the most complex phenomenon in the known universe is the human brain and its intricate neurological system—highly evolved organs that presumably serve the most important of life functions, the perpetuation of the species.

We know that through millions of years of evolutionary history each species has evolved within a specific environmental niche, and that its centers of intelligence and reproduction reflect the survival possibilities available in that niche.[2] As the human species has extended its purview around the globe, its most important environmental niche has remained the interpersonal realm, the world of intersubjective emotional engagements in which intelligence, sexuality, and intimacy skills are developed (Greenspan & Shanker, 2004; Hedges, original manuscript). For this reason, our exponentially expanding understanding of our neurological complexities has far-reaching implications not only for our intelligence, but also for our sex and sexuality.

What follows is the briefest description of six well-known approaches to brain and neurological functioning—each of which has significant implications for sexual functioning.

---

[1] The story of the discovery of brain and neurological functions was told variously by Cozolino, 2002; Damasio, 1994, 1999, 2003; Edelman, 1993; Edelman & Tononi, 2000; LeDoux, 1996, 2002; Lewis, Amini, & Lannon, 2000; Pert, 1997; and Siegel, 1999, 2007.

[2] It no longer makes good sense to talk about the "theory" of evolution. The evolution of the species is as much a fact today as the orbit of Earth around the sun—although, as we know, there was also a lot of loud right-wing religious controversy for centuries over the fact of the Earth orbiting the sun. Dr. Francis Collins, eminent geneticist and head of the Human Genome Project—himself a devout conservative Christian—in the 2006 book, *The Language of God*, declared that the evidence for evolution that is now available from numerous scholarly disciplines is so absolutely overwhelming that evangelical creationist Christians make themselves look foolish. Worse, they end up betraying their young people, who will someday become educated as scientists so that they will have no choice but to renounce their blind religious dogmas. Fresh interpretations of ancient texts are now what is called for, said Collins.

The Split Brain and Localization

Early brain studies were based on injuries to the head that were the result of war or accidents. When an injury to a certain part of the brain produced a certain kind of deficit, it was assumed that the missing mental function was localized in that part of the brain. For example, left-brain functioning became identified as having to do with speech and logic, while right-brain functioning became identified as having more to do with physical activity and emotion. The bridge connecting the two sides of the brain was known to be larger in women than in men and often thought to account for women's generally greater capacities for multitasking. Much has been learned (and continues to be learned) by studying contrasts in functioning between the right and left sides of the brain (Schore, 1999, 2003).

The Triune Brain

Paul MacLean (1997), an evolutionary neuroanatomist and senior research scientist at the National Institute of Mental Health, has argued that the human brain is comprised of three distinct subbrains, each the product of a separate age in evolutionary history. Using MacLean's model, we can understand the brain as having developed in three concentric layers. The first ("reptilian") is the inner layer of the brain stem, which controls automatic biological functions, such as the circulation of blood, breathing, sleeping, and the contraction of muscles. The second ("mammalian") layer is the limbic system, which controls emotions. And the third ("primate") layer is the large cerebral cortex, which controls the cognitive functions of conscious thought—observing, planning, organizing, responding—and the creation of new ideas. The first two layers of the brain are referred to as the "old brain." The third is referred to as the "new brain" or the "cognitive brain" and is possessed to limited degrees by other primates, dolphins, and whales. The old brain functions mostly outside of awareness, primarily concerned with environmental survival. However, in humans the old brain obtains information not so much from direct perception of the external environment as from images, symbols, and thoughts that are generated by the new brain. The new brain processes information and impressions directly from cognitive experience. It searches for the logic of experience, the cause-and-effect relationships that make sense of sensory stimulation arriving from the human intersubjective environment. The wisdom of the human race is embedded primarily in culture and language that is passed down the generations through intersubjective emotional engagements. The new brain discriminates subtleties that distinguish one person's intentions from another's. It differentiates my mental activities from yours, the inside from the outside, and the now from then. The new brain moderates the instinctual reactions of the old brain—a capacity that has the ever-present possibility of changing human destiny. This triune view of our brains has been helpful to neurological researchers in many ways and is often used by sex researchers.

The Reentrant Brain

Nobel Laureate Gerald Edelman has long been interested in studying the complexities of consciousness. Using stunning new technologies, it was his genius to discover that more important to consciousness than the bridge that connects the two sides of the brain—in fact, more important than *any* single part of the brain—are the ever-changing patterns of neural activity integrated throughout the entire brain by way of "reentrant reactions," the ability of two (or more) brain regions to simultaneously affect each other. He spoke of consciousness as a "dynamic core … a process, not a thing or a place, [which is] defined in terms of *neural interactions*, rather than in terms of specific neural location, connectivity, or activity" (Edelman & Tononi, 2000, p. 144). An interesting consequence Edelman found that is particularly apt for our present discussion of human sexuality is that "the exact composition of the core related to particular conscious states is expected to vary significantly from person to person" (Edelman & Tononi, 2000, p. 144)—a fact borne out experimentally by brain-imaging studies. That is, the very ways each person organizes experience of self, of others, and of sexuality is highly idiosyncratic and ever shifting in different relational contexts.

The Synaptic Brain

Ever since neurons were discovered in the late 19th century, it has been known that they have a wide variety of ways of communicating with each other. The simplified metaphor is of tiny tendrils reaching out to exchange chemical substances called neurotransmitters where tendrils meet other synapses. As our knowledge of neurotransmitters has grown, we have discovered that there are many neural substances produced in many different places in our bodies and brains traveling at near light speed to other places, thus creating untold complexities in our overall neurological functioning. The metaphor now is more of a cosmic soup filled with billions of spaceships (neurons) simultaneously sending out and receiving multibillions of message substances (neurotransmitters) through carefully selected channels and ports. Each message type is intended for only a certain set of doors in certain locales in various parts of the body that will let it in. Whatever it is we mean by "mind" and "self," then, resides in the incredibly complex system of synaptic connections and neurotransmitter flows, which are *stimulated by interpersonal relationships*. The basic hardware of the neuron system can be thought of as genetically determined. But, the software and the many programs that follow—including gender- and sexuality-relevant software—become established by unique synaptic connections and neurotransmitter routes that *are the result of complex relational learning experiences*. That is, who we become personally, neurologically, and sexually is cocreated by the needs of the body and the mind in coordination with interaction opportunities provided by the human relational environment. In our species, the intersubjective environment of available intimate relationships turns out to be the most important environmental source of who we are and who we will become.

Neuroscientist Joseph LeDoux, in his books *The Synaptic Self* (2002) and *The Emotional Brain* (1996), maintained that we are each responsible from long before birth for constructing a self, a sense of personal agency, that is essentially made up of how our flow of neurotransmitters comes to influence migrations of neuronal connections in response to our early relationship strivings. For our purposes here, the important point is that whatever we come to call "ourselves" is an *ever-shifting inner world of neuronal connections that are in constant interaction with the inner worlds of neuronal connections of our most intimate relationship partners*—from before birth and throughout our lives. Our "synaptic selves" are the direct genetic heritage of our limbic and neocortical brains. The people we are in intimate contact with participate in our ongoing mental development in mutually interpenetrating ways so that we can no longer claim our brain or our sexualities as simply and uniquely our own. According to this view, we are relational beings inextricably tied to one another by the necessities of our interpenetrating synaptic selves. For a lifetime, our intimate relationships continuously have an impact on us and actually change our brains and our neurological systems to determine who we are as social and sexual beings.

The Cluster Brain

Perhaps the most complex of the many ways scientists have come to think about our brains and neurological systems has been outlined by M. Marsel Mesulam in terms of a brain made up of *clusters of functions*. Rather than considering our brain as divided by parts that can be visibly seen—such as right-left, triune, reentrant, or synaptic—the cluster approach considers how many *complex functions* have evolved in various interactive fields over millions of years given whatever genetic hardware and environmental niches become available to each species. That is, the telling features of our brains are not what can easily be seen or physiologically measured but are *clusters of evolved functions*—the primary being the reproductive function, in all of its multifaceted complexity. Clusters of functions are intricately connected to clusters of other functions operating not only throughout the brain and nervous system but also throughout our entire bodies and extending to various fields of environmental influence—*the most important being our intimate intersubjective interactions.*

For example, since as a species we had to develop group and family life to survive in a hostile world, crucial survival functions have evolved that use the overall connective possibilities of our entire interrelated brain and nervous system in coordination with our interpersonal and intersubjective possibilities to coordinate functional relationships between clusters of brain activity and myriad interpersonal environmental forces. Sex, the chief survival function, certainly operates in this infinitely complex, ever-shifting functional milieu.

Candace Pert (1997), National Institute of Health biological researcher, added to the list of overall neurotransmitters the many peptides, or "molecules of emotion," that originate mainly in our guts, suggesting yet more primitive "brain" functions that preceded in evolution even our reptilian ancestors and add to the complex cluster view of brain and neurological functioning.

This view of brain and neurological system as clusters of functions involving our entire bodies, as well as our interactive intersubjective environments, is more in keeping with what physicists are calling quantum, chaos, or 11-dimensional cosmic realities (Green, 1999, 2004) that are now believed to fill our universe. We have no idea how our scientific knowledge about ourselves and our brains and neurological systems will unfold in the future. But, the cluster brain theory is the most likely candidate for future research because of its infinite possibilities. The cluster approach takes the human reproductive function to levels of complexity never before imagined. But, there are even more elusive complexities to consider.

The Transcendent Brain

Joseph Chilton Pearce (2002), in *The Biology of Transcendence: A Blueprint of the Human Spirit*, summarized recent research into the functioning of the prefrontal cortex—long recognized as the fourth brain, not even 400,000 years old in its structure, functions, and currently understood significance. Immediately behind the ridge of our brow (the exact location of the oriental third eye) lies the prefrontal cortex, the most recent of brain additions. Behind the prefrontal lobes lies the rest of our neocortex, our new or primate brain.

MacLean (1997) knew about this fourth brain, but technology at the time of his theoretical research could not establish definitively that the prefrontal cortex actually "did" anything, actually performed any clear-cut functions. He knew that it was somehow involved in intimate relationships and social learning, so he called the prefrontals the "angel lobes," attributing to them our "higher human virtues" of love, compassion, empathy, and understanding as well as our advanced intellectual skills. We now know that the link between the three older brains and the prefrontal cortex is the orbitofrontal loop behind the orbit of the eyes. This link has been established as determining a person's relationships and mental capacities in life. Neuropsychologist Alan Schore (1999, 2003) described how the orbitofrontal linkage is entwined with the care a toddler receives and how this, in turn, determines the lifelong shape and character of that child's worldview, mind-set, sense of self, impulse control, and ability to relate to others—in short, a person's intersubjective capacities and tendencies.

It is of interest to note that, according to Pearce (2002), primary prefrontal growth and usage develops rapidly immediately after birth—at the exact time when intersubjective relationships are key in guiding brain development. Neuropsychologist and psychoanalyst Cathearine Jenkins-Hall (personal communication, November 2, 2007) described the neurological effects of the early relational process:

> During the first couple of post-natal years, brain cells migrate to form cell assemblies that ultimately form the neural scaffolding that supports various neuropsychological functions. The redundant brain cells or those brain cells that are irrelevant/neutral to that particular cell assembly get pruned away.

The assumption now is that the prefrontal cortex serves to organize the other brain centers in terms of relational possibilities that are available in the infant's early interpersonal environment. Then, at about age 15, when the majority of the threefold brain has completed its development, the secondary stage of prefrontal growth begins with a major growth spurt of new neural material—again presumably coordinating the complex web of intimate social connections developing in the mature brain through midadolescence as sexual and social activities expand. The end result is a prefrontal system that is thoroughly and dynamically connected to every part of the brain—every module, gland, lobe, hemisphere—which makes for the machinery by which, through the prefrontals themselves, we can actually *regulate and monitor our brain's neural structures*—and thereby our intersubjective and sexual engagements.

> In their early primary stage, then, the prefrontals unfold not so much from their own inherent capacity for development, as the older brain systems do, but more *through their influence on the unfolding of these earlier*

evolutionary systems [emphasis added]. The prefrontal lobes parallel the growth of the other systems because they have an important task at hand. Their main objective at this time is to govern each module or lobe of the threefold brain in its sequential unfolding in such a way that each older system forms according to the [anticipated intersubjective] needs of the prefrontals in their secondary stage of development during mid-adolescence. The task of the [early developing] prefrontals is to turn the unruly reptilian brain, old mammalian brain, and neocortex into one civilized mind that it may access later. It is only when this has occurred that the secondary prefrontal stage can unfold as designed. (Pearce 2002, p. 43)

The immediate implication for sex and sexual functioning of this two-phase development of the prefrontal cortex is evident. At the exact moments when infantile and adolescent intersubjectivity are blossoming, the prefrontal cortex is rapidly expanding to take advantage of the sensual and later sexual interpersonal developmental lessons taught by the intersubjective environment. In adolescence, we are clear that this intersubjective development is tied to sexual development. When we later consider infant development, it will become equally clear that early intersubjective patterns of sensuous interactions with caregivers set the biological and psychological foundations for what will later become sexualized interpersonal experiences.

But wait, there is yet more—the heart–brain interaction.

Electromagnetism is a term covering the entire gamut of most energy known today—from atomic molecular waves to radio waves, microwaves, infrared waves, ultraviolet waves, X-rays, gamma rays, and visible light waves. A heart cell is unique not only in its pulsations but also in its receptivity to and production of strong electromagnetic energy—in the form of signals that radiate to and from all parts of the body and into the environment beyond. Recall the famous high school biology experiment with two beating frog hearts that had been experimentally dissected? When finally one heart died, stopped beating, it could be stimulated back to life by putting the other beating heart into close proximity. We now even have defibrillators in our airports to stimulate regular heartbeats in those who have become overanxious or overtired—giving people a new lease on life. Theatergoers know only too well the restorative effects of cheering hearts for Tinkerbell, E.T., and Elliot (*Pete's Dragon*).

The heart's capacity for reception and transmission of electromagnetic waves, due to the electromagnetic sensitivity of glial cells, *gives the heart its own form of intelligence.* According to Pearce (2002), the intelligence of the heart is not verbal, linear, or digital like head intelligence. Rather, heart intelligence is more of a holistic capability that responds in the interest of the total well-being and life-sustaining continuity of the organism. The heart, the traditional seat of love and emotion (as well as sexuality), sends to the emotional system of the brain an intuitive prompt for appropriate response and in turn receives an ongoing relay of vital messages. Pearce summarized what he took to be the heart-brain-body connections:

- The electromagnetic field of the heart is holographic and draws selectively on the frequencies of the world, our solar system, and whatever is beyond.
- Through glial action, our neural system selectively draws the materials needed for world structuring from the electromagnetic fields as coordinated by and through the heart.
- Our emotional–cognitive brain makes moment-by-moment qualitative evaluations of our experience of the resulting world structure, some of which we initiate in our high cortical areas and others that form automatically and instinctually in the old mammalian brain.
- The dialogue between our heart and brain is an interactive dynamic in which each pole of our experience—heart and brain—gives rise to and shapes the other pole to an indeterminable extent. No cause-effect relationship can be implied in such an infinitely contingent process.

We have little idea at this point how the emerging information from the new field of neurocardiology will affect our thinking about brain structures and clusters of brain and neurological functions—including the reproductive function. But, it is estimated by researchers that a sizable number of cells in the heart—perhaps up to 60%—are neurons, the same kind of cells that are found in the brain. Concluded Pearce (2002):

Nature's economical habit of building new evolutionary structures on the foundations of older ones has led to our current magnificent potential. ...

We have within us this ... three-way connection among our emotional-cognitive brain, our prefrontal lobes, and our heart-brain. Here in this set of connections lies our [possibility for psychological/spiritual] transcendence. ... Whatever language or rationale it might take, our task is to discover—or rediscover—these three potentials and align them so that we come into transcendent dominion over our life. (p. 73)

In the present context, I take "transcendent dominion over our life" to mean aligning ourselves as much as possible with our functional emotional intelligence and sexuality to free ourselves from our individually and collectively constructed just-so stories about sex, sexuality, gender, and gender identity.

I cannot emphasize enough the enormous implications that these new theories of brain and neurological functioning hold for our understanding of sex, gender identity, and sexual functioning. The 19th-century view of human sexuality as parallel with sexual instincts of other animals has by now totally collapsed. Likewise, the 20th-century notion of our brain and neurons working like a telephone switchboard governing our sex by relaying stimulus-response messages from place to place in our bodies has been totally obliterated.

Biologists and physicists now tell us that we have evolved over millions of years in a universe made up of 11 space–time dimensions—although our conscious primate perceptions inform us only of four dimensions (Green, 1999, 2004). Cutting-edge brain theories, such as the ones reviewed here, attempt to make sense of massive data now rapidly becoming available through our new technologies. Theories like reentry, synaptic, cluster, and transcendent make clear how incredibly complex our intelligence and its central reproductive function are to have successfully evolved through 4 million years and 11 dimensions of space–time.

The bottom line is that we simply do not know how any human being's sexuality develops. But, by now we do know that all of our personal and cultural theories about sex, sexuality, gender, and gender identity are truly local myths—just-so stories that are long overdue to collapse. I believe it is our task as psychotherapists to listen to individual just-so sex stories, as well as to professionally generated just-so sex theories, and to try to untangle whatever limiting meanings have become attached to them. The theoretical perspectives and psychotherapeutic encounters in this book are intended as listening guides, as possibilities we can entertain that will expand our capacities to be alive to our own and to our clients' sex lives.

PART 1

PERSPECTIVES FOR CONSIDERING SEX, SEXUALITY, GENDER, AND GENDER IDENTITY

1

SEX, SEXUALITY, GENDER, AND IDENTITY

The Natural/Religious/Biological Perspective

Plato's myth of the first humans with four legs, four arms, and two heads who were cleft in two by divine intervention, thus leaving male and female beings forever searching for their other halves, expresses the widespread belief that humans are naturally divided into two sexes with heterosexual motivation—although Plato did make room for some beings attracted to their own sex.

Despite tolerance for sexual variations in both antiquity and cross culturally throughout time, the hierarchical orders of the Greek city-states and later nation-states have generally supported a heterosexual orientation that ensures a distribution of wealth and inheritance rights according to what has been considered a natural principle of heterosexual patriarchal dominance.

We note, for example, that the orderly procession by twos into Noah's Ark *does not* include any creatures sporting lavender fur collars, waving rainbow flags, or riding motorcycles—much less any creatures representing other minority community banners like those we now see flying in Internet chat rooms. The ark is decidedly heterosexual—dominated by male ordering. It is certainly fair to say that religious doctrines and governing powers around the world for at least 6,000 years have generally supported some form of natural or God-given heterosexual patriarchy based on male dominance and female submission, with other forms of sexual interest and curiosity generally repressed or subverted.

Biological science both before and after Darwin affirm the natural occurrence of male and female forms as essential for reproduction, with intersexed and other "queer" forms of sex and sexuality generally considered aberrant. The science patriarchy teaches that natural selection must involve exclusively male and female forms—and that other deviant tendencies quite naturally die off. But, such dogma at this point in the development of our knowledge simply makes no sense.

The year 2005 marked the centennial of the publication of Sigmund Freud's *Three Essays on Sexuality* (1905/1975) and its iconoclastic shattering of historical innocence regarding human sexuality. While Freud sought to establish a biological basis for the sexual and aggressive drives, at all times he was mindful of the wide variety of biological, as well as culturally constructed, psychological sexual experiences. According to Steven Marcus (1975), in the forward to Freud's three essays:

> In its disclosure to the world of the *universality* and *normality* [emphasis added] of infantile and childhood sexuality in all its polymorphously perverse impulsiveness, Freud's *Three Essays* was bringing to a close that epoch of cultural innocence in which infancy and childhood were regarded as themselves innocent, as special preserves of our lives untouched by desires, strivings after selfish pleasure, twinges of demonic perversity, [and] drives toward carnal satisfactions. ... Some considerable measure of the odium that was attached for years to Freud's name has to be understood in this light. In the name of truth and reality, he undertook to deprive Western culture of one of its sanctified myths. Cultures do not as a rule take kindly to such demythologizings, and it should come as no surprise that of all of Freud's findings those that have to do with infantile and childhood sexuality were resisted with the most persistency. (pp. xx–xxi)

Freud's seminal 1905 essays assume a *universal and natural biological bisexuality* (Freud, 1905/1975). His position holds that any and all of the many biological, cultural, and individual variations of sexual curiosity, interest, and activity are *universal interests* that all humans are capable of pursuing. In other words, we are much more complex sexual beings than had ever before been imagined.

Despite early feminist bashings of Freud, later reconsideration reveals that he, perhaps more than any other Victorian liberal, is to be credited for paving the road not only for equality between the sexes but also for a recognition of all forms of sexuality as essentially natural and universal. Said Freud (1905/1975): "Psychoanalytic research is most decidedly opposed to any attempt at separating off homosexuals from the rest of mankind as a group of special character" (p. 145). For example, in Adrienne Harris's reading of Freud's 1924 essay on a case of female homosexuality, we find that

> Freud traces out the view that sexuality and identity can never be simply some hard-wired, constitutionally driven forms but, rather, that the formation of sex and identity operates like the rules of grammar. ... [Following Chomsky, she states that] any human experience of sexuality and identity is built on a unique and particular sexual sentence in which elements of subjectivity, action, and object are never inherent or inevitable. ... The play of sexual forms and symbolic meanings for bodies, selves, and acts are the radical core of Freud's theory of desire and gender. (Harris, 1991, in Mitchell and Aron, 1999, p. 310)

Harris (1991, in Mitchell and Aron, 1999) points out the "golden possibilities" in Freud's unsettled, wondering, open register and speculated on how little we know of whom and why we love. "It would seem that the information received by our consciousness about our erotic life is especially liable to be incomplete, full of gaps, or falsified" (Freud, 1924, pp. 166–167). Harris adds that, "Freud makes a pitch for a hermeneutic method for psychoanalysis as opposed to prescriptive and predictive scientism" (p. 313), and that Freud maintains that "sexual object choice is achieved, not given. Any individual contains and, in some forms, retains multiple sexual needs and objectives. Only a reflective, psychoanalytically-based study of an individual's history yields some understanding of the relative potency of homosexual and heterosexual libido" (pp. 312–313). Following Freud, Harris argues for reading gender identity as a complex, multiply figured, and fluid experience. ...

> Gender may in some contexts be as thick and reified, as plausibly real as anything in our character. At other moments, gender may seem porous and insubstantial. ...
>
> For some individuals gendered experiences may feel integrated, ego-syntonic. For others, the gender contradictions and alternatives seem dangerous and frightening and so are maintained as splits in the self, dissociated part-objects. Any view of sex, object choice, or gender that

grounds these phenomena as categories of biology or "the real" misses the heart of Freud's radical intervention in our understanding of personality. Gender, then, and the relation of gender to love object *can be understood only by acts of interpretation.* (pp. 302–321, emphasis added)

Thus, Freud's *clinical* interest in sex and sexuality lies in analyzing, breaking down, or deconstructing relationally based psychological complexes that develop in early childhood. Psychological complexes arise from internalized conflicts in infantile sexual desires and engagements. Later, he formulated patriarchal culture as in perpetual conflict with polymorphic sexual drives and implicitly endorsed heterosexual development as the ideal cultural norm (Freud, 1938).

Subsequent psychological studies have generally followed Freud's lead in being open to a plurality of naturally occurring variations of sex, sexual identity, and sexual orientation (Jung, Hillman, & Kettner, as cited in Downing, 1991, pp. 111–130)—so much so that we now have another potential problem on our hands: Psychotherapists today, in their eagerness to be open-minded regarding their clients' sexual interests, desires, and orientations, can easily forget that, while biologically based, all sexual curiosities and interests are also a product of cultural, familial, and individual constructions that need to be carefully scrutinized in therapy for their personal meanings. As such, *all* psychodynamic constructions of sex, sexuality, gender, and gender identity—all just-so stories—are a potential focus for therapeutic study, and none can be considered as necessarily permanently fixed.

To summarize, while the natural/religious/biological perspective historically has been characterized by doctrines that have privileged the heterosexual patriarchal order, psychologists since Freud have continued to expand this perspective toward naturalizing and universalizing (although not necessarily condoning) all expressions of human sexual interest and desire. The sex life of any particular person coming to our consulting rooms may be intertwined with any and all of the themes developed in the listening perspectives under discussion.

The Infant–Caregiver/Erotic Interaction Perspective

The past three decades have seen the emergence of a community of baby watchers, ingeniously researching every possible aspect of infant life that they can define and observe. Summarizing recent infant research from a dyadic systems point of view with an eye to shedding light on intimate adult interactions, and therefore adult sexuality, Beebe and Lachmann (2003) developed three principles of salience for considering infant-caregiver interactions and lifelong attachment issues:

1. Moment-by-moment ongoing self and interactive regulations
2. Disruption and repair of interactive connections
3. The special impact of interactive moments of heightened affect

Beebe and Lachmann propose that affectively charged expectancies based on these three principles of self and other mutual regulatory interaction are stored in infancy as prototypical or foundational presymbolic representations that later evolve into relational interactive possibilities that form the foundation of adult relationships and sexual engagements. This point of view is consistent with 50 years of somewhat differently formulated attachment research (Fonagy, 2001) as well as relational psychotherapy research (Benjamin, 1988, 1995).

Of special interest in considering the origins of mutual sexual regulations are the infant studies that involve both mimicry and affect mirroring—that is, the parent's use of facial and vocal expression to represent to the child the feelings the parent either mimetically reflects or assumes in interactions with the infant. Research indicates that the image of the caregiver mirroring the internal experience of the infant comes to organize the child's emotional experience. Thus, the self not only is open to environmental influence, but also is *constituted* through its interactions with the mirroring social environment. The caregiver's mirroring display is internalized and comes to represent an internal state, but it can do so only in certain conditions, which include sufficient emotional attunement, together with signaling to the infant that the affect the caregiver is expressing is not the caregiver's but the child's.

Infant researcher Ed Tronick (cited in Beebe & Lachmann, 2003) has suggested that, in the process of mutual regulation, each partner (mother and infant or therapist and patient) affects the other's "state of consciousness" (state of brain organization). As each affects the other's self-regulation, each partner's inner organization is expanded into a more coherent, as well as a more complex, state. In this process, each partner's state of consciousness expands to incorporate elements of consciousness of the other in new and more coherent forms. While these processes of mimicry and affect mirroring have been defined and studied in infancy in a variety of ways, they have also been demonstrated to be lifelong processes characteristic of intimate intersubjective relating. (The effects of mimetics as such are discussed more fully in a further perspective.)

Further studying the psychological impact of early interactive formations, Jessica Benjamin, in her studies of the erotic in psychotherapy (1988, 1995), uses a metaphor of a "space" in which two subjects negotiate relatedness. She formulates this relational space as an emblem for the feminine, in counterpoint to phallic penetration as an emblem for the masculine. Benjamin (1988) linked presymbolic representations of movement in space, transitional and reciprocal experiencing, and being alone in the nonintrusive presence of the other to the unfolding of woman's desire, to an intersubjective space that allows the self to come alive, to become absorbed with internal rhythms rather than reacting to or being excited by penetrations and impingements. This quality of internal preoccupation that can emerge in the space of intersubjective relatedness contrasts with the image of phallic penetration in the erotic experience of becoming recognized and known. For Benjamin, the feminine/maternal relational dimension includes interpersonal space that allows for "a mutual awareness of affect, a reciprocal impact on each other, interacting contours of intensity and kinetic timing, and a complex and idiosyncratic choreography of turning toward and away, all of which become internalized interaction schemas that affect later intimate relationships" (1988, pp. 160 ff.).

In considering the implications of infant research for understanding the establishment of erotics in adult relationships, Benjamin (1988) said: "These internalized schemas lead to expectations of closeness vs. distance in relating, of matched and met vs. violated and impinged upon experiences, and of an erotic dance [each schema being] fundamental to mutual attunement and pleasure in adult sexuality as well as to movements and mutual empathy in the analytic relationship" (p. 160). Benjamin views these early sensual experiences of mutual attunement as becoming internalized as interactional or intersubjective schemas. When they reappear in later intimate relationships, including the therapeutic relationship, she refers to them as *erotics of transference*.

Benjamin (1988) wrote extensively on the importance of mutual recognition in intimate relationships, moments when mutual attunement between separate minds and bodies is achieved. "In erotic union this attunement can be so intense that the separation between self and other feels momentarily suspended [and] *a choreography emerges that is not reducible to the idea of reacting to the outside*. In erotic union the point is to contact and be contacted by the other—*apprehended as such*" (p. 184, emphasis added). Benjamin also said:

> In erotic union we can experience that form of mutual recognition in which both partners lose themselves in each other without loss of self; they lose self-consciousness without loss of awareness. ... This description of the *intersubjective foundation of erotic life* offers a different perspective than the Freudian construction of psycho-sexual drive phases, for it emphasizes the tension *between interacting individuals* rather than that *within* the individual. (pp. 27–29, emphasis added)

The Origins of Human Sexuality: Two Just-So Stories

While infant research, as well as current attachment and intersubjective theory, are now able to draw clear connections between internalized infant–caregiver interaction schemas and later erotic interactions in intimate adult relationships, these connections have long been a topic for study by psychoanalysts. Almost as an aside, let us review briefly the theoretical work of Freud and Laplanche on the topic of early established interpersonal dynamics that make their appearance in later erotic life.

In addressing the topic of the development of sexuality, Freud attempted a distinction between the biological and the psychological aspects of sex. He took the position that parental responsiveness sets up a series of interactions (now studied as attunement/misattunement, rupture/repair, mutual empathy [or lack of it], and mutual affect regulation [or failure of such]). In "Instincts and Their Vicissitudes" (1915), Freud formulated the first infantile instinctive position as "primary sadism"—activity that is indifferent to the outcome, to whether the other is being hurt. Next comes a perception of the other's pain through primary identification or mimicry (A. Balint, 1943) and an understanding of that pain. Once the infant internalizes the pain of the other (establishes an internal position that Freud called "primary masochism"), the infant can willfully inflict pain on the (m)other. This intentional sexual position Freud labeled "sadism proper." According to Freud, the many processes, engagements, and reengagements of these essentially sadomasochistic dynamics become internalized as the intrapsychic world of early object relations. In this formulation, primary sadism is biological and instinctive, whereas the internalization or identification with the other's pain, primary masochism, is psychological. Likewise, sadism proper as a later development is psychological. This is Freud's story of the origins of psychological sexuality.

The French psychoanalyst Laplanche (1976) relabeled Freud's first instinctual step simply "aggression." At the second (object-relations) step, during which pain in the other is perceived and aggression is incorporated and through primary identification internalized as masochism, we have the first sexual position (i.e., masochism)—an alloy of eros and aggression. This move toward *reflexivity*, into role reversibility, simultaneously creates (a) unconscious sexual fantasy, (b) early object relations, and (c) "the sexual"—whether the fantasy or interpersonal enactments are active or passive. Thus, according to Freud and Laplanche, three steps are involved in the early development of sexuality: (a) the *real* movement toward and interaction with the other is instinctive, (2) the psychologically internalized aggressivized sadomasochistic exchange constitutes "the sexual," and (3) both comprise the erotic of a person's developing "sexuality."

In my opinion, both of these early formulations of sexuality and the erotic are meritorious and serve to give us pause for thought. But, they also serve as excellent examples of theoretical just-so stories—theoretical formulations in the third person about the nature of human sexuality that lack the force of first-person sincerity and anxiety that are so crucial to understanding any person's sexual life. These formulations illustrate the historical interest in making sex a study for objective scientific scrutiny—an approach with severe limitations in the listening task of intersubjective psychotherapy today.

But, whether we choose to follow the infant researchers or the psychoanalytic formulations of Freud and Laplanche, an important perspective on the development of adult sexuality involves the foundational affective and sensual impact of early infant–caregiver interactions on the later selection and maintenance of intimate relationships. Any person coming to our consulting room is likely to be struggling in one way or another with basic affect–interaction issues in the establishment and maintenance of his or her intimacy and sexual life.

The Personal Identity Perspective

We often speak of personal and sexual identities without always being clear about what these are. *Identity* was conceptualized by Erikson (1954) as (a) a consolidation of ego structures connected with a sense of continuity of self, (b) a consistent overall conception of the world of others, and (c) a recognition of identifiable consistency by the interpersonal environment and the perception by the individual of this recognition (i.e., "social confirmation"). Roy Schafer (1976) said that one may speak of identity or identifications in the sense of making possible a "high degree of consistency in certain modes of subjective experience and behavior; on the basis of identification, specific acts of desiring, thinking, and doing other things, along with specific emotional modes associated with these actions, may be in evidence much more regularly and readily than they would be otherwise" (p. 192).

Virginia Goldner (1991) spoke of identity in general and of sexual identity in particular as problematic concepts in that identity structures tend to provide magical solutions to complex conflictual personal issues by providing an "I am" statement and a belief system that spares us further conflict and thought.

Jacques Lacan (1938/1977) considered a mythical moment when the human child looks into the mirror and says, "That's me." In that instant of identity, the child simultaneously betrays personal, somatopsychic, kinesthetic experiencing and accedes to the human realm of mirrored symbolization so that full-bodied self-experience is never again the same. Therefore, whatever our human genetic or instinctual proclivities might have been in regard to sexuality, we are forever barred from knowing them by the fact of our acceding to an identity in an imaginary and symbolic system that begins channeling us and our evolving passions long before we even have the capacity to say "That's me" or "I am."

But, whether we consider the symbolic function of the "That's me" of early childhood or the more complex symbolic equations and identity symbolizations of later childhood and adolescence, we do know that our potential for free and easy spontaneous and creative expressions of ourselves in our personalities and in our sexualities tends to become progressively curtailed as we continue to grow in relation to the demands of the mirroring human symbolic and sociocultural environment. This is a momentous tragedy of human existence: that the beauteous spontaneity and creative sensuous expressions of early childhood become socially bound and channeled in our personalities before the 10th year of life—before our full capacity for sexual passion has even arrived.

In psychotherapy, we spend years attempting to dismantle those identifications and symbolizations of self and other that constrict us and limit our sexuality. It is no wonder in psychotherapy that all manner of sensual and sexual scenarios are regularly a part of transference–countertransference experiencing. Human sexuality—unlike sexual expressions in other species, which are more or less direct, reflexive, and instinctual—is heavily weighed down by the cultural-symbolic systems that precede our individual existences and that channel and mold what comes to be experienced as gender relevant and sexually stimulating to each person.

Benjamin (1995) summarized decades of thinking about gender identity development in a clarifying sequentially ordered schema:

1. **Nominal or core gender identification** represents the earliest sense of belonging to a gender group, an identity that serves as a backdrop for future developments, as a baseline against which to refer later experiences.

2. **Early differentiation of identification** then occurs in the context of separation-individuation from the mothering parent, an event that may have a gender marker for boys, although both sexes generally continue to elaborate both gender identifications as aspects of the development of self.

3. **In the overinclusive (or preoedipal) phase,** children of both sexes participate in a variety of cross- as well as same-sexed imaginary elaborations of self—in full narcissistic enjoyment of the ability to be everything.
4. **Gender (or oedipal) complimentarity** then develops, which serves to polarize male-female identities into distinct culturally ordained versions of gendered selves.
5. **Gender (or postoedipal) flexibility** optimally develops to lessen the rigidity of the previous binary gender complementarities, especially if there has been rich imaginative elaboration in the earlier overinclusive preoedipal stage.

Benjamin's (1995) developmental schema elaborates a position taken by Person and Ovesey (1983), according to which "gender differentiation, evolving through separation conflicts and identifications, *defines and gives weight to the genital difference* [emphasis added], which then assumes great (if not exclusive) symbolic significance in the representation of gender experience and relations" (p. 127). In contrast, earlier theories of gender identity had held genital difference to be the motor of developing gender and sexual identity. Such theories fail to account for the rich symbolic diversity that clearly exists in the wide range of adult sexualities. Simple awareness of genital difference cannot possibly be the great shaper of all the conflictful richness that will later become known as one's sexuality and one's gender identity.

Rather, favorable development through the long processes of attachment and separation-individuation from the primary maternal identification as well as a multitude of trial identifications, with both sides of the gender divide, lead to the grandiose position of being able to be everything one wishes to be genderwise. The abrupt realization that the world dictates differently, that it requires identities that match one or the other of the binary cultural models, then forces the child's inner richness of developed identities into rigid molds that correspond to binary genital difference as culturally defined. Confusion, shame, guilt, dissociation, and repression mark those individual desires and identities that cannot be meaningfully or appropriately housed in the "proper" heterosexual gender mold. Individual desire is required to submit to cultural demand, at the price of loss of considerable personal richness. Those who suffer the most in this way are undoubtedly individuals with transgendered and gender-varied identities (Caghan, 2010).

The reason this way of considering personal identities is so important in our consulting rooms is that it allows us a way of accounting for the wide variety of sexual identifications that people in fact experience consciously and unconsciously. This view also allows us to consider the many ways multiple gender identities emerge from the child's many interactional experiences of sameness and difference with important caregiving others in early self-development.

The Perspective of Dissociation, Otherness, and Multiple Selves

When two people approach one another hoping for a significant personal or sexual relationship, they each bring a host of self and other definitions and expectations with them that tell them who they are, how they are to be with each other, and what they can reasonably expect from each other. From this, we can quickly see that the relationship stage is set for disaster. Each relating partner has all of these accumulated ideas, fantasies, and reflections of what we each believe to be real for us and how life in relationships is "supposed to" be. But in fact, we have no idea whatsoever what to expect from each encounter with intimate relating partners.

In sitcoms, social conventions get people through. In nonpersonal relationships, such as business transactions, ritualized speech and behaviors get people through. But in intimate relationships—in or out of psychotherapy—we do not have the slightest idea what will happen in the next *now moment* (D. N. Stern, 2004).

British psychoanalyst Wilfred Bion advised approaching each intimate encounter "without memory or desire" so that we two can be as fully together in the now moment, as free as possible from the burdens of the past or the future (Bion, 1977). We know only too well that living relationships in the present is a major challenge. We are forever dragging in something from "memory or desire" to wreck the gift of possibility in the present moment. Suffice it to say that the identities, selves, and personal orientations we take to any relationship are burdened with a lifetime of instructions, emotions, fears, hopes, and other baggage from the past. This is, of course, true for our relating partners as well.

I want now to introduce into our consideration of sexuality the idea of strangeness or "otherness" in ourselves and in our partners. In our standard and familiar versions of ourselves and our personal and sexual identities, we do our best not to notice many aspects of our full potential selves that do not quite fit within our official versions of ourselves. For a lifetime, we have worked to disown various parts of ourselves that do not fit our accepted sense of self. Yet, these disavowed, disowned, dissociated aspects of who we are nevertheless have a way of showing up at inconvenient times, when we are least expecting or least wanting to deal with them. The same can be said for those aspects of our partners that the partners have disavowed for a lifetime or that we have chosen not to notice in them.

Disowned, disavowed, and dissociated parts keep cropping up to confuse, perturb, or often even frighten us. Psychologists speak of these unwanted, unrecognized, uncomprehended, and unformulated parts that feel alien or strange in ourselves or in our partners as "otherness" (D. B. Stern, 2010). In the course of growing up, we all experience social pressure to be certain ways and not to be other ways—say, for example, to be a boy and not a girl. Our heads then become filled with notions of what it means to be a boy and what it means to be a girl. So, in a given intimate interaction I may feel swept away with feelings of passivity, weakness, or dependency that are feelings that girls and not boys—not I—are supposed to feel. The leaking through into consciousness of "girl feelings" then feels strange, not okay, "other" to myself. This is a simple example, but consider how often we experience unwanted angry or sexual feelings or other thoughts and fantasies that have that same not-me or other-than-me sense about them. We experience them as alien or other to the self-experience we have constructed or desired in the moment.

In addition, psychological studies now make clear that we do not have simply one self but multiple selves or self-states (Bromberg, 2006; D. B. Stern, 1997, 2010). To put it in the simplest terms, we are one person on Saturday night and another on Sunday morning, one person with a client at work and another with a frustrating spouse or child at home. Psychologists for many years spoke of identity or self as a unitary thing that we possess as something consistent and comprehensible. But, we do not think that way anymore. We know that from birth onward we experience multiple self-states that are often contradictory and that switch from moment to moment, hour to hour, day to day. Yes, we may have a sense of "me, myself, and I" that goes forward with a certain sense of continuity in time, but we also know that we are subject to frequent shifts in self-states that basically change who we are in the world for the time being. We now recognize that multiple dissociated self-states are the norm, that we have all developed many frames of mind that appear at separate moments and in differing relational contexts—some of them quite ugly, some of them quite crazy, many of them quite enjoyable, and many of them not very comprehensible.

At any given moment in time with a relating partner, we are living in a certain self-state with a particular version of who we are and what we want activated in the present relational context. Yet other, unwanted aspects of ourselves keep popping up, keep clamoring to be heard. Perhaps the situation can bear an appearance of the dissociated self-state. Or, perhaps we are in a situation for which recognition or approval of a dissociated self-state—whether by ourselves or by our relating partner—would be intractable. In the moment, we simply need to move forward. We are clear on what we think should happen, but some part of us or our relating partner is surprisingly out of line. What now? This is the central dilemma that faces us all the time in relationships: how to be consistent, sensible, reliable, or whatever when some unruly thought, feeling, or fantasy is tugging in some other direction.

Confusing self-states do not happen in sitcoms. Yes, someone may be speaking a dilemma of not knowing what to do or talking about a conflict over something, but the media are grossly inadequate at representing our most frequent kinds of momentary relational confusions when a half dozen different directions are blipping on the screen, demanding our attention all at once, while our active self at the moment is bewildered, frightened, or horrified at some or all of the blippings.

Let us move to some sexual examples because our sex lives are so poorly understood by ourselves, and otherness plays such a large role in sexuality. How many times have we been moving toward a sexual encounter when for no good reason at all we found we were not in the mood, were tired, or had other things to do? What about when during a sexual interaction a picture, fantasy, or sensation suddenly occurred that was quite out of place or even shocking to our sensibilities? Or, how about when our partner let out some sort of completely inappropriate exclamation? And on it goes. The bottom line is that when we have given ourselves over to a mutual sexual encounter, a certain interpenetrating dance—a coordinated choreography—begins that causes two to go off on some "strange" trajectory together, one that may contain thoughts, words, or fantasies that in our everyday versions of our selves we would find outlandish or otherwise frightening or unacceptable. At the moment of orgasm, intense and perhaps forbidden images and sensations flash and then disappear as quickly as they arrived. So much of what we experience in our sexual selves is "strange" or "other" to our ordinary selves—not only our parts, but also our partner's parts. The sexual selves with which we interact may be, for example, quite desperate and dependent or quite ruthless and incongruent with our selves that at other times are secure, loving, and considerate of each other (Frommer, 2006).

In any given situation, we may be generally comfortable with how we are experiencing things and where we are going with our partner. But, in all kinds of intimate relationships there is always a strange otherness lurking just around the corner—both in ourselves and in our partners. At times, this strangeness is experienced as elusive, mysterious, and exciting. At other times, this strangeness in ourselves or in our partner may be confusing, distressing, or frightening. Being in intimate relationships—psychotherapeutic or otherwise—offers the possibility of learning somehow to represent in the relationship these strange experiences of otherness in ourselves and in our relating partner—and in so doing creating some mutually transformative now moments.

The Postmodern Social-Constructionist Perspective

Galileo with his telescope, Newton with his falling apple, and Einstein with his space–time relativity have all led us through the 20th century with the hope of discovering finally the grand unified laws of the natural or God-given universe around us. This so-called modern attitude toward truth, certainty, and reality holds that there will come a moment in human history when the great mysteries of the universe will be ours to behold with clarity once and for all.

Pioneering sexologists once held the modernist view that the truths of human sexuality would someday become objectively and definitively understood (Kinsey, Pomeroy, & Martin, 1948; Kinsey, Pomeroy, Martin, & Gebhard, 1953; Masters & Johnson, 1966). But, that was before the incredible diversity and complexities of human sexuality began to become understood. In recent years, the "modern" hope of ultimately knowing everything has faltered seriously. That is, we now know that there are many contrasting, competing, and even conflicting ways to view and to interact with the infinite realities of the known universe, and that at the incredibly complex level of human existence, many realities, many truths, and many perspectives are now deemed essential for multidimensional understanding—an approach nowhere more important than in the study of human sexuality.

The postmodern social-constructionist position was clearly stated as early as 1966 by epistemologists Berger and Luckmann:

> Man is biologically predestined to construct and to inhabit a world with others. This [socially constructed] world becomes for him the dominant and definitive reality. Its limits are set by nature, but once constructed, this world acts back upon nature. In the dialectic between nature and the socially constructed world the human organism itself is transformed. In this same dialectic *man produces reality and thereby produces himself.* (p. 183, emphasis added)

Thus defined, *modern* is the commonsense attitude that objectively true certainties can ultimately be discovered and controlled, while *postmodern* is the attitude that all knowledge is a product of various kinds of perspectives and subjective constructions—individual and collective. In postmodern social-constructionist thinking, while we may no longer be able to know things with certainty, we can certainly generate interesting and useful perspectives from which to view and to interpret all that we do encounter. With regard to constructing gender, psychologist Nancy Chodorow (2002) argued that

> Individual psychological meaning combines with cultural meaning to create the experience of meaning in those cultural categories that are

important or resonant for us. … [A]n individual, personal creation and a projective emotional and fantasy animation of cultural categories create the meaning of gender and gender identity for any individual. … Each person's sense of gender is an individual creation, and there are thus many masculinities and femininities. Each person's gender identity is also an inextricable intertwining, virtually a fusion, of personal and cultural meaning. … Gender cannot be seen apart from culture. (p. 237)

The postmodern constructionist view is that we are forever limited to defining certain vantage points, operational definitions, and perspectives that aid us in focusing our curiosity, collecting data, and formulating ideas—theories about what our observations *mean* to us rather than theories about how things really are. The postmodern constructionist search to understand human erotics and sexualities involves the study of a complex array of personal ever-shifting meanings as they become enacted and understood in dynamic relationships, not in finally unearthing the biological or psychological truths about sex and sexuality. That is, in exploring the many complex, affective, and interpersonal aspects of anyone's sexuality, therapists must be able to do more than simply explore the behavior and personal narratives (the just-so stories) put before them. Rather, through the interpersonal engagement of the therapeutic relationship itself, the client and therapist have the possibility of (a) coconstructing new, more encompassing interpersonal narratives; (b) engaging in novel interpersonal erotics; and (c) mutually creating fresh meanings of their experiences and their sexualities (Hoffman, 1998; D. B. Stern, 1997, 2010). The social-constructionist perspective allows us to consider how cultural constructions create cultural realities, including definitions of gender identity and sexual orientation that become internalized early in life and manifest as transference, resistance, and countertransference in psychotherapy.

The Race/Ethnicity/Sexuality Perspective

In *Race, Ethnicity, and Sexuality* (2003), sociologist Joane Nagel observes that from multicultural studies comes a newly emerging awareness about "the power of sex to shape ideas and feelings about race, ethnicity, and the nation … and how sexual images, fears, and desires shape racial, ethnic and national stereotypes, differences, and conflicts … how sex matters insinuate themselves into all things racial, ethnic, and national … [and] how ethnic boundaries are also sexual boundaries…" (p. 1).

Nagel writes:

> Ethnicity and sexuality join together to form a barrier to hold some people in and keep others out, to define who is pure and who is impure, to shape our view of ourselves and others, to fashion feelings of sexual desire and notions of sexual desirability, to provide us with seemingly "natural" sexual preferences for some partners and "intuitive" aversions to others, to leave us with a taste for some ethnic sexual encounters and a distaste for others. Ethnicity and sexuality blend together to form sexualized perimeters around ethnic, racial, and national spaces. (p. 1)

Currently developing cross-cultural studies are demonstrating how ethnic and sexual boundaries converge to mark the edges of what are being called ethnosexual frontiers. Ethnosexual frontiers are constituted not only by ethnic identity variations but also by sexual identity variations and the interactions between ethnic and sexual identities.

The often hidden-from-view connections between sexuality and ethnicity can be inferred from such things as the sexual messages in racial slurs, the not-quite-whispered subtext of racial discussions, and "in ethnic stereotypes, national imaginings, and international relations" (Nagel, 2003, p. 2). Ethnosexual connections exist in

- artistic depictions of men and women of various ethnicities
- fears and fantasies implicit in racial stereotypes
- rules for contact between ethnic groups
- men's and women's places in different societies
- ethnic attitudes toward desire and disgust
- beliefs regarding characteristics and potencies of ethnic and immigrant peoples
- appetites and aversions toward ethnic individuals
- sexual overtones in ethnic cleansing, genocide, and war efforts

Despite universal historical claims of essential or biological differences between "us" and "them," we now know that there is more

DNA variation within than between the so-called racial groups, thus reducing social constructions of race to historical ploys for dominance. As Derald Wing Sue (2005) remarked, "White people are not our enemy, but the doctrine of White Supremacy is." As an example of the way sexual ideologies construct ethnic others as *inferior* to the accepted norm—that is, as oversexed, undersexed, perverted, or dangerous—Judith Halberstam's (1998) research has shown that currently in the United States dominant white middle-class ideas about acceptable masculinity and male sexuality define African American and Latino men as excessively masculine and oversexed and Asian men as insufficiently masculine or undersexed.

Another example from multicultural studies reveals how boundaries are universally maintained by ethnic groups in the tendency to construct "our group" as vigorous (usually our men) and pure (usually our women), while "those others" are generally constructed as sexually depraved (usually their men) and promiscuous (usually their women) (Nagel, 2003, p. 10).

Ethnosexual boundaries often constitute exotic destinations and erotic locations that are surveilled and supervised, policed and patrolled, and regulated and restricted from both sides but with boundaries that nevertheless are constantly being transversed by individuals seeking links with stimulating ethnic Otherness. Nagel's (2003) work defined various kinds of ethnosexual adventurers, sojourners, settlers, and invaders. She researched the worldwide sex industry created by multinational military operations and international tourism, an industry that appeals to the erotic excitement of the ethnosexual frontier. She also cited the Internet as offering the latest titillating adventures in ethnosexual encounters.

Researchers in ethnosexual history are now suggesting that the primary binary in human thought—whether in families, clans, tribes, or religious, ethnic, national groups—is between Us and Them, *not* between male and female. That is, gender identities are secondary to and participate in constructing in- and out-group identities. Judith Butler (1993) raised the question

What would it mean if, instead of viewing sexual differentiation as more fundamental than other forms [of social differentiation] ... , we considered the disjunctive ordering of masculine/feminine as taking place not only through a heterosexualizing symbolic, with its taboo on homosexuality, but through a complex set of racial injunctions that operate in part through a taboo on miscegenation? Does reproduction of a racialized version of the species require and reproduce a normative heterosexuality in its service? (p. 167)

And, how do we account for the much greater flexibility in ethnosexual boundaries in homosexual communities? These are all questions that point to the social construction of both sexuality and ethnicity.

In psychotherapy, beyond what is consciously and explicitly presented, therapist and client have the task of being alert to how many different kinds of ethnicity and sexuality are embedded in each of their conscious and unconscious histories and how in the therapeutic relationship itself new erotics are continuously mutually coconstructed based on the ethnic and sexuality dimensions that both client and therapist bring to the relationship.

The Perspective of Mimetics

Following our consideration of sexual identities and ethnosexual realities, we are in a position to consider the place of mimetics, imitation, in the development of sexual practices and gender identities. The multimillion-dollar-an-hour Internet pornographic industry and a seemingly endless number of sexual meeting Web sites leave little doubt about the powerful role mimetics plays in sexual excitement, sexual practices, and gender definitions.

In her book *The Meme Machine* (1999), biologist Susan Blackmore integrates several decades of research into the evolution of "memes," the cultural replicators that parallel genes. Mimetics are heavily involved in cultural and ethnic practices and identities, as well as sex, sexuality, gender, and gender identities. Says Blackmore:

> For more than three thousand million years, DNA has been the only replicator worth talking about in the world. But it does not necessarily hold these monopoly rights for all time. Whenever conditions arise in which a new kind of replicator *can* make copies of itself, the new replicators

will tend to take over, and start a new kind of evolution of their own. Once this new evolution begins, it will in no necessary sense be subservient to the old (Dawkins 1976, pp. 193–194). Of course, memes could only come into existence when the genes had provided brains that were capable of imitation—and the nature of those brains must have influenced which memes took hold and which did not. However, once memes had come into existence they would be expected to take on a life of their own. (p. 4)

Blackmore (1999) points out that since the early days of Darwinism analogies have been drawn between biological and cultural evolution. But, "truly Darwinian explanations require more than just the idea of accumulating changes over time. The whole point of a memetic theory of cultural evolution is to treat memes as replicators in their own right. This means that memetic selection drives the evolution of ideas *in the interests of replicating the memes, not the genes*" (p. 4). Blackmore's work considers the various reasons why certain aspects of human behavior and activity are selectively chosen for imitation, citing biologist Daniel Dennett as saying, "The first rule of memes, as it is for genes, is that replication is not necessarily for the good of anything; replicators flourish that are good at replicating" (p. 4). Any piece of behavior, idea, attitude, emotion, or practice can serve as a meme to be selectively imitated.

For Blackmore (1999), as for biologists Dawkins and Dennett whom she quotes, memetic evolution means that people *are truly individually different*—both culturally and sexually. The human capacity to imitate complex activity and emotion creates a second-level replicator that acts in its own interests and can produce behavior that is memetically adaptive but biologically maladaptive. Considering memes as second-level replicators with a job that, like DNA, is simply to keep replicating allows us to understand why so many seemingly strange cultural and sexual variations exist all over the planet.

All primates are imitators. But, humans have taken imitation to abstract levels of values, symbols, heroes, rituals, and practices. Once a thought, feeling, or behavior is imitated, it can easily, blindly, and militantly perpetuate itself for any of myriad reasons. Cultures, ethnicities, sexualities, and gender definitions and identities evolve based on selective mimetics over long periods of time in specific social contexts. Individuals are born into complex mimetic networks, which like complex language networks, are gradually acquired over long periods of time through daily immersion in a web of interactive relationships.

Thoughts, feelings, and behavior acquired in mimetic networks are highly resistant to change because human imitation serves to construct living human realities. We have all been "carefully taught" to live within the limits of reality, and this includes the limits of our culturally, ethnically, and sexually constructed mimetic realities. This means that a psychotherapist trying to understand an idea, practice, ritual, or value in the mimetic soup of another is inevitably bound to fail in many regards. As therapists, then, simply understanding cultural, ethnic, and sexual variations cannot possibly be our goal. Rather, we must ask ourselves how we can best position ourselves so that those who live in other mimetic systems than our own can begin to represent, elaborate, and achieve their own understandings of what they are thinking, feeling, or doing in their own lives and relational contexts.

The Perspective of Trauma and Transgenerational Ghosts

Psychotherapy as we know it today effectively began with Freud's realization that neurotic symptoms were the direct result of childhood sexual trauma. But, Freud subsequently based his psychotherapeutic *technique* not so much on the direct effects of the actual trauma as on the ways in which the trauma was internally experienced and stored in memory by the person involved. We have since come full circle to realize that both the direct effects and the internalizations of traumatic experience have an impact in different ways on people's ongoing psychological and sexual lives. Since the posttraumatic effects of actual sexual trauma on individuals have been widely studied and written about (see especially Davies & Frawley, 1994), the perspective for clinical listening I want to introduce deals more with the transgenerational transmission of trauma.

The great psychological controversy of the 19th century concerned which was more important in human development, nature or nurture.

Freud believed that his most significant discovery was that more important than either nature or nurture in human beings was a third force: the progressive elaboration from birth of an "internal world." Each stage of our emotional–relational development is molded not only by the genetic and constitutional load we bring into the world with us but also by how we experience and construct in memory each unfolding interpersonal encounter. We may joke about perceiving the proverbial glass as half empty or half full, but at some level we know that our early character formation influences all of our subsequent perceptions and projections. We construct ongoing subjective worlds based on how we have experienced relationships in the past. Further, the psychological makeup of significant others of our childhoods greatly influences the construction of our subjective internal worlds.

The central concept of psychotherapy is "transference"—by whatever name we choose to call it. Psychotherapy teaches us that we all carry within us internalized ghosts from the past that influence how we live our present relationships. That is, the central assumption of therapy is that early conditioning in the context of emotionally significant relationships and dynamically impactful experiences heavily influences the ways we construct our subsequent perceptions and lives.

The theories and practice of psychotherapy, as well as contemporary neuroscience[1] support our professional belief that in emotionally significant relationships later in life, people can learn to focus on and to alter their relational patterns and behaviors. But, the internalized ghosts of our past lives, as well as ghosts of our parents and ancestors, often persist in haunting us. These ghosts are destined to appear in the transference, resistance, and countertransference of psychotherapy.

There are three kinds of ghosts or psychological internalizations that can be said to inhabit our internal worlds:

1. **An individual internalization** would be a way we each organize our perceptions and projections based on emotionally significant experience from our personal and familial past—such as abuse, trauma, success, or privilege.

---

[1] See Cozolino, 2002; Damasio, 1994, 1999, 2003; Edelman, 1993, 2006; Edelman & Tononi, 2000; LeDoux, 1996, 2002; Lewis et al., 2000; Pert, 1997; Siegel, 1999, 2007.

2. **A positional internalization** refers to a way we may psychologically organize our experience based on some condition of the sociocultural position we were born into or came to occupy—for example, social class or racial prejudice; gender or sexuality bias; or handicapped, immigrant, or refugee status.[2]

3. **A transgenerational internalization** is a psychological organization or orientation based on experiences our parents or ancestors may have suffered but that persists in haunting our present—for example, the possibility of poor self-esteem carried by an African American individual based on generations of maltreatment. Racial hatred, religious intolerance, class prejudice, and white guilt are all sustained through internalization and transgenerational transmission. Attitudes of ethnic or racial superiority, supremacy, or privilege are further examples of transgenerational transmission or haunting. Sexual practices, sexual boundaries, gender definitions, and gender identities may all be significantly impacted by transgenerational haunting.

It can be said that internal world attitudes are introjected in three stages:

1) Something new or foreign (good or bad) occurs in or to me.

2) I turn myself (consciously or unconsciously) into that which this new "thing" has done to me; that is, [through imitation, introjection, or identification] I appropriate it into myself in order to understand and/or to master it (the so-called role-reversal identity).

3) I can become aware of what has occurred (i.e., of the internalization) and how it has affected me. Making conscious those unconscious internalizations that have blocked my ongoing life processes allows

---

[2] Maher and Tetreault (1996) defined positionality as suggesting "that rather than being composed of any fixed 'essence' or individual identity, we all develop amid networks of relationships that themselves can be explored, analyzed, and changed, as long as people understand that they are not simply individuals, but differentially placed members of an unequal social order" (p. 163).

me to continue internalizing other experiences that may allow me
more flexibility and vitality. (Abraham and Torok, 1994, pp. 14–15)

In 1975, Hungarian psychoanalyst Nicolas Abraham introduced the
concept of the "transgenerational phantom," moving the focus of psychoanalytic psychotherapy beyond the individual because it postulates
that some people unwittingly inherit the secret "psychic substance" of
their ancestors' lives. "The 'phantom' represents a radical reorientation
of Freudian and post-Freudian theories of psychopathology, since here
symptoms do not spring from the individual's own life experiences but
from someone else's psychic conflicts, traumas, or secrets" (Abraham,
1975, in Abraham and Torok, 1994, p. 166).

The terms *phantom*, *ghost*, and *revenant*, as used by Abraham and
Torok (1994), derive from folklore giving psychological substance to
age-old beliefs, according to which only certain categories of the dead
return to torment the living: those who were denied the rite of burial
or died an unnatural, abnormal death; were criminals or outcasts; or
who suffered injustice in their lifetime. In Abraham's view,

> The dead do not return, but their lives' unfinished business is uncon-
> sciously handed down to their descendants. [In therapy] laying the dead
> to rest and cultivating our ancestors implies uncovering their shame-
> ful secrets, understanding their nameless and undisclosed suffering. ...
> [U]nsuspected, the dead continue to lead a devastating psychic half-life
> in us. The phantom represents the interpersonal and transgenerational
> consequences of silence. The idea of the phantom concerns itself with
> the unwitting reception of someone else's secret. Though manifest in one
> individual's psyche, the phantom eventually leads to the psychoanalysis
> in absentia of several generations (parents, grandparents, uncles, et al.)
> through the symptoms of a descendant. ... Abraham studies the unwit-
> ting transmission of secrets by one generation to another and sees the
> phantom as a function of the individual life experiences of the person
> who transmits it to his or her descendants. (N. Rand in Abraham &
> Tarok, 1994, pp. 166–169)

A specialized version of transgenerational haunting has appeared
recently in Françoise Davoine and Jean-Max Gaudillière's *History
Beyond Trauma: Whereof One Cannot Speak, Thereof One Cannot Stay*

Silent (2004). Through detailed case histories of hospitalized psychotics the authors trace how social traumas—breaches in cultural history for selves, parents, and ancestors—create severe pathologies in individuals and blind spots in cultures that live on in the symptoms of individuals.

The special difficulty of therapeutic work with transgenerational phantoms lies in the patient's horror at violating a parent's or a family's guarded secret, even though the text and content of the secret are inscribed within the patient's own unconscious. Abraham believes that

> The horror of transgression, in the strict sense of the term, is com-pounded by the risk of undermining the fictitious yet necessary integrity of the parental figure in question. ... [T]he words used by the phantom to carry out its return ... refer to the unspeakable. ... [P]hantom words [can] determine the choice of hobbies, leisure activities, or professional pursuits. One carrier of a phantom became a nature-lover on weekends, acting out the fate of his mother's beloved. The loved one had been denounced by the grandmother (an unspeakable and secret fact) and, having been sent to "break rocks" [*casser les cailloux* = do forced labor—Trans.], he later died in the gas chamber. What does our man do on weekends? A lover of geology, he "breaks rocks," catches butterflies, and proceeds to kill them in a can of cyanide. (Abraham, 1975, in Abraham & Tarok, 1994, pp. 174–175)

Recent attachment research clearly demonstrates the operation of transgenerational phantoms in the mechanisms of biologically based and psychologically molded human attachment. According to Marone (1998):

> Parental functions are organized by the parents' representational systems, defenses, and strategies, and their manifestation through family scripts, which in turn were formed under the influence of their own parents' representational systems. ... There is now ample and robust empirical support for this hypothesis. Identification with negative and or abusive aspects of the parents plays an important role in intergenerational transmission of disturbance. (pp. 135–139)

As a clear example of how transgenerational haunting operates, bell hooks, in her book *killing rage: ending racism* (1995), raises questions about negative habits of being that may have emerged as forms of political resistance ... in the days of extreme racial apartheid. ... For example, dissimulation—the practice of taking on any appearance needed to manipulate a situation—is a form of masking that black folks have historically used to survive in white supremacist settings. As a social practice, [dissimulation] promoted duplicity, the wearing of masks, hiding true feelings and intent. While this may have been useful in daily relations with all-powerful white exploiters and oppressors ... as a paradigm for social relations it has undermined bonds of love and intimacy. ... By not addressing our psychological wounds, by covering them, we create the breeding ground for pervasive learned helplessness and powerlessness. This lack of agency nurtures compulsive addictive behavior and promotes addiction. ... If this reality is not considered then the root causes of genocidal addiction may remain unaddressed. ... Similarly, young black children would not be emotionally crippled by psychological problems that emerge from low self-esteem, caused by the internalization of racist thinking, if African-Americans had institutionalized progressive mental health-care agendas that would address these issues so that they would not be passed from generation to generation. (pp. 142–144)

Further illustrating transgenerational phantoms is the now-classic book *Ghosts From the Nursery: Tracing the Roots of Violence* (Karr-Morse & Wiley, 1997). Psychoanalyst Selma Fraiberg coined the phrase *ghosts in the nursery* to refer to "the tendency of parents to bring to the rearing of their children the unresolved issues of their own childhoods" (Karr-Morse & Wiley, 1977, p. ix). *Ghosts From the Nursery* further demonstrates how violence is transgenerational—that children learn violence and its potential in the context of family violence. "[M]urderers and other violent criminals, who were once infants in our communities, are always accompanied by the spirits of the babies they once were together with the forces that killed their promise" (Karr-Morse & Wiley, 1997, p. ix).

Neurological findings[3] demonstrate that the brain evolves in infancy through significant emotional relationships with caregivers. "In order

---

[3] See Cozolino 2002; Damasio, 1994, 1999, 2003; Edelman, 1993, 2006; Edelman & Tononi, 2000; LeDoux, 1996, 2002; Lewis et al., 2000; Pert, 1997; Siegel, 1999, 2007.

to understand the tide of violent behavior in which America is now submerged, we must look ... to the cradle of human formation in the first thirty-three months of life [including nine months in utero]. ... It's not the finger that pulls the trigger, it's the brain; it's not the penis that rapes, it's the brain" (Karr-Morse & Wiley, 1997, p. 195).

Writers interested in intergenerational transmission of trauma hold that the transmission is not simply from parent to child but may occur within entire societies and cultures. "Many present-day conflicts cannot be fully understood without first understanding how historical hurts and grievances survive from generation to generation as 'chosen traumas'" (Volkan, 2004, p. 47). "Large groups tend to hold on to mental representations of events that include a shared feeling of success and triumph among group members. Heavily mythologized over time, such events and the persons appearing in them become elements of large-group identity. "Chosen glories" are passed from generation to generation through caretaker-child interactions and by participation in ceremonies that recall the past success. ... In times of stress or war-like situations, leaders often reactivate chosen glories in order to bolster their group's identity" (Volkan, 2004, p. 47).

The role of the chosen trauma—the collective mental representation of an event that has caused a large group to face drastic common losses, to feel helpless and victimized by another group, and to share a humiliating injury—is to sustain large-group identity and its cohesiveness. Psychoanalyst Vamik Volkan (2004) notes that:

> There is far more to this transgenerational transmission of massive trauma than children mimicking the behavior of parents or hearing stories of the event told by the older generation. Rather, it is the end result of mostly unconscious psychological processes by which survivors deposit into their progeny's core identities their own injured self-images. ... In order to gain relief from feelings of shame and humiliation, the inability to be assertive, and the inability to mourn, a Holocaust survivor, for example, deposits his or her image of him or herself as a damaged person into the developing personal identity of his or her child; thus, the parent's self-image "lives on" in the child. ... Then the parent unconsciously assigns to the image of him or herself that is now in the child specific tasks of reparation that rightfully belong to the survivor: [such as] to reverse shame and humiliation, to turn

passivity into activity, to tame the sense of aggression, and to mourn the losses associated with the trauma. (pp. 48–49)

What is then passed to the offspring is not the traumatized person's memories of the event because memory can belong only to the survivor of trauma and cannot be transmitted. Deposited parental self-images are the elements by which the representation of traumatic history can be passed from person to person, as Volkan holds (2004).

Since all the injured self-images that various parents in a traumatized group transmit to their children refer to the same event, a shared image of the tragedy develops [and] a new generation of the group is unconsciously knit together. ...

[W]hat is essential is this marker's unseen power to link the members of the group together in a persistent sense of sameness through history. (p. 49)

Cross-cultural research in attachment, neuroscience, and infant intersubjectivity confirms that individual, positional, and transgenerational phantoms inhabit our inner worlds, informing us who we are and how we are to be in our intimate relationships and in the world. Sexual practices, as well as gender definitions and gender identities, are subject to all sorts of ghostly limiting internalizations. The task of the psychotherapist cannot be to have a knowledge of all of the types of personal, familial, and cultural haunting experienced by diverse peoples. Rather, our task is to provide a setting maximally conducive to the emergence of internal ghostly representations in the symbols, words, and actions that are projected into transference, resistance, and countertransference. After all, it is the exposure to the light of day that phantoms cannot survive.

The Intersubjective Perspective

I am a subject, an agent of my desires, thoughts, and actions. You are a subject, an agent of your desires, thoughts, and actions. When we come together for an intersubjective engagement over a period of time, something else begins to happen that affects us both. Intersubjective theories provide different ways of thinking about our shared intersubjective experiences.

In recent years, psychotherapists from divergent schools of thought have begun to formulate various kinds of relational views of self-development. These formulations rest on the belief that the human mind emerges from and continuously exists within interactional processes, rather than being simply constructed or conditioned as a separate or isolated mind-self.

The central theoretical construct of intersubjectivity theory is the *intersubjective field*, defined as "a system composed of differently organized, interacting subjective worlds" (Stolorow, Brandchaft, & Atwood, 1987, p. ix). Robert Stolorow and his colleagues used *intersubjective* "to refer to any psychological field formed by interacting worlds of experience, at whatever developmental level these worlds may be organized" (Stolorow & Atwood, 1992, p. 3). "The concept of an intersubjective system brings to focus both the individual's world of [personal] experience and its embeddedness with other such worlds in a continual flow of reciprocal mutual influence" (p. 18). The subjectivity of sexual experience is a critical aspect of the intersubjective field.

Some writers see the intersubjective and relational perspectives as replacing the traditional (Freudian) intrapsychic psychological perspective. Others (myself included) view the two perspectives as complementary—one highlighting the psychological dimension that develops *within* individuals, the other highlighting the psychological dimension that develops *between* individuals. Most relational theorists now view both perspectives as essential to our understanding of ourselves and others.

Intersubjective theory generally distinguishes two subjects in the process of interacting and recognizing each other from one subject observing or influencing another. The main experience of intersubjectivity is one of being with rather than one of observing and interpreting. Sameness and difference exist simultaneously in the tension of intersubjective mutual recognition (Benjamin, 1988, 1995). The goal of psychotherapy in this view is for both participants in the context of a mutually evolving, coconstructed intersubjectivity to come to recognize each other and to know themselves more fully in order to attain more flexibility, creativity, and passion in living and loving.

While the topics of subjectivity and intersubjectivity have interested philosophers for several centuries, it has only been during the past few decades that the development of subjectivity and the maintenance of intersubjectivity have been scrutinized in a wide range of multidisciplinary studies, including infant research, neurobiology, and relational psychotherapy. Philosopher Jürgen Habermas, in "A Theory of Communicative Competence" (1970), speaks about "the intersubjectivity of understanding" to mean both an individual capacity and a social domain. Infant researcher Colin Trevarthen (1980) observes in early infancy a phase of "primary intersubjectivity" characterized by mutual sharing of intent as an effective psychological activity. Infant researcher D. N. Stern (1985, 2004) sees intersubjective relatedness as a crucial step in self-development as the infant becomes able to share subjective experiences, especially affective ones. Further, Stern (2004) came to consider the capacity and drive for intersubjective communication as innate and present from birth.

An historical fulcrum in considering the development of intersubjectivity is psychoanalyst-pediatrician Donald Winnicott's (1969) article, "The Use of an Object." In a schematic, Winnicott says that "object relating" *precedes* "object usage." That is, early relating to another (a love "object") occurs without fully recognizing the psychological separateness of the other. However, the later object usage entails perceiving the other as an independent external being (not as a projective entity of one's own mind). The child comes to recognize the other as a separate entity, a person in his or her own right and then to use that person (at first ruthlessly) for his or her own purposes. Winnicott's idea is that the internalized other established in early object relating must be destroyed by the child before the real external other can be recognized as surviving separately outside and then "used" for interactions, growth, reflections, and pleasure—and internalized for intersubjective experiencing.

Psychoanalyst Jessica Benjamin (1988) formulated a sequence of theoretical stages for the development of intersubjectivity:

> *Primary recognition* is to affirm, validate, acknowledge, know, accept, understand, empathize, take in, tolerate, appreciate, see, identify with, find familiar … love [the other]. (pp. 15–16)

Mutual recognition includes ... emotional attunement, mutual influence, affective mutuality, sharing states of mind. ... Research reveals infants to be active participants who help shape the responses of their environment, and "create" their own objects. (p. 16)

Actual interpersonal interaction is the development of the self *within* relatedness and interpersonal interaction. The accent here is on the self that is affected by the other's recognition or lack of such so that the child feels either confirmed or denied in his/her sense of agency and self-esteem. (p. 18)

Intersubjective mutual recognition occurs when the individual grows in and through the relationship to other subjects. ... The other whom the self meets is also [recognized as] a self, a subject in his or her own right ... we are able and need to recognize that other subject *as different and yet alike*, as an other who is capable of sharing similar mental experience. (pp. 19–20)

Mutual recognition, "the necessity of recognizing as well as being recognized by the other, is crucial to the intersubjective view; it implies that we actually have a need to recognize the other as a separate person who is like us yet distinct" (Benjamin, 1988, p. 23), and that we have a need to be recognized as like but separate, different and distinct. "This conscious pleasure in sharing a feeling introduces a new level of mutuality—a sense that inner experience can be joined, that two minds can cooperate in one intention. ... Awareness of the separate other enhances the felt connection with him: this *other* mind can share *my* feeling" (p. 30).

The intersubjective perspective has enabled us to move our ideas about sexuality beyond the essentialist or naturalist drive conceptualizations that have been elaborated in the traditional intrapsychic perspective. Intersubjectively considered, various sexual interests, curiosities, and identity orientations become elaborated in relation to significant others early in life and then later manifest in different interpersonal and intersubjective contexts. According to Benjamin (1993):

My premise is that recognition of the other is the decisive aspect of differentiation. In recognition, someone who is different and outside shares a similar feeling; different minds and bodies attune. In erotic union this attunement can be so intense that self and other feel as if momentarily "inside" each other, as part of a whole. In my view, the simultaneous desire for loss of self and for wholeness (or oneness) with the other often described as the ultimate point of erotic union, is really a form of the desire for recognition. In getting pleasure with the other and taking pleasure in the other, we engage in mutual recognition. *Understanding desire as the desire for recognition changes our view of the erotic experience. It enables us to describe a mode of representing desire unique to intersubjectivity.* (p. 126, emphasis added)

Intersubjective theory and practice thus point to the ways we now try to grasp the subjective meanings—especially sexual meanings—of the unconscious in terms of communication between ourselves and the other person in the room. Intersubjectivity theory acknowledges

1. The unknowability and uncertainty of the meanings of all interpersonal encounters
2. The sense of the multiple possibilities of interpretation in any given moment
3. The realization of the likelihood that we will communicate our subjectivity (whether we wish to or not)
4. The possibility of speaking from our own responses and doubts *within* the therapeutic situation

These features of the intersubjective perspective lead us into a related area of study—a perspective focusing on the psychotherapy relationship itself.

The Relational/Thirdness Perspective

A large and influential international, multidisciplinary group of theorists and therapeutic practitioners led by Stephen Mitchell and Lewis Aron from New York University have collaborated to develop a "relational" perspective. Paying homage to Freud, Ferenczi, Sullivan, Levenson, Ghent, and Foucault, this group generally embraces the infant–caregiver, personal–identity, postmodern, social–constructionist, ethnicity, and intersubjectivity perspectives as previously discussed.

Noting the numerous difficulties encountered over the years with Freud's biologically based instinct approach to sexuality, Mitchell, in his relational approach (1988), reversed the classical formula—that internalized object relationships transferred into adult relationships memorialize infantile sexual conflicts—to read that interactive adult sexuality expresses early relational configurations.

Heavily influenced by the feminist accent on the historically destructive male-subject/female-object dominance/submissive split, the relationists emphasize that the human mind is not monadic but dyadic in nature. Vitalizing dynamic human relationships are seen as constituted by coconstructed intersubjective erotics—that is, by interpersonal interactions, dances, or idioms that are formulated as a "third" force or vector mutually created by and influencing both participants.

There are several general features that characterize the relational approach:

1. Symmetry exists between the two separate and equal subjectivities who engage each other toward achieving mutual recognition (and negation) in the intersubjective field of psychotherapy and psychoanalysis. Yet asymmetry also characterizes the therapeutic situation, in that the therapist can be seen as an experienced expert, facilitator, and leader—although at times the asymmetrical roles can also reverse.

2. The co-creation of a mutually-achieved rhythm and harmony of relating and the emergence of a co-constructed set of relational realities evolves in the therapeutic relationship that is rich, complex, and often confusing and contradictory.

3. Mutually-engaged ego and self boundaries are in constant flux between fruitful and dangerous interpenetrations. The emergent sense of the importance and reality of the relationship itself (often referred to as "the third") can be fruitfully studied by the therapeutic dyad.

4. Numerous dialectics of personality formation—for example, oedipal/preoedipal, narcissistic/object love, depressive/manic affective

splits, passive/active participation, and masculine/feminine gender attributes—may all be mutually experienced and worked through in the relational context.

5. A full array of developmentally-determined relational patterns becomes mutually engaged and worked through in the transference/countertransference matrix.

6. Internalized personality functions and structures featuring increased flexibility, expanded horizons, and novel possibilities of relating are thought to emerge from the relationally-centered treatment process. (Hedges, 1983/2003, pp. xxii ff.)

My Relatedness Listening Perspectives Approach

In a series of books and articles, I have developed a "listening perspectives" approach that aids in framing different developmentally based qualities of internalized interpersonal relatedness experience as they arise in the here-and-now therapeutic relationship (Hedges, 1983/2003, 2005). Both the listening perspectives approach and relational psychotherapy abandon entirely the naïve view that we can ever objectively consider how things "really are" or that the human mind can ever be studied in isolation from the intersubjective fields in which human beings live.

The listening perspectives way of approaching the psychotherapeutic situation encourages us as professional listeners to experience ourselves as living human participants involved in a full emotional relationship with someone endeavoring to experience and to express his or her life experience. This listening perspectives approach further encourages us to formulate our work in terms of theories that enhance the listening and speaking possibilities within a living, breathing, here-and-now relationship, rather than with theories that seek to reify or personify psychological concepts or to capture the "true nature" of the human mind as objectively defined.

I have defined four general perspectives for listening to people in psychotherapy. These perspectives, listed next in order of increasing complexity, borrow developmental metaphors to describe various relational possibilities.

Schizoid

I. **The organizing experience:** Infants require certain forms of connection and interconnection to remain psychologically alert and enlivened to themselves and to others. In their early relatedness they are busy "organizing" physical and mental channels of connection—first to mother's body and later to her mind and to the minds of others—for nurturance, stimulation, soothing, and evacuation. Framing organizing patterns for analysis entails studying how two people approach to make connections and then turn away, veer off, rupture, or dissipate the intensity of the connections.

Oral

Overt
need or
disavowed
oral.

II. **The symbiotic experience:** Toddlers are busy learning how to make emotional relationships (both good and bad) work for them. They experience a sense of merger and reciprocity with their primary caregivers, thus establishing many knee-jerk, automatic, characterological, and role-reversible patterns or scenarios of relatedness. Framing the symbiotic relatedness structures for analysis entails noting how each person characteristically engages the other and how interactive scenarios evolve from two subjectively formed sets of internalized self and other interaction patterns.

Sense
of
Self +
other

Pre-
Oedipal

III. **The self-other experience:** Two- and 3-year-olds are preoccupied with using the acceptance and approval of others for developing and enhancing self-definitions, self-skills, and self-esteem. Their relatedness strivings use the mirroring, twinning, and idealizing responses of significant others to firm up their budding sense of self (Kohut, 1971). Framing for analysis the self-other patterns used for affirming, confirming, and inspiring the self entails studying how the internalized mirroring, twinning, and idealizing patterns used in self-development in the pasts of both participants play out to enhance and limit the possibilities for mutual self-to-self-other resonance in the emerging interpersonal engagement.

Oedipal

IV. **The independence experience:** Four- to 7-year-olds are dealing with triangular love and hate relationships and are moving toward more complex social relationships. In their relatedness, they experience others as separate centers of initiative and themselves as independent agents in a socially competitive environment. Framing the internalized patterns of independently interacting selves in both cooperative and competitive triangulations with real and fantasized third parties entails studying the emerging interaction patterns for evidence of repressive forces operating within each participant and between the analytic couple that work to limit or spoil the full interactive potential.

Figure 1.1 graphically portrays the way relational psychotherapy is considered using a listening perspectives approach. The two lower ovals depict ways to listen to four levels of relatedness complexity in the subjective worlds of client and therapist, respectively. The large upper oval depicts the third vector or force thought to be operating in intersubjective and relational theory—the third or the transference-countertransference matrix.

The four different relational frames or self-and-other listening perspectives encourage mutual surrender (Ghent, 1990; Maroda,

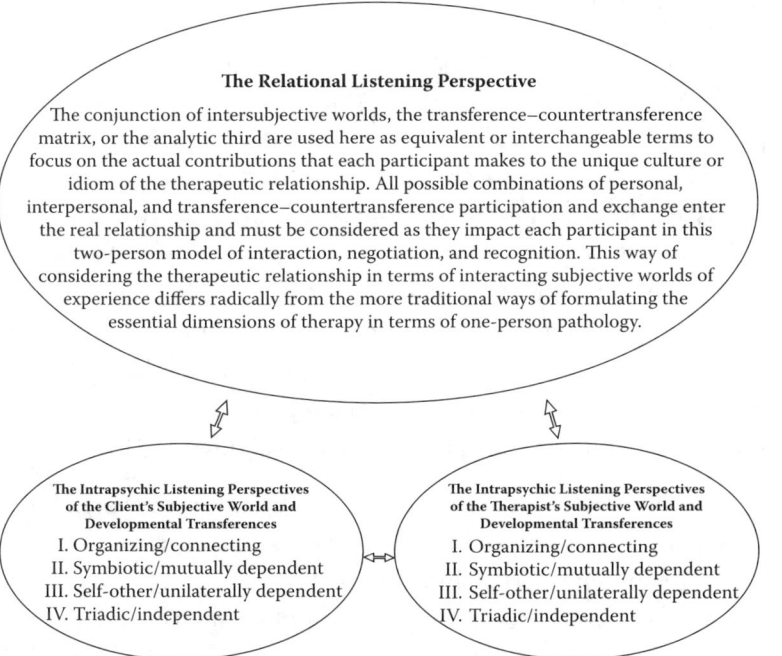

Figure 1.1   Listening perspectives and transformational relationships—the leading paradigm of psychoanalytic psychotherapy.

1999) to a process in which different modes, styles, or patternings of internalized self-and-other possibilities are active at different moments in the ongoing therapeutic relationship—or perhaps predominate during different phases of the therapeutic work.

With a relational lens, we are in a position to realize that the erotic dynamics, imagery, and experiences brought from the infantile pasts of both participants are necessarily replicated or enacted in some form or another in the therapeutic relationship for the limiting internalized object relations structures of sex, sexualities, gender, and gender identities of both participants to become known and therapeutically worked through.

The "thirdness" highlighted by relational theory fosters the tension required for interpersonal space to exist in which partners can simultaneously play, create, and recognize each other. This relational space for recognition and negotiation is what Benjamin (1988) suggested as the emblem of femininity to contrast with phallic assertiveness as the emblem of masculinity. Relational psychoanalyst Muriel Dimen (2003) holds that

> *Sexuality has become a relation, not a force* [emphasis added]. If, with Freud, we thought that your sex is what makes you who you are, now we think that who you are shapes what sex you are and what sex you like. [In relational psychotherapy and psychoanalysis] clinical attention is less often on how the anatomical distinction between the sexes influences the psyche. More commonly we think about meaning, not biology. We [now] wonder how the intrapsychic, interpersonal, and cultural significance of the anatomical distinction inscribes [any person's] desire. The self, we now think, is born in relationship, not in the continuously flowing impersonal excitement—libido—located by Freud beneath psychic processes and structures. (p. 157)

Psychotherapists working within a relational framework thus consider sexuality as something that is actively and continuously cocreated between people in relationships rather than a state of being, identity, or orientation. Each person's expressions of sexuality bear a history of internalized relationships in which tension has been imperfectly held and balanced, thus leaving each person with unbalanced internalized schemas of expectation. The past schemas of both client and therapist come under scrutiny as the erotics of the psychotherapy relationship emerge. The evolving dynamics or erotics of the mutually cocon-structed therapeutic relationship allow the possibility for the open-ing of new space and new tensions in which the dance of thirdness can appear and be jointly negotiated toward mutual regulations and transformations. My relational listening perspectives approach affords an opportunity to frame for psychotherapeutic scrutiny four distinctly different types of self-and-other transferred relatedness possibilities, along with whatever erotic dynamics may be present in the psycho-therapeutic relationship stemming from each type of relatedness.

In conclusion, what becomes manifestly clear is that we can no longer simply take anyone's stated sexual orientation or gender iden-tities at face value in life or in psychotherapy. The series of perspec-tives offered here for listening to a person in psychotherapy seeks to illustrate sex, sexuality, gender, and gender identity in their manifold richness. These perspectives on sexualities also serve to illuminate the multiplicity of all the whos we are and all the whos we can yet become in all of our interpersonal encounters.

PART 2

PUBLISHED ACCOUNTS OF SEX IN PSYCHOTHERAPY

2

SEXUALIZED THERAPEUTIC ENCOUNTERS

You are about to enter the private sex lives of a number of psychotherapists and their clients as known in the workspace of the psychotherapeutic consulting room. While Freud (1912a, 1912b, 1915) acknowledged that loving and even sexual feelings toward patients on the part of the therapist are an inevitable part of psychotherapy, he prescribed only consultation and more personal analysis for the therapist. For this reason, it was not until the 1950s in London that countertransference—feelings of the therapist toward the client—begin to be seriously studied as a vital source of information about what is going on in the therapeutic relationship.

The reports of sexualized therapeutic encounters that follow are organized into my four developmentally based relatedness listening perspectives, which were briefly described in Chapter 1. Each of the four listening perspectives is introduced here with a repeat of the brief paragraph describing the kinds of relatedness that are attended to in this perspective followed by a listing of the listening parameters involved. As mentioned, my listening perspectives are explicitly constructed and ordered according to developmental metaphors of increasing relatedness complexity.

Internalized relatedness patterns from the lived past of each participant, as well as novel configurations emerging from the interpersonal engagement of therapy (the "third"), are an expectable focus of discussion as the therapeutic relationship unfolds (Hedges, 2005). Emotional honesty about and limited disclosure of affective experience on the part of the analyst is an expectable part of the emerging therapeutic relationship (Maroda, 1999). The development of a personal creative style of relating that, like postmodern art, integrates a variety of ideas and interventions into the specific therapeutic exchange is another expectable aspect of the emergent dialogue (Johnson, 1991). A multiplicity of ways of viewing and working together with the internalized patterns of both people, along with the emerging configurations of interaction characteristic of the couple, are also expected (Stark, 1994, 1997).

The four relatedness listening perspectives that follow are based on developmental *metaphors* of how a growing child potentially engages and is engaged by others in interpersonal interactions that build internal habits, structures, or patterns of relational expectation during different age periods. Differential framing secures for psychotherapeutic study the structures, patterns, configurations, or modes of internalized interpersonal interaction that have characterized the past interactions of both participants and that are transferred into and resisted conscious awareness and expression in the current mutually developing therapeutic relationship. Relatedness listening perspectives thus formed do *not* represent a developmental schema per se but rather serve to identify a general array of relatedness possibilities lived out each day in various ways by all people.

Relational psychotherapists rightly or wrongly have been repeatedly criticized on the basis that there is little *systematic* attention to transference, resistance, and countertransference in relational work. In contrast, the relatedness listening perspectives have been explicitly defined for the purposes of bringing out the unconscious transference/resistance and countertransference/counterresistance relatedness dimensions perennially at play in the therapeutic relationship.

The relatedness listening perspectives approach considers psychotherapeutic concepts valuable and viable only insofar as they are formulated specifically within a human listening (relational) context. Psychotherapeutic knowledge cannot be about a thing, the human mind, but rather exists as a body of thought about how people are able to achieve mutually enlivening, consciousness-raising experiences in an emotionally alive and emotionally stressful therapeutic relationship (Friedman, 1988).

In recent years, there has been considerable discussion regarding so-called countertransference disclosure. The field of psychotherapy inherited from Freud the "blank screen" model that effectively foreclosed any personal emotional involvement or disclosure on the part of the therapist. Recent analysis showed that what was foreclosed was in fact the therapist acknowledging, or perhaps even knowing about, his or her necessarily participatory role in the process. The point has been repeatedly made that in fact therapists are emotional participants, and that their clients know a great deal about them that can be effectively made use of as therapeutic grist for the mill. The question remains what kinds of disclosure are therapeutically appropriate under what circumstances (Aron, 1996; Hedges, 1996; Maroda, 1993)?

The following vignettes illustrate some points of view on therapist disclosure of sexual responsiveness. This issue is revisited in the final case study of Charles in Part 3 of this book.

Some Relational Countertransference Issues

Maroda: On Speaking Erotic Feelings

Psychoanalyst Karen Maroda considers the question of whether it is ever appropriate for the therapist to speak to a patient of the therapist's erotic feelings toward the patient (1994). Gorkin (1985, 1987) notes that the sexualized countertransference is a seriously neglected topic. Maroda agrees with Gorkin and further endorses his position that disclosure of erotic feelings is not generally a good idea because of the high level of anxiety that it usually provokes in the patient. But, she holds that there are exceptions to everything.

Maroda (1994) cites as an example a case with an impasse reported by Atwood, Stolorow, and Trop (1989). The patient, Alice, was a 36-year-old Asian woman who had been ignored by her father because he had wanted a boy. She developed an erotic attachment to her therapist and demanded that he acknowledge that he found her attractive and sexually exciting.

> Her demands for a concrete affirmation of her sexual self became increasingly strident. The therapist, feeling enormous pressure, finally did acknowledge that she was an attractive woman whom many men would find appealing. The patient became furious at what she felt was a lukewarm response. She continued to demand that he simply acknowledge that he felt sexually excited by her. She reiterated her awareness that they would actually never do anything sexually, but she still wanted

him to demonstrate that he was interested and excited. In reaction to her increasing demand, the therapist became more emotionally disengaged and adopted a more intellectual stance, inquiring into why she was feeling so needy at this time. The patient became even more incensed and felt that he was abandoning her and that she should leave him. It was at this point that the therapist sought consultation in an attempt to understand what had happened between them. (p. 562)

Maroda (1994) believes that the situation described is a classic impasse, and that it calls for an effective response from the therapist.

Alice is focusing on her therapist's sexual interest in her, with the importance of her attractiveness being over-determined by her history. Her conviction that her therapist is sexually attracted to her is rooted in reality, since Alice is not psychotic. ... Alice is very probably correct in her belief that her therapist is sexually attracted to her and she is telling him in no uncertain terms that she needs confirmation. ... [It] is impossible from the information given to ascertain whether Alice's fixation on obtaining the admission of sexual arousal from her therapist is based solely on her need for affirmation of her female sexuality or whether it also represents a displacement of some other emotional response that she believes her therapist has withheld. ... When a patient is as frustrated and as focused on erotic aspects of the therapy relationship as Alice was, I would certainly want to consider seriously that there were underlying contributing factors and that the erotic attachment might well be serving as a defense against hostility or other repressed material. [But] regardless of what underlies it, once a crisis and impasse of this intensity exists, the patient needs a personal and emotional response to it. Before disclosing something as potentially anxiety-producing as sexual arousal, I would definitely discuss the impasse with the patient and attempt to discover any and all meanings that it has. ... Telling the patient that you know the situation is critical and he obviously needs something from you that he is not getting, responds to the patient's needs and feelings, and begins transforming the impasse into a joint effort at resolution. (p. 136)

But, Maroda (1994) feels that even discussing the impasse may not respond to the patient's needs, that the patient will feel falsely placated and become angry again, thus reinstating the impasse.

With Alice, the therapist was distant and defensive at first, but after consultation he could discuss the impasse with her by stating his desire to be emotionally responsive in the face of his not being professionally comfortable answering her questions. Alice's acceptance of the therapist's professional stance was her contribution to resolving the impasse. Says Maroda:

> But as I read the case I wondered how long her acceptance would last. Would Alice really be able to accede to her therapist's refusal to answer her questions or would the impasse take hold again later? If Alice renewed her demands for her therapist to admit his sexual interest in her, I believe he would have had no choice but to do so. Alice had already stated that she knew that their professional relationship did not allow any acting out of sexual feelings and that she had, in fact, accepted this limitation. She simply wanted him to admit what he felt anyway. Undoubtedly such a disclosure from her therapist could be highly sexually stimulating to Alice, but I believe this would pass if the therapist was not being seductive. Furthermore, the problem of sexually stimulating the patient is less severe than frustrating her to the point of dealing with a lengthy impasse or, worse still, a premature termination. (p. 137)

Maroda (1994) believes that Alice may have been one of those rare exceptions—someone who actually needed her therapist to acknowledge that he found her sexually attractive. Maroda advises caution and recommends careful exploration and consultation regarding the meanings of such requests, in tandem with making clear that *acting* on erotic feelings is never appropriate. "When a patient repeatedly demands to know the truth regarding the therapist's feelings, *no matter what the truth is*, I think he has a right to be treated respectfully and given an answer" (p. 138). Maroda's stance marks a courageous approach to dealing with the inevitable sexual feelings that arise from time to time on the part of the therapist.

Davies: Love in the Afternoon

I am here reminded of the wonderful case study contributed by Jody Messler Davies, "Love in the Afternoon" (1994). Her client had an intense dread of sexual stimulation in himself, but especially of perceiving arousal in others. At a decisive moment, Davies stood against the character scenario of his childhood by telling him that she indeed had sexual fantasies about him. This precipitated a storm of indignant outrage reminiscent of the frequent storms of outrage that the client's mother had frequently directed at him. The client had often recalled how as a boy, following delicious afternoons in mother's bed snuggled up against her body with her reading exciting stories to him, mother would realize that he was in a pleasurable ecstasy, intensely enjoying his time with her, and then become outraged. Dynamically, mother would seduce the boy with delicious incestuous relating, and then when she sensed he was enjoying and feeling aroused by the relating, she would become indignant and angrily push him away. Little wonder that he had been totally unable to sustain sexual relationships as an adult. Davies's client had continued to regale her with tantalizing sexual imagery for some time, which she had been deflecting. But, as her analytic curiosity allowed her to consider what this was all about for him, she found herself having sexual fantasies—and at a critical juncture told him so. His sudden indignant outrage served momentarily to frighten and shame her, replicating how cruelly his mother had raged at and shamed him—and perhaps also signaling his realization that the delicious but perverse scenario with his therapist was crumbling, slowly coming to an end.

In my view, her intervention was directly to the point and did serve to bring a long-festering internalized erotic scenario directly under analytic scrutiny. She dared to stand against the scenario by declaring that all of his sexual talk and imagery was indeed having an erotic impact on her, whether he wanted to think so or not. Although his instantaneous rage and outrage were momentarily intimidating to Davies, in the confrontation she spoke what the boy's child-self could not speak: that he was stimulating her, and that it was both titillating and invasive. And that in raging and shaming her, he was attempting to blame her for a mutually stimulating situation that he was deliberately instigating and in which she was participating. In role reversal, he had given her in the countertransference the untenable position that he had been victim to in childhood. Her speaking up for herself, and therefore against what was happening, gave voice to the client's child-self and unmasked the perversity of it all.

Aron: Dominance and Submission

Lewis Aron (1996) describes a man who had for some time been associating about sadomasochistic interactions, sexual fantasies of anal penetration, and feelings of abuse, dominance, and submission. Aron interpreted his client's idea that he (the therapist) was dominating him, controlling him, and expecting him to submit. The client then expressed his belief that Aron *did* want him to submit, that this is what he always felt his therapist wanted from him. Aron replied, in a way he hoped conveyed an attitude of musing or thinking aloud, "The entire psychoanalytic therapy is a sexual conquest for me, in which I become excited by your submissions" (p. 178). He left it ambiguous regarding whether it was the client's belief or the therapist's experience, both in an attempt to avoid dismissing the client's thoughts as projections and simultaneously to open himself up for possible countertransference interpretations. He may have learned something about himself and about the analytic interaction that he had not known before.

> As I tell the client that I derive sexual excitement from dominating him, I may recognize some excitement in my tone of voice, excitement that I perhaps had not been aware of. Or I may realize that my interpretation has a more aggressive or penetrating quality than I previously realized. … It is not that I expect that my client will regularly interpret something dramatically new to me. After all, if I had no idea that I was susceptive to issues of dominance and control, I believe it would be quite unlikely that I could hear my client's associations as interpretations and make good use of them. What occurs more commonly is that the client will cue me in to some conflictual area that I do know about but was not sufficiently aware of at the moment, in the present analytic context. The client serves as my therapist by helping me to work through a conflict that was previously worked on in my own personal psychoanalytic therapy. There are risks and complications in this approach but the fact that thinking in terms of mutuality is complicated and hazardous does not mean that it is to be avoided. (pp. 178–179)

These three clinical examples of Maroda, Davies, and Aron serve to alert us to the importance at times of openly acknowledging the presence of sexual feelings in the consulting room. They further illustrate how seasoned therapists can move forward in this work in the most thoughtful and professional manner possible.

Developmental Listening

Psychotherapists have had a keen interest in developmental theories since Abraham (1924) defined the psychosexual stages, Erikson (1959) set up the stages of ego development, and Mahler (1968) put forth her separation-individuation theory of development. The assumption of these early attempts at developmental listening was that symptoms and transferences in adult psychotherapy could be traced back to the individual's developmental experiences in infancy and childhood. Jacobson (1954, 1964) shifted the paradigm from considering individual growth experiences to looking at the ways children in their early years come to *internally represent* their worlds of self and other and how those internal representations serve as silent guides in subsequent relational experiences. Following in her footsteps, Kernberg (1976, 1984) saw the building blocks of personality as (a) a representation of self, (b) a representation of other, and (c) an affect state linking them.

I located four main watersheds of self and other experience that have emerged from a century of psychoanalytic listening and theorizing. But, following contemporary philosophers of the mind such as Ryle (1949), Wittgenstein (1953), Searle (1992, 2004), and Rorty (1979, 1989), I have taken the position that theorizing about the nature of the unitary mind only serves to reify and personify *processes* that are always ongoing, fluid, and interpersonal. Abandoning scientific objectivity in favor of systematic subjectivity and intersubjectivity, I have taken the position that the only theories that are valuable to therapists are those about how to listen to and to be emotionally present with the narrations put forward by people who choose to talk with us about their lives (Hedges 1983/2003, 1992, 1996, 2005).

Thus, the four relatedness listening perspectives are derived from self and other developmental considerations and define an array of relatedness possibilities from the least complex (I) search for connections, to (II) the establishment of reliable channels of mutual attunement, through separation and individuation to (III) the firming up of a cohesive sense of self, to (IV) the highly complex capacity for fully ambivalent triangulated experiences of self and other. The liberating twist of the listening perspective approach is not to be found simply in the overall reorganization of familiar clinical concepts; rather, a profound shift of mental organization on the part of the therapeutic listener is required—a mental shift from looking for what is "really there" in the speaker to experiencing what is happening in the intersubjective field of mutual and reciprocal influencing. The sexual vignettes in Part II are ordered along this axis of self and other experiencing.

3

THE PERSONALITY IN ORGANIZATION

The Search for Relatedness

This perspective for therapeutic listening is based on an appreciation of the many features of human intrauterine life and the neonate's rich experience potentials in the first few months after birth. During this period of human life, an infant organizes sensorimotor and cognitive–affective channels toward the human environment. The earliest learning experiences of *organizing* mind/body channels for sustenance, comfort, safety, stimulation, and intelligibility provide a foundation for the development of subsequent patterns of relatedness.

Traditionally, persons functioning primarily or periodically in mental states rooted in early organizational experience have been referred to as psychotic, autistic, schizophrenic, schizoaffective, manic-depressive (bipolar), or paranoid-schizoid. But, all humans have experienced this period of primary organization of psyche. All physically normal infants organize channels for reaching out and contacting the environment pre- and postnatally. Infants work to bring needed features of the environment to themselves by various means. All future somatic and psychic developments depend on how this process goes and how the body and psychic modes developed during this period serve to expand or to limit and constrict possibilities in ways specific to the infant and to the possibilities offered it by the immediately available facilitating environment.

Most long-term psychotherapy sooner or later focuses on the primary relatedness modes that form the foundation of a person's basic somatic organization and emotional life. I call this the "organizing" period, with its organizing issues, aspects, or features that remain embedded in body structure and in personality. This listening perspective is designed to orient the psychotherapeutic listener to the ways in which foundational organizing patterns (forms, modes, styles) can be discerned and responses made to them. The exact ways in which people search for and find satisfying relatedness and the ways in which people learn to accept defeat or to expect a loss or breaking of human contact are the focus of study in this listening mode. This perspective thus has applications not only for people formally diagnosed with some sort of psychosis but also for the deepest layerings of learned experience of all people, which serves to determine an individual's fundamental orientation to the environment. Parallel work by Bromberg (2006) and Stern (2010) focuses on these normative gaps of interpersonal connection in terms of "dissociation" and "unformulated experience," respectively.

Précis: Listening to the Search for Relatedness—The Organizing Experience

Developmental Metaphor

Infants require certain forms of connection and interconnection to remain psychologically alert and enlivened to themselves and to others. In their early relatedness, they are busy organizing physical and mental channels of connection—first to mother's body, then later to her mind and the minds of others—for nurturance, stimulation, evacuation, and soothing. Framing organizing patterns for analysis entails studying how two people approach to make connections and then turn away, veer off, rupture, or dissipate the intensity of the connections.

Psychotherapeutic Parameters

Traditional diagnosis: organizing personality/psychosis
Developmental metaphor: ±4 months from birth—focused attention versus affective withdrawal
Affects: connecting or disconnecting, but often appearing as an inconsistent, generalized, or chaotic clamor to a casual observer
Transference: connection versus disconnection, rupture, discontinuity, and disjunction

Resistance: to connections, to channels that are organizing or promise consistent bonds

Listening mode: connecting, intercepting, linking

Therapeutic modality: a focus on withdrawal, constriction, or destruction of links that results from mutually connecting or from mutual engagement—interception as a goal

Countertransference: fear of intensity of psychotic anxieties that arise from interpersonal and intrapersonal connections; withdrawal and defense

While my listening perspectives are based on developmental *metaphors* referring to various levels of complexity of relatedness, adults in therapy are not infants or children and do live in bodies that are fully sexualized, so that after puberty many early or organizational-level relational experiences become expressed in sexual terms. What follows is a series of vignettes that illustrate how sexuality expressed within the organizing experience can be handled.

Searles: Love in the Countertransference

Psychoanalyst Harold Searles, staff psychiatrist at the Chestnut Lodge inpatient facility in Maryland, broke the taboo on talking about sexual feelings in his now-classic 1959 article, "Oedipal Love in the Counter-Transference." Searles reported that since he had begun doing intensive psychotherapy some 9 years previous, he discovered that with every one of his hospitalized patients who had shown major improvement he had experienced romantic and erotic desires and fantasies. He reported that such feelings have generally persisted for long periods of time and were accompanied by a variety of other feelings, including frustration, separation anxiety, guilt, and grief—feelings he reported as being a part of his own analysis some 5 years before. He reported that the first few times he experienced erotic feelings toward a patient, he reacted with anxiety, embarrassment, and guilt. His training, as well as the psychoanalytic literature of the time, moved him to hold suspect any strong feelings on the part of the analyst toward his patient, especially sexual feelings. He therefore remained convinced for a long time that he had an unusual propensity for exploiting analytic patients for the purpose of grappling with his own unresolved Oedipus conflicts.

But, contrary to the usual professional opinion of his time, Searles (1959) had come to believe through his years of experience "that there is a direct correlation between, on the one hand, the affective intensity with which the analyst experiences an awareness of [erotic] feelings … and, on the other hand, the depth of maturation which the patient achieves in the analysis" (p. 183). He emphasized that it is the analyst's own inner awareness of these intense feelings that is the important thing, not directly expressing them to the patient. He did, however, acknowledge that more deeply disturbed patients generally do need more direct affective expressions than better-developed patients. He gave an example:

> An … experience of this sort … occurred in approximately the twelfth month of my work with a 50-year-old, single woman who was suffering from schizophrenia with marked depressive features. Thus far I had seen her to be a drab, colourless, wraithlike individual devoid of any capacity to arouse romantic or erotic feelings in anyone. I was therefore astonished upon awakening, one morning, to remember that I had had a sexual dream about her. From now on I began seeing her with new interest, and it was not long before I began to discern previously-unnoticed little evidences of seductiveness on her part. In the ensuing several months, she progressed to the point where she was so attractively feminine a person that it would not be difficult for any man to think of her in sexual terms, and sexual conflicts which had played an integral role in her schizophrenic breakdown came now into the therapeutic investigation. I found every evidence, subsequently, that my sexual dream about her had constituted a most valuable landmark in a deepening, and eventually successful, therapeutic relationship. (p. 184)

Searles (1959) reported that erotic feelings experienced toward a patient of one's own sex are likely to be particularly anxiety provoking.

> During my first two years of work at Chestnut Lodge, I was seeing a paranoid schizophrenic man in his middle thirties, a sensitive, highly intelligent, physically handsome man who manifested a gratifying

improvement over the course of our work. But after about eighteen months, I began growing uneasy at the intensity of the fond and romantic feelings which I had come to experience toward him, and particularly alarmed during one of our sessions, while we were sitting in silence and a radio not far away was playing a tenderly romantic song, when I suddenly felt that this man was dearer to me than anyone else in the world, including my wife. Within a few months I succeeded in finding "reality" reasons why I would not be able to continue indefinitely with his therapy, and he moved to a distant part of the country. To be sure, he had been voicing a persistent desire to make this move, all through our work together; but I am certain that it was my anxiety about these recently-recognized responses in myself that caused me to find, now, that it somehow made excellent sense for him to leave here. Subsequently, upon carefully examining the detailed notes I had kept concerning his case, I saw many indications that I had fled from going further, with him, into the exploration of the intense fondness which had prevailed, behind a screen of mutual rejection, between himself and his mother. For many months I had endured from him such sarcasm, scorn, and rejection as he and his mother had characteristically directed at one another; but I was unable to brave the fondness which now came up in the transference. (p. 185)

Four years later, after the completion of his personal analysis, in which Searles (1959) had become more familiar and at ease with various kinds of erotic feelings, he reported on therapy with a man in his early 40s diagnosed as paranoid schizophrenic:

After an initial two-year period in which negative feelings seemed clearly to predominate in the transference and the countertransference, I began finding myself feeling surprisingly fond of him, and to be having not-infrequent dreams of a fond and sexual nature about him. One morning, as I was putting on a carefully-selected necktie, I realized that I was putting it on for him, more than for any of the several other patients I was to see that day.

He referred to us, now in the third and fourth years of our work, as being married, and at other times expressed deeply affective fantasies of our becoming married. When I took him out for a ride in my car for one of the sessions, I was amazed at the wholly delightful fantasy and feeling I had, namely that we were lovers on the threshold of marriage, with a whole world of wonders opening up before us. ... When I drove home from work at the end of the day I was filled with a poignant realization of how utterly and tragically unrealizable were the desires of this man who had been hospitalized continually, now, for fourteen years. But I felt that, despite the tragic aspect of this, what we were going through was an essential, constructive part of what his recovery required; these needs of his would have to be experienced, I felt, in however unrealizable a form at first, so that they could become reformulated, in the course of our work, into channels which would lead to greater possibilities for gratification. And I felt a solid sense of personal satisfaction that I was able, now, to go through feeling-experiences with a male patient which years before, even in much lesser degree than this, would have scared me away. (p. 185)

Searles (1959) wrote that erotic feelings of the therapist have four potential sources:

1. The analyst's feeling responses to the patient's transference, that is, the reciprocal feelings of love to the patient's past loving experiences
2. The countertransference in the classical sense—the therapist responding to the patient in terms of transference feelings carried over from a figure out of the analyst's own earlier years
3. The appeal that the gratifyingly improving patient makes to the narcissistic residue in the analyst's personality, the Pygmalion in him, as it were
4. The genuine reality of the analyst–patient situation in that the nearer a patient comes to the termination of his analysis, the more he becomes, per se, a likeable, admirable, and lovable human being

Searles (1959) concludes his consideration of erotic countertransference feelings by linking them to the many unresolved feelings of love and sex that are transgenerationally transferred to children from their parents' own past sexual and incestuous experiences. Searles' work illustrates the complexity of sexual feelings in psychotherapy and their possible source.

Ogden: Split-Off Homoerotic Brutalization

In the first session with Mr. D, San Francisco psychoanalyst Thomas H. Ogden (1997) was informed that his new client had been terminated by six previous analysts.

> The patient carried himself and spoke in a way that conveyed a sense of arrogance, aloofness, and self-importance; at the same time, this deportment had a brittleness to it that made readily apparent that the patient's superior tone of voice and demeanor thinly disguised feelings of fear, worthlessness, and desperation. (p. 35)

Mr. D declared he would never be the one to speak first in a session, and that if Ogden attempted to wait him out the session would be wasted in silence.

> Mr. D's presentation of himself intrigued me and stirred feelings of competitiveness in me. He had thrown down the gauntlet and I would prove myself to be more adept and agile than the previous six analysts. In the initial interview I was also aware that I was unconsciously being invited to take the role of a suitor and that there was a fantasied homosexual sadomasochistic scene that was already beginning to take shape in the transference-countertransference. At the same time, I recognized that the fantasy of entering into a competitive game protected me from fully feeling the deadly seriousness of the intense contempt and hatred that I was encountering. In addition, the narcissistic/competitive fantasy protected me from feelings of being trapped in the web that Mr. D was already beginning to spin with his imperiously controlling, instructions regarding the way in which the analysis was to be conducted. I imagined that long years of isolation awaited both of us if we were to undertake analysis together. (p. 36)

Ogden (1997) responded to the gauntlet by saying that Mr. D seemed to envision the analysis as one or the other of the participants brutalizing the other until the one being brutalized could not stand it any longer and quit, and that he had no interest in brutalizing, being brutalized, or participating in Mr. D's brutalization of himself. He agreed to be the first to speak in each hour, but only when he had something to say, and that it might take a bit of time each session for Ogden to locate his experience and have something to say, but he would not attempt to wait him out. Mr. D seemed to relax on finding that Ogden had managed to find something to say that was not a sadistic attack or a compromise position.

> At the outset of each of the meetings with Mr. D, I attempted to find words to convey what it felt like being with him in that particular moment. I (silently) hypothesized that both the fantasies and feelings about brutalization and the fantasies reflecting manic excitement (competition) in the transference-countertransference represented forms of defense against the experience of inner deadness, which deadness was symbolized by Mr. D's feeling that he had nothing in him with which to begin the hours (to begin his story). I would have to be the one to bring life to the analysis (to create history) each time we met. Almost always as I began the hour, I had the conscious fantasy that I was giving the patient and the analysis mouth-to-mouth resuscitation. I chose not to tell Mr. D about this fantasy directly in order not to demean him nor to prematurely address the homosexual aspects of the transference-countertransference. (pp. 37–38)

Ogden (1997) reported his struggle not to sound rote, hackneyed, or clichéd at the beginning of the hours so he would not add further to Mr. D's lifelessness. On one occasion, he told Mr. D that he found himself imagining attempting to lure him into trusting him, but that he realized that this not only would be futile but also would be destructive since any "winning" on his part would be an alienating theft. In response, Mr. D described his continual vigilance in combating theft—burglar alarms, safes, antitheft devices. Although this comment was said in direct response to Ogden's remark, there was no acknowledgment of that, and Ogden was left feeling that there was nothing human holding the hours together.

Mr. D had chosen not use the couch. Six months into therapy, Ogden (1997) thought for a moment that he saw tears in Mr. D's eyes but could not be sure. He said to Mr. D that whether there were tears or not, what had happened reflected the sadness of their situation.

> Mr. D sat quietly for a minute and said that he had not been moved by my "little speech." He then returned to his silence. After about five

minutes, I said I thought that what had just happened between us must reflect something basic to his experience. I had felt sadness, part of which was no doubt my own, something attributable to my own sense of extreme loneliness in being with him. I added that nonetheless I felt that in part I was feeling something for him, in his stead. I said that I had in the past tried to talk with him about it, but that his replies had always made me feel as if I were either crazy or stupid or both. I said that if I were not in a position to feel some confidence in my ability to differentiate between what feels real and what does not, I would find it a great strain to have my perceptions drawn into question in such a fundamental way. I told him that it would surprise me greatly if at important points in his life, he had not felt this type of strain in relation to his own ability to differentiate which parts of his experience and perceptions were real and which were not. It seemed from my experience in being with him that he must have felt powerfully assaulted in his efforts to hold onto a conviction about the truth of what he thought, saw, felt, heard, and so on. (pp. 39–40)

Ignoring what had just been said, Mr. D commented that the only accurate word that had been spoken in all these months was "brutalized" in the first session. Although he had not been beaten or abused as a child, he nonetheless felt that he had been brutalized in subtle and not-so-subtle ways. He was, however, not interested in talking about his childhood. Ogden (1997) reports that this exchange was the closest they had come to talking with each other, and that in the ensuing weeks Mr. D became "increasingly antagonistic and disparaging of me and the analysis" (p. 40). Ogden ventured an interpretation:

I told him that I thought that his having acknowledged feeling understood by me, if only in my use of that single word, had led him to feel that things between the two of us had become wildly and dangerously out of control. I said that I thought that what currently appeared on the surface to be his brutalizing me felt to me more like an effort to protect me by getting me to throw him out. I added that I suspected that if I did not soon terminate our meetings he would end the analysis as the only way he felt he had at his disposal to protect me from what he feared to be his endlessly escalating brutalization of me. (p. 41)

During the following 6 months, Mr. D turned his chair each session so that its back was to the analyst. Ogden (1997) formulated that during the foregoing period Mr. D had in fantasy put him into the fragile remainder of life and hope he possessed. It was Ogden's job to speak and feel for him around his profound sense of loneliness and sadness while Mr. D sadomasochistically attacked him for imagining he could safeguard their lives in the face of his brutality.

> Extreme splitting of the brutalized and brutalizing aspects of the patient had been a necessary condition for any form of relatedness to me to be sustained. In the course of the analysis, the patient began to experience for himself the rudiments of sadness and compassion for the aspects of himself which he had projected into me and had experienced through me. (p. 42)

Ogden (1997) chose to call this encounter "sadomasochistic" and "homoerotic," thus recognizing the essentially sexualized nature of the interaction involved, even though there is no direct mention of sex. My reading of his text suggests that the erotic exchange being replicated dated to the patient's sensual organizing experiences in earliest infancy that were somehow brutalized. His capacity for relationships was severely stunted by his primary identification (A. Balint, 1943) with the brutalizing other, who has foreclosed any possibility of communicative exchanges that could lead to symbiotic, bonding, or secure attachment experiences. By working to establish any kind of communicative connection whatsoever with his patient and then seeking to interpret the compulsive need to rupture that connection—to break the links, as it were—Ogden gradually moved Mr. D from disorganized attachment toward an attachment position in which relationship growth experiences toward maturity and mature sexuality could become possible.

Moss and Zeavin: Having a Man

> Ms. A entered analysis 5 years ago, a 35-year-old woman troubled by a sense that she was "not as happy as she might be." At that time she was single and having a series of unsatisfactory and transient sexual relationships with men. She characterized her desire in terms of her need to

have these men want her. Her focus would be on getting them to want to have sex with her, which seemed to quiet her own wanting for a time. Frequently, these liaisons would cease after one encounter, and Ms. A would be bewildered and alarmed, feeling "as though I am nothing." (Moss & Zeavin 1999, p. 206)

Psychoanalysts Donald Moss and Lynne Zeavin (1999) reported that over time in therapy Ms. A's self-esteem stabilized, and she realized that her desire was totally organized around getting a man, so that often she would find herself with men she did not even like. Having a penis inside her made her feel fuller initially, but when the man did not call, that meant she was not wanted. Despite great strides and economic successes at her job, not having a relationship with a man was seen as evidence of her inferiority to other women who *did have*. In transference, her analyst *had*—men, babies, a kind of vital internal substance. In comparison, she felt herself "full of shit." On the other hand, a less-than-perfect man mirrored her own failings, her own inferiority. If other women did not want what he had, then how good was he, and how good was she?

Shadowing Ms. A's conscious preoccupying fantasy of getting and having a man is her wish to be at the center of a woman's attention and from there to receive her approbation. Her orienting heterosexual fantasy of getting a man, therefore, is linked to a homosexual fantasy in which she establishes an erotic tie with a woman against whom she can prove herself superior. She must outdo all others, and she must succeed in this outdoing for all time; otherwise she feels herself to be nothing. The analysis has revealed the painful wish to be first: first with her mother and then—that repressed wish's derivative expression—first with a man. Longing for a woman has been replaced in consciousness with longing for a man. And the longing is to be wanted, to be all important, to be so valuable and so superior that no one will ever be able to outdo her. What Ms. A visits and revisits in her recurrent disappointment is the hope that she possesses what it takes to win. What she ultimately wants is her mother's love. She wants to fill the mind of the mother. ... The interworkings of envy, longing, and narcissistic fragility in this woman might well, to a naive eye, appear to be the consequence of intractable penis envy.

Such an interpretation might be equivalent in this case to Freud's attribution of disappointment in his case of the female homosexual. Disappointment figures largely in Ms. A, as it does for Freud's young woman. Both women might be understood to want something from their mothers that is unforthcoming. While each has developed a different manifest solution, the underlying fantasy content seems to be a hybrid of heterosexual desire and homoerotic longing. ... Each retreats from both her own body and some of her own objects so as to maintain a fantasy that the mother is still accessible: that *her* love and *her* body will be renunciation's reward. (pp. 209–210.)

My view of the dynamics reported in this case is that, despite their more advanced developmental appearance, the compulsive need to search for fulfillment and then somehow to avoid or rupture that possibility stems from the organizing level of relatedness experience. The content, whether of being first with mother, a man, or the analyst, neatly sets the stage for repeated ruptures for which she can disown responsibility.

Buchanan: Ensnared by Eros

My Introduction

The ebb and flow of the connection/disconnection dimension is to the organizing experience what verbal free association is to the neurotic experience. That is, the ability to free associate and the developing ability to sustain interpersonal connection are both ultimately unattainable goals that serve as perceivable backdrops against which glitches in the processes can be noted and studied. In the following account of a countertransference experience, an attractive, seductive man succeeds in temporarily pulling the rug out from under his newly licensed therapist by creating sexual arousal, first in himself and later in her. At one point, he almost stops his therapy because he is failing to ensnare her in an emotional connection through the only means he feels he has at his disposal: Eros.

Paradoxically, as the therapist permits herself to succumb to the arousal that for this patient spells connectedness, it gradually becomes clear how his lifelong passion of stimulating himself and women has backfired, repeatedly leaving him in a lost, lonely, and untransformed organizing state. His erotic stimulations function to destroy rather than to create connections. Here, we watch his erotic maneuvers nearly destroy again his hope of someday feeling human.

Freud (1905/1975) has taught us not only that sexuality is ubiquitous but also that it takes myriad forms. The analytic engagement reported here not only confirms Freud's correctness but also points to forms and transformations of sexuality not dreamt by Freud. Therapists tend to be unable or reluctant to discuss therapeutic involvements that include physiological arousal. Here, a courageous and emotionally available therapist skillfully is led into Eros's tender trap—and what a nightmare for her it is—a trap that nonetheless appears therapeutically essential.

During 40 years of supervising and consulting on difficult cases, I have had frequent occasion to review therapeutic work in which the sexuality of the therapist has become somehow stimulated or engaged in response to the client's erotic transference or projective identifications. National studies reveal that the overwhelming majority of therapists (87%) report experiencing sexual attraction to clients (Pope, Keith-Spiegel, & Tabachnick, 1986). Further studies make it clear that sexuality in therapists is poorly addressed in training programs (Pope, Sonne, & Holroyd, 1993). The complexities of a newly licensed therapist trying to deal with powerful erotic/psychotic projections into the countertransference are amply illustrated in the study that follows.

Ensnared by Eros

Contributed by Suzanne Buchanan

I have real relatedness with Tom. We are bonded, have a language, jokes, topics of interest, and in general, a way we are when we are together. We eat and drink, laugh, cry, get angry or sad. We suffer together. We endure together. And we enjoy each other—and all this within the therapeutic hour. We are as real together as we know how to be. In addition to being real together, there are times when we are able to observe the interaction that takes place between us as observers, commenting on the process, trying to understand what is going on. Oftentimes, that understanding takes the form of trying to understand the past in the present. This activity is of much more importance to me than to Tom. Just being together is enough for Tom. We never know what can happen. As the relatedness evolves, there is always that sense of being in uncharted waters.

Tom began therapy with a focus centered on stress reduction. When we first began, he was in a state of complete exhaustion or collapse. His stress level was extreme and included bleeding ulcers. Our time together centered on his telling me about his anger and frustration with his job, his relationships, and life in general. He talked a lot about how his back and neck hurt. He was suffering from migraine headaches, long-term lower-back pain, sleeplessness at night, and extreme sleepiness during the day.

For me, the work was not stimulating. He was a nice man who used words in a fun way, and his sense of humor was enjoyable. I felt empathy for his suffering and said so. We began a course of relaxation exercises. Often during these times, Tom would go into a deep sleep. I felt that he trusted me and that this was a good indicator of his comfort with me. I was also comfortable with him.

At some point during the year, it felt like we were stuck, like he and I were merely doing more of the same. He was making headway in stress management. He was much more relaxed, a lot less angry, and he was feeling considerably better. I found myself wondering, "Now what?" I did not sense that we had reached the end of our relating, by any means. Although his stress symptoms were lessened, I sensed that in time something more would come up.

Tom was a toucher. He found ways to stand just close enough to come into contact with me. He asked for a hug. He was able to pick up the fact that I was also a toucher and said so. I did not think too much about it at the time. Hugging seemed to me a ritualized way of greeting and parting, a lot like handshaking. I did not realize then the significance of touching or the possible danger or importance of it.[1]

One day, he came and told me he was going to stop coming to therapy. I was surprised. I felt we had a really good connection. I

---

[1] Note that the treatment occurred in Southern California, where touching and hugging are a greater part of everyday life and psychotherapy than in many other locales.

sensed that what we were doing and would do was important, yet he was terminating. I felt disappointed and confused. With seemingly nothing to lose, I asked, "Tom, how do you feel about me?"

Heretofore, the interaction had been nonstimulating. Surprisingly, this man who had not said too much to me of a personal nature began to tell me everything he liked about me, from the top of my head to the tip of my toes, and it was far from nonstimulating: In essence, he was the most seductive man I had ever met. I felt as if he had made love to me—and yet I had all my clothes on. It was exciting. I thought to myself, "Wait a minute. Should I be feeling this way? I am enjoying myself and him, and I feel confused." I had heard mention of something called sexual countertransference, but I had no personal notion of what that meant. Did I really want to mention this to my mentor/consultant? I had my doubts. Perhaps I could just go over the rules with Tom. This was probably some kind of brief, passing experience. At this point, I began to question the meaning of touching in this relationship.

Well, Tom decided to stay in therapy because he wanted to, because he was enjoying me, and he made it clear his interest was in me and not in therapy. Somehow that seemed okay. I knew that relatedness was the issue, and that "therapy" was a word that did not mean anything to him. I told him that what we were doing was therapy, and that not everyone did therapy the same way. My mentor, Dr. H,[2] managed to give me some understanding of sexual transference and countertransference as potentially useful. I began to see that sexual feelings could be an expectable and acceptable part of therapy under certain conditions. However, I experienced embarrassment, which I hated admitting. I sometimes felt guilty and uncomfortable about the strong sexual feelings and ideas about Tom that I found myself experiencing.

Tom just accepted how he felt and said that being with me was why he came, and that he was not in agreement with my explanation about the potential role of feelings or their appropriate limits in therapy. We jokingly called it my "psychobabble." I had

---

[2] Lawrence Hedges.

carefully explained to him that I understood how close he felt to me. And since he was a man with adult genitalia, of course that sense of closeness might register in his body as sexual attraction and arousal. I informed him that after an outside consultation I had found that this was not all that unusual. I assured him that there was a lot we could both learn about him by studying such feelings. He laughed a little and said that if I needed to think that way, that was okay. However, in his words, "I am a dirty old man who would like to jump your bones."

When I asked Dr. H how long Tom's response could go on this way, he said it could be some time. The reason was that while Tom seeks connections through sexual stimulation, at some level he also knows how to use sexuality to avoid or to rupture possible connections. This cycle of search and rupture, connect and discon-nect, *is* Tom's organizing level transference that he seeks to work out in therapy. The question is, can he do it?

Uncharted waters always have surprises. One day, I was attempting to get into my office with a teapot full of water in one hand and the keys in the other when Tom showed up. When he was standing right behind me, I looked up at him. Suddenly, he kissed me on the lips. I was horrified—not because he had kissed me, but because my lips responded. *Now* what is going on? So far, the uncharted waters have yielded up excitement, enjoyment, and now responding lips. Now, I not only questioned touching in the present; I also talked with him about not misunderstanding or misreading the touching in the past. I was careful to explain that it would be unethical and unthinkable that I could ever become involved with him. I also told him to feel free to express his feel-ings and fantasies. He did so with real feeling.

Sessions continued, and what I seemed to be seeing right before my eyes was a man falling in love with me. I found responsiveness within myself. I was learning to enjoy him more and more. One day, he did verbalize that he loved me, and he guessed he could never have me. I was feeling close to him and fond of him and sad. I said so.

It had become our custom to sit in two wing chairs that had an ottoman between them. And at the close of a session in the second year of therapy, Tom leapt from his chair. His knees landed on the ottoman between us and both his hands took hold of the ends of the arms of my wing chair. His face came close to mine. He had pinned me in so that I could not move. He had surprised me. Yet, the movement was so like that of a very young boy that I found myself saying, after what seemed a long time, "Tom, I am not comfortable with this." He did not respond right away, but in time he removed his hands and himself, remarking, "I have to make you more comfortable with me."

Tom is the first client I ever dreamt about. The theme was one of not being safe. To return to Dr. H he told me that at the worst I might need to terminate the relationship if the transference became overly intrusive or threatened to become violent. The wing-chair episode could be the beginning of something violent, so extreme caution with the transference was in order. I felt reassured by Dr. H's advice and his availability to me. I felt sad thinking about terminating what had become for me a very meaningful relationship.

I began the next session with Tom by recounting the wing-chair experience. I spoke of how I felt about our last session and of what I needed from him in the future: "We don't need me being afraid of you. If I'm afraid of you, I won't be able to listen to you. What happened in our last meeting frightened me. I am not saying you're a "bad boy." But if I am worried about what you might do, I can't be tuned in to you. You must stay in your chair. You must not touch me or startle me. I want to work with you. I don't want to let you do anything that would make me have to end our relationship. I know you have intense feelings. There is a difference between intense feelings and actions. So from now on, stay in your chair. You must not touch me or startle me."

Tom's response was, "You don't need to be afraid. I need your approval. You remember I told you how frustrated I am, but I would rather have that frustration than not see you. We have such good nonverbal feeling."

What a relief. It would have broken my heart to have to end that there. And so, the uncharted waters continued. Things slowed down for awhile. The contact was mostly visual, but it still seemed sexually stimulating to me. I was thinking about this man between sessions. I sometimes avoided his looking at me. He was clearly enjoying me in erotic ways. I wanted him to use me in the way he needed to, but what was all this sexual stimulation, and what were those many thoughts about him between sessions? This felt confusing.

He said he kept thinking that one day I would give in, and that he would never tell, that the rules are stupid. His hope was that one day I would let down the final wall. He asked if this was going to be unrequited love. I answered, "Yes." It felt tragic to me. I went to Dr. H. He said move away from the tragic sense and back to work. This was the first connection Tom had ever experienced that was near safe. We did not know yet why he must experience it as so erotic.

I had a long period of time [with Tom] in which I felt frustrated, sexually aroused. I knew it was up to me to keep that wall up, to be there for Tom in the way that was best for him. This was hard. Sometimes I felt such intense longing for him that it was confusing. I felt embarrassed, silly, and guilty.

In an attempt to divert his attention while maintaining our relating, I introduced jigsaw puzzles. It turned out to be a very good idea, something we both enjoyed doing. I also thought it quite a good idea to sublimate some of those sexual feelings we each were having. I was feeling quite good about what I had done. But one day, I was horrified to realize that I had cleverly introduced a way that to Tom virtually concretized the sexual act via puzzle pieces—so much for sublimation.

Well, we are still enjoying puzzling, as we have come to call it. Over time, the way we puzzle has grown to include more than just working in the same area of the puzzle; it includes my handing him pieces as I notice what he needs or might need. Now, we have added another dimension of working parts of the puzzle while each of us is in our own little space, much like parallel play. Puzzling is still a warm, pleasant experience for both of us, a closeness without words.

One day during session, he was looking into my eyes, and I was looking back. I was feeling closer and closer to him. He was in his wing chair and I was in mine; suddenly, I felt myself merged with this man. It felt wonderful. I was struggling to say something, and finally I asked him, "Tom, where are you?"

"Inside you," came the answer.

It was time for session to end, and I needed to hurry to get in my car and attend the weekly case conference group of which I am a member. My legs were weak; I was stumbling and lightheaded and feeling completely undone. Tom and I walked down the stairs to our respective cars. He remembered the no-touch rule. At the next session, he commented on how hard it had been, knowing that he was not supposed to touch me in the face of how much he wanted to help me. He knew how unorganized and out of charge of my own body I felt—uncharted waters and more surprises, and back to Dr. H.

At our next meeting, I told Tom I thought things were moving too fast. I hoped the roller-coaster ride was not disturbing him too much. I recognized that he was choosing to bare his soul to me, and that I was choosing to be open to it. I said, "Why would we want to stop that? We are finding out about parts of ourselves. Girlfriends and fucks are a dime a dozen, but what we have is very, very special. Now, we talk all we want about anything, and it is rather nice that we have this law to keep us safe. Our being together sets off things in you and in me. It has sent me in a lot of different directions. As you know, I am seeking consultation, and I want you to know that I have support from other professionals. I'll be okay. We have a very special relationship. Things happen in our relationship that don't happen other places. You know that mothers give birth to sons and have very special relationships. I am not saying that mothers never have sexual thoughts about their sons or sons about their mothers, but it is always fundamentally impossible for mothers and sons to have sex without it being destructive to both. Our relationship is special. To destroy this unbelievable thing we have developed would be very wrong. It's like incest. We have no choice but to keep going. This intensity of feeling could last a long time, or it could come and go. We will do whatever we need to keep being together. I know you are suffering greatly. I, too, am suffering in my own way. Yet, hope is increasing, our connection is good, and we are finding ways to process disconnections as they occur. Dr. H. says that when near-overwhelming feelings occur on either side, we need to consider how they disrupt our flow, our harmony together, and serve to throw us back into that lost and lonely place we know so well. I want to know myself, and you want to know yourself, and we are finding out about parts of ourselves." So, on we went to more uncharted waters and more surprises.[3]

The intrusive sexual transference continued. There were times when I think I managed things well, and there were other times when I visualized newspaper headlines telling some sordid story about me because I had let that wall give way inappropriately. I am thankful for Dr. H and his continual belief that I could do this the right way, and for his suggestions and direction and all his under-standing and empathy for both myself and my client.

At one point, Dr. H mentioned another therapist who might talk to me about having had a similar experience. We were able to meet, and he had much empathy. What a relief to know that what was going on was happening not only to me.

Once before we left the parking lot, Tom warned me to drive carefully. I asked him, "What would you do if something happened to me?" The look on his face was one of pure panic and told me all I needed to know. He had told me often of how much he liked "we." What we were doing together seemed important to me, and, despite arousals, I understood that what was happening was not adult sexuality. Tom had had a dream earlier in treatment of stand-ing between two buildings with a woman. The buildings had no doors and no windows, no way in and no way out. The male-female togetherness was the only vestige of connection, the only possible bridge between two walled-off souls. This was the essence of his experience.

The sexual nature of the countertransference has currently been waning for me. Perhaps I am avoiding experiencing it. It was

---

[3] One frequent form of countertransference to the organizing experience is that the continued rupture of connections stimulates the therapist's organizing level of expe-rience in the countertransference (Hedges, 1994b, 1994c, 2000b).

powerful, confusing, frustrating, and at times disruptive to my functioning. Tom still mentions sexuality, but the power of it is not so overwhelming to me any longer. That sense of "we-ness" is still there and growing even in new ways. Someday, I hope Tom and I will understand and be able to verbalize about our voyage in a clear way. As of yet, we are not there, and the waters are still largely uncharted.

Tom had another dream, one of being where several roads were under construction, yet there was no road that would take him to any destination as they were all unfinished. Roads connect people and places. I asked if it were okay that the roads were still being constructed. He said, "Yes—I think that is where we are." Life-giving connections are being built for Tom, and that is enough for him. We are together doing the building. The threat of destructive sexuality has subsided as construction proceeds.

It feels like the right thing for both of us to be doing. I cannot imagine it being possible to do this building together without uncharted waters or without surprises. There is a unique reality within our therapeutic hours together that just does not exist anywhere else for either of us. It is a special reality of attachment, closeness, comfort, play, struggle, and sometimes suffering. There is no real clear-cut blueprint for us. We have and are still creating a reality that is building structure and meaning into both of our existences—to such an extent that neither of us will ever be the same.

I am becoming more and more aware that if I stay present and am open, he can find me. What he needs is to find me in his search for relatedness. Theory is a helpful guide, and as a therapist, I have great regard for theory. Human beings need other human beings who can be present not only with theory but also with real aliveness, so that the search for relatedness results in usable human contact. That search can take many different forms. Sexual transference and countertransference is one of those forms. It was the way in which we initiated contact and began to study the breaks in contact that eventually opened the way to other forms of human contact. We are all in search of human contact all our lives. When contact is empathic and timely, it permits the transformation of our relatedness possibilities from concrete and disruptive forms into increasingly abstract, symbolic, coherent, and cooperative forms.

There are times of wonder when another person meets us in our search, and out of the contact comes relatedness. Our forms and ways of searching for relating can be limited, and they can expand. Our early experience with Mother limited each of our searches for relatedness in some way or another. We then look a long time for another human being who can meet us in our search for relatedness. I am grateful that I was open to Tom in his search for relatedness. I would not have wanted to miss any part of it.

I have come to believe that erotic or sexual energy was for each of us the channel open on an unconscious level that permitted us to connect and to have that connection displaced toward other kinds of connection. It was the way we had of connecting and developing relatedness. I think it has opened other ways of relating. The importance of this connection is that such an interaction was needed to establish relating and a deep bond. Out of this bond came "we," and out of "we" will come "self" and "other" in some more differentiated way.

After I read this part of the chapter to Tom, he made it clear that his feelings for me were as strong as ever, that nothing had changed for him. He continues to express his feelings and wishes and his desire for me. He says that I know more about him than anyone, and that he enjoys being with me more than anyone. I recently told him that I thought when he was young he gave up on being loved, and that he then withdrew; he went inside himself and created an internal world of excitement. He confirmed that this could be true. I went on to say that I thought there were two Suzannes for him, the one in his created internal world who was perennially arousing and the one in the external world who shared our times together. He agreed. During our sessions, he has experienced both the Suzanne in the room and the Suzanne in his internal world. We discussed how impossible it is at times to know the differences between the two experiences. Was it that he got overstimulated and then withdrew from contact, or that he was understimulated and withdrew into private stimulation?

Tom had a critical mother. He knows he is safe from criticism from me. Tom experienced some kind of early failure to be loved in a way that would permit him emotional growth. Tom has never been able to be involved with any woman in an integrated way involving sex and closeness. He does not know how to initiate contact this way. In his fantasies of sex with me, he says, "You want it as much as I do." He tells me he would never do anything unless I wanted him to. These comments remind me of the primary infant bond in which the infant experiences Mother as passively merged with his own desire, a bond in which the infant is the one that needs to be loved and cared for.

My thinking at this point is that in some way Tom's primary love became overeroticized. Tom still desperately wants to be touched. This early primary longing and yearning to be touched is equated with love and is mixed with his biologically adult sexual desire. There is a confusion or fusion between his fantasy world of sexual fulfillment and the features he perceives in the external world.

In time, when enough psychic roads are built, we can expect that Tom will be able to connect with people in ways through which he can be integrated and find fulfillment in his external world rather than through his fantasized fulfillments—which, in fact, are not fulfilling but excruciatingly painful, as his beginning complaints indicated. For now, we can appreciate the constriction of his connections and the gradual expansion of symbiotic bonds in which psychic stimulation can empathically proceed between two people.

Tom's compulsive attempts to destroy the continuity of our connecting, our relatedness, with invasive hypersexuality have served throughout his life to ensure that no transformation of his early internal world would occur. His pattern now slowly gives way to sustained and sustaining relatedness.

My Commentary

Sexually sensitive interactions from psychotherapeutic work have seldom been reported in our literature—and even more rarely in this uncertain and courageous manner. Training programs seldom, if ever, include courses designed to explore the sexuality of people training to be psychotherapists. Issues of erotic transference and countertransference are not given an appropriate place in our training programs. As a profession, our neglect of studying sexual feelings in the therapeutic situation has no doubt contributed to the state of affairs in which the largest single cause of malpractice suits involves accusations of a sexual nature. The seemingly impenetrable wall of silence about sexual feelings in the therapist marks a taboo that is slowly being broken down by studies such as Pope et al.'s *Sexual Feelings in Psychotherapy* (1993) and Hilton's (1993) "Sexuality in Psychotherapy."

Traditionally trained therapists, with limited training in and understanding of the nature of primitive transference and expectable countertransference responsiveness to early developmental issues, no doubt would experience difficulty with the foregoing vignette. They might ask such questions as: Wasn't Suzanne being sexually provocative herself in the early stages? How clear was the therapist about her own boundaries? Did Suzanne get her own sexual and merger issues worked out in her own therapy? Didn't she actively participate in creating a mutually seductive situation? I submit that this kind of Monday morning quarterbacking completely misses the point of what is happening in this sort of therapeutic relationship. People who get stuck on such questioning are not equipped to consider the vital nature of this kind of work with organizing experience. These questions do not help us consider therapeutic work that has a strong impact on early layerings of personality formation.

I find more often than not that it is the less-experienced therapists who dare reach out to organizing-level clients in deeply personal and life-giving ways. In a certain sense, it may be their naïveté and inexperience that allows them to be so courageous. And, it is not surprising that in their eagerness and awkwardness they often get themselves into various kinds of pickles. More experienced therapists tend to be frightened by the obvious dangers such clients present and horrified by the intense relatedness they demand. These therapists thus tend to remain content not to work transformationally with primitive personality issues.

My book *Facing the Challenge of Liability in Psychotherapy: Practicing Defensively* (Hedges, 2000a) won the Gradiva Award for the Best Book of the Year from the National Association for the Advancement of Psychoanalysis. In that book, I detail aspects of primitive transferences that can potentially lead to false accusation against therapists and how therapists can proceed safely with this kind of work (Hedges, 2000a, revised in 2007). In my books, *Working the Organizing Experience: Transforming Psychotic, Schizoid, and Autistic States* (1994c) and *In Search of the Lost Mother of Infancy* (1994b), I consider in theory, with numerous case examples, exactly how this work can be safely and effectively accomplished. In my book *Terrifying Transferences: Aftershocks of Childhood Trauma* (Hedges, 2000b), 12 therapists submitted casework that illustrates how organizing-level transferences and countertransferences can be explored.

For our purposes here, the crucial aspect of this vignette is that it allows us to think about the ways a sincere and well-intentioned therapist who is receptive to deep personality issues may become emotionally involved and then derailed if not guided by theory and consultation. People dealing with organizing-level issues have a lifetime of experience in making sure that meaningful and potentially helpful human contact *does not occur.* Yet, like Kafka's characters, they continue to search in myriad ways for just the life-giving contact they compulsively foreclose once they get close enough to sense it (Hedges, 1983/2003). The very way in which they approach relatedness often ensures that it will not occur. The internalized "psychotic mother" transference crops up, and suddenly "something happens" to breach the connections, to break the link. What might have been usable contact is suddenly rendered useless. Such was the way with Tom's intense and intrusive sexuality—his lifelong way of making sure that he would never be able to connect to anyone. But, Suzanne foiled him. She stood steady in the midst of her own psychic and somatic confusions, found consultative help, and slowly moved his seductive manipulations into a place that enabled them to be seen for what they were: desperate attempts learned early in his life to foreclose useful but potentially terrifying contact. The dream of Tom and a woman (maleness and femaleness) standing between two closed-off buildings might be understood not only as a potential locus of linking but also as a transference representation of how the gap between two is created or sustained.

The story of Tom and Suzanne continues from here, with much working through yet to accomplish. Tom must find additional ways to ally himself with Suzanne in the therapeutic task of noticing how each potential contact is spoiled by the intrusion of overstimulation. He must come to understand how he perennially deprives himself of growth-producing experiences by trying to get her to be seductive with him and how he succeeds in alienating her through his seductions. Freud used the words *seduction* and *trauma* interchangeably to indicate that damaging human trauma is the result of stimulation that overwhelms the person's currently operative ego processes. Suzanne shows us how she allowed herself to become overwhelmed, traumatized to the point of threatening the ego processes required for maintaining a therapeutic stance. She then sought ego supports to help her perceive, integrate, and develop creative and usable responsiveness to Tom's lifelong self-destructive dilemmas. Did any of us imagine, when we decided to become psychotherapists, that such demanding requirements might be someday made of us? I think not. But, the choice later becomes clear: Write people off as untreatable or roll up your sleeves and go to work.

4

SYMBIOSIS AND SEPARATION

Mutually Dependent Relatedness

From the earliest beginnings of psyche, channels are organized on the basis of response from the mothering person's body and personality. We can clearly observe the "Mommy-and-me" dance that is forming in the mutual cuing behaviors being established by the third or fourth month of life. These psychological tendrils of mutual relatedness were *metaphorically* termed "symbiosis" by Margaret Mahler (1968). These *internal states* that characterize the symbiosis of the infant are believed to evolve according to growing expectations of attuned and misattuned interactions. In the symbiotic exchange that the infant overlearns, the response of each partner comes to depend on the response of the other. Peaking by the 12th to 18th month, the symbiotic mutuality, the dyadic responsiveness or forms of symbiotic exchange, remain strong through the 24th to 30th months. I follow Mahler's explicitly intended use of the term *symbiosis* as a set of internalized interaction patterns that the infant develops in relation to early caregivers. Basic character and body structure date from early in this period, as the constitutional and personality variables of the infant come into play with the environment, creating the first sense of psychological familiarity and stability.

The possible dimensions for construction of the merged dual-identity dance of the evolving symbiosis are defined and limited by the foundations of the available connect and disconnect modes that were laid down in the physical and psychical patternings established during the previous organizing period. The particular emotional and behavioral patterns established in this primary-bonding relatedness are thought to follow us throughout our lives (as character structures) as we search for closeness, intimacy, security, familiarity, physical security, and love. If some people's stylized search for security and love seems strange, perverse, addictive, or self-abusive, we can only assume <u>that the adult</u> <u>search replicates in some deep emotional way the primary bonding pat-</u> <u>tern that the infant and toddler experienced in the symbiotic exchange</u> <u>with his or her caregiving others.</u> This listening perspective has been developed for use with what has come to be referred to broadly as "borderline personality organization" and the various "character disorders" (Kernberg, 1976) and is essentially a way of understanding various aspects of the preverbal interaction patterns that were established during the symbiotic and separating periods of human development.

All well-developed people evolved interactional patterns or scenarios related to basic emotional bonding or symbiotic experience. I define *scenario* as a listening device for highlighting the interactive nature of the early bonding experience as it manifests itself in the replicating transference based on an analytic re-creation of relatedness forms, patterns, and modes of the symbiotic period. These patterns become transferentially replicated in some form when any two people attempt to engage each other emotionally. The (almost "knee-jerk") emotional dance that forms in any relationship can be studied in terms of an interaction, drama, or set of scenarios that unfold based on deeply entrenched ways each participant has established for experiencing and relating intimately with others. This listening perspective seeks to bring under scrutiny the predominantly preverbal engagement patterns and body configurations that mean attachment, bonding, and love—regardless of what individualized forms those patterns may take. The notion of symbiosis should by no means be construed as searching for or finding harmony and bliss. Rather, it is conceptualized as reflecting or representing the exact and idiosyncratic emotional relatedness patterns as recorded in the child's body/emotional experience during the bonding period (roughly 4 to 24 months, peaking at 18 months).

Précis: Listening to Mutually Dependent (Symbiotic) Experience

Developmental Metaphor

Toddlers are busy learning how to make emotional relationships (both good and bad) work for them. They experience a sense of merger and reciprocity with their primary caregivers, thus establishing many knee-jerk, automatic, characterological, and role-reversible patterns or scenarios of relatedness. Framing the symbiotic relatedness structures entails noting how each person characteristically engages the other and how interactive scenarios evolve from two subjectively formed sets of internalized self-and-other interaction patterns and then coconstructing ways of speaking about what is happening.

Psychotherapeutic Parameters

Traditional diagnosis: borderline personality organization/ character disorders

Developmental metaphor: 4–24 months—symbiosis and separation–individuation

Affects: split "all good" and "all bad"—ambitendent

Transference: replicated preverbal dyadic interactions or scenarios

Resistance: to assume responsibility for differentiating, for renouncing the scenarios

Listening mode: interaction in replicated scenarios, followed by standing against them

Therapeutic modality: replication and differentiation— reverberation

Countertransference: participation in reciprocal mother and infant positions—a "royal road" to understanding merger relatedness

The following vignettes illustrate the ways clients engage therapists in symbiotic scenarios that tap into the therapist's own early scenarios and vice versa. What parallel work (Bromberg, 2006; Stern, 2010) often refers to as "enactments" can be seen in both the organizing-level and symbiotic-level spontaneously relating of client and therapist before they have discovered ways to put words and symbols to the ways they have found to be with each other.

Rosiello: Disavowed Love as the Erotic Countertransference

In her book *Deepening Intimacy in Psychotherapy*, clinical social worker Frances Rosiello (2000) takes a strong stand in favor of the therapeutic effectiveness of allowing her patients to experience their feelings deeply—including their sexual feelings. In numerous case vignettes, she demonstrates how deep body and feeling states cannot be simply spoken by her clients until and unless they have been encouraged first to know about them by experiencing them in the psychotherapy relationship. For example, she speaks of Sean, a handsome, 6-foot, 4-inch blond man in his early 40s with Irish blue eyes and a terrific body.

> He quickly fell in love in the treatment and asked if he could take me for a walk through the park, since he wanted to point out his favorite places. He added that he hoped we would end up, bodies intertwined, making love in a secluded spot. This was quite moving—countertransferentially—in that I felt very emotionally and sexually stimulated by his passions. (p. 7)

Traditional technique suggests the need to interpret his wishes as infantile longings and unconscious needs. But her experience with Sean had demonstrated that genetic interpretations were experienced as restricting his expressive freedom—as though she were building walls around him. He would react with narcissistic injury whenever she interpreted his feelings toward her as incestuous wishes. Rosiello (2000) views verbal interpretations as part of the blank-screen model that sees therapeutic action as inevitably motivated by abstinence. But, Sean was powerfully immersed in his feelings toward her, and his immersion could easily be traumatized by emotional abstinence. "This clinical material clearly poses the question of therapeutic action. Is therapeutic action facilitated by Sean's knowing the information that would make up my interpretation, or is therapeutic action facilitated by Sean's emotional experience in the erotic transference?" (p. 7)

Continuing her emphasis on therapeutic action through the experience of feelings, Rosiello (2000) begins her discussion of her client Benjamin with a dream of her own:

> The dreamer, a woman, is lying in the middle of a bed.
> On her right is a young boy with blond hair. He is fast asleep and faceless. A man begins to get into bed on the side where the boy is sleeping and repeatedly kisses the woman. The man wants to get closer to the woman and walks around the bed to the other side. They begin to kiss and the dreamer feels frightened they'll go too far. In a moment, they

are seated on a bench and the woman says, "We can't do this. I'm your analyst." (p. 29)

Ben had been in treatment for many years with Rosiello (2000) and early on had established an erotic transference that they were both able to speak about openly. Ben expressed many emotions—loving, warm, and tender intimate feelings, sometimes along with feelings of sexual desire that aroused him in session. The dream seemed to represent that the boy in her patient was an obstacle to the man she desired. Two previous girlfriends while Ben was in treatment strongly resembled his therapist, and in time he became convinced that his girlfriends were substitutes for his therapist, and that he occupied a very special place in her life.

> While Ben was dating his most recent girlfriend, his narratives became full of sensual exploits, erotic positions, and details of manipulations with sexual toys. He spoke of a new-found freedom in being allowed to tell formerly forbidden stories to me, a receptive woman. He would look up from the couch and gaze lovingly, saying he had never felt so safe in expressing his emotions and experiences and how lucky he was that he had me. This treatment facet culminated when he turned onto his stomach and asked me to come lie beside him as he slowly played with the fringe on the carpet a few inches from my feet.
>
> I was engaged, mesmerized, and erotically stimulated. During this period, Ben became my favorite patient. I could barely wait for him to enter my office so I could fantasize about him while he spoke about his sexual exploits. I nearly basked in his regret when he wished I was in his bed and of his fantasy of spending the day having sex. At the end of his sessions, he would sit on the couch and remind me that his relationships with women were in lieu of our dating, and he would often end with declarations of love and desire. (p. 31)

Rosiello (2000) reported a conscious awareness of allowing Ben to nourish her narcissism, but also that she did not feel lost in the countertransference. She mirrored his narcissism, enjoying his enjoyment of feeling loved and in love with a woman he experienced as his intellectual equal and who was comfortable with his sexuality. As she began writing an essay on erotic transferences and countertransferences, she became aware that she could write about the patient's love and sexual desire for the analyst, and she could write about the analyst's sexual arousal to the patient's erotic material, but that she really could not write about falling in love with the patient. For her, "It was just a sexual arousal. I reminded myself of an adolescent boy, 'It's just testosterone'" (p. 32). What only slowly dawned on her was that she was considering the erotic countertransference simply as the presence of sexual stimulation but not in terms of love.

Rosiello (2000) reported beginning to worry that maybe there was something wrong with her because she did not feel love for Ben, then maybe that she needed to get back in therapy, then maybe that she was permanently broken because she could not love him. It finally occurred to her, "It's ridiculous to think I have never been in love with a patient," and it was that night that she had the dream in which she desired Benjamin and found a way to love him while still being his analyst. She wondered why it took so long to see this—and whether it was the case that she was comfortable with sexual feelings but not with feeling love.

> I believe a part of the answer has to do with our sense of surrender to a patient. I felt comfortable when Ben was mirroring my narcissism; I was idealized, and in that idealization I was in charge. … On the one hand, I was treating the patient in a contemporary relational manner—by creating a milieu for a mutually experienced eroticism in the analysis, albeit a sexual eroticism—which then led to intimacies as well as an expression of the patient's innermost thoughts. And on the other hand, I was adhering to Freud's notion of abstinence when it came to experiencing my own feelings of love for the patient. (p. 33)

The day after her dream, Rosiello (2000) reported feeling open and flirtatious, which Ben must have sensed because he declared more openly than ever, "You have something with me that you don't have with anyone else. I know I'm your favorite patient." She felt his words more deeply than ever before and silently enjoyed his tender expressions. She reported being able to feel sexual stimulation freely in response to erotic transferences of a number of her clients, but never before had she consciously been aware of love. She interprets her countertransference:

With hindsight, I believe my disavowed feelings *were* my erotic countertransference and I believe Benjamin's erotic transference was a mirrored reflection or manifestation arising from my dissociated feelings. In other words, Benjamin unconsciously experienced something about me that was out of my awareness and he unknowingly enacted it as a means of communicating his experience of my feelings—and as a consequence, his emotional resonance with my subjective experience influenced his erotic transference development. (p. 34)

In Part 3 of this book, I report a similar phenomenon in which my countertransference response to Dora clearly had an impact on the way she unconsciously organized her erotic transference to me.

Rosiello: Performance of Affect and Gender

Rosiello (2000) tells the story of her treatment of Angelo, a transgendered MTF (male to female) who identified as lesbian and took great care in all the details of his makeup, hair, and attire. Rosiello uses the pronoun "he" because he came to his session after work usually dressed as a man, although occasionally he appeared for therapy looking striking in what he called his "androgynous look."

After his father used to beat him, he would insist that the young child kiss him and tell him how much he loved him and how great a father he was—teaching Angelo the importance of performance, that there is nothing real, no naturalness in the world. One particularly telling episode in his session occurred one day when Angelo brought a tape recording made at Christmas time when he was 3 years old. His father ordered him to sing a holiday song, then constantly interrupted, bellowing out: "That's not the right word, Angelo," "What's the matter with you? Sing it right," "Don't you know anything, Angelo?" "Sing it this way, Angelo." When the recorder was turned off, Angelo and Rosiello sat in stunned, tearful silence. But, she said, the remarkable thing was that he *did* sing for his father, and he *did* incorporate all his corrections—performing on command as a 3-year-old.

In the transference, Angelo seems to never get enough from me, he constantly questions my opinion about his behavior, perhaps eliciting, expecting, and/or fearing verbal sadism or my rejection. Do I think he's feminine? Is his face too masculine? Does he do what other women do? Aren't women supposed to be demure, and what do feminists think about this or that? ... My subjective experience of countertransference is that I feel quite exhausted after our sessions. I feel that every part of me has been tugged for, pulled intellectually, emotionally, and physically. For instance, once when I had injured both my knees and had some stiffness walking, Angelo noticed, left his chair, sat at my feet and began stroking my shins. I remember saying to myself, "Oh, please just go back to your seat and stop doing that." Perhaps in this moment I played one of my own performances, since I feared a reaction or an interpretation would humiliate him and repeat his father's sins. I had it in my mind that he used to stroke his mother to make her feel better when she was depressed and also stroked his father after he beat him, and so told him I didn't think I shaved as frequently as he did. He laughed and returned to his chair. ... He asked if I had minded his touch and then wondered why I never wanted a hug after sessions. The thought of being entitled to one's own reaction to another's touch was novel to him. (Rosiello, 2000, p. 103)

In considering the dyadic scenarios mutually engaged in by Angelo and herself, Rosiello (2000) muses on how much energy it takes to perform affect and to perform gender. She asks: Is there any essential difference in performing the expected affect or the expected gender? Should she perform the affect he expects? Angelo's performances of both affect and gender felt natural and real, presumably due to a lifetime of having to perform for others. But, she thoughtfully asks, in the final analysis, does it really matter if the level or quality of emotional performance or gender performance is real? Her work teaches us a humility about our feelings and interactions as therapists—stemming as they do from childhoods fraught with confusion and conflict.

Orbach: A Countertransference Rape Fantasy

Psychoanalyst Susie Orbach (2004) presents an experience that demonstrates how powerful countertransference body experiences can be in psychotherapy. Forty-eight-year-old attorney Rob started therapy during a breakdown. Unable to sleep for weeks, he was depressed and anxious about being anxious. He was able to perform well in the courtroom only if he could find some love or sexual interest to keep him mentally involved in the actual scene.

> In the course of our time together Rob revealed a wide range of sexual activities. He frequented call-girls, picked up prostitutes for dangerous car rendezvous around the King's Cross red-light district, and engaged in consensual sex so close to the edge that it took a great deal on my part to be curious rather than frightened. Indeed, of course, I did become frightened. I found myself one day in a perfectly ordinary session suddenly fearful that Rob would rape me. I felt my body being pulled apart and tearing. I was so scared that time held me in a pincer. I became rigid, started to sweat, cursed myself for not having an alarm alert in my room before I could find a way to still my momentary psychosis. After the session, as I replayed the rape scenario occurring in my body, I was stunned at the level of brutality and the visual acuity of a scene of bodily fluids, teeth, and fight coursing through my body. (p. 20)

Orbach (2004) reported that Rob had talked about "transgressive" sex in a pseudoliberated way during sessions. He reported that his various sexual pursuits soothed and terrified him, giving him a sense of being rooted but out of control physically. "With a consideration of the stark physicality of my body counter-transference in my awareness, we could get much further than the formulation that his sexual activity was a vehicle for anxiety if I took the savagery I experienced as a clue to his terror and his search for another body, for a body that could respond, a body that didn't collapse, a body that could meet his body" (p. 21). In studying this role-reversal symbiotic scenario, Orbach formulated that Rob had three modes of body experience: a body full of love and tenderness that could be seen and received, a performing body that could be confirmed as worthwhile, and a sleaze body that could be confirmed as foul, disgusting, and full of hatred.

> In court, Rob entered the performing body. He sought in the eyes of the jury, who watched him [with] the admiration and pleasure, the acceptance and recognition, that he had failed to see reflected in his parents' eyes when he was growing up. In sexual pursuit he entered the giving body, the body full of love and tenderness, the body he could love for himself because

he could be loved by another. In the third mode, the degraded body, the body in the sleaze of a paid sexual encounter or on the sexual edge, he was propelled by a physical force going at the crash barriers, looking for a kind of containment that could meet his body hatred. (p. 22)

Orbach (2004) formulated that in her body countertransference feeling of being the victim of a savage rape she was caught in Winnicott's (1971) position of the mother of early object relatedness whose fantasy must be destroyed before the mother who can be used for growth can be seen and given a response. She felt that her body was receiving Rob's hatred and aggression, and that she must manage her alarm and allow herself to be disturbed but not to collapse. For him to be able to relate to a body in the room, she felt required to receive the challenge to her physical integrity while remaining rooted in her own body. That is, in Winnicott's terms, she needed to be able to endure and survive the emotional destruction Rob must foist on her in the transference replication.

> Rob could only put together a body for himself via a violent encounter with another and yet on-the-edge and dangerous sex failed for him because *he* had to hold the boundary. He couldn't go the full destructive route. Via my body counter-transference, I think he gave me the chance to enter into the sense of desperation and need for a body which could be destroyed and yet survive. (p. 25)

Mitchell: The Horror of Surrendering

Freud (1937) taught us that for a man to take in something from another man is psychically equivalent to surrendering to homoerotic longings, femininity, and the loss of male potency. But, Steven A. Mitchell (1997), founder of the Relational Psychotherapy movement, pointed out from our modern point of view that perhaps all men in one way or another long to be liberated from the burdens of socially constructed male-gendered identity.

To illustrate this thesis, Mitchell (1997) recounts an analysis he conducted with an artist who had gotten into a stalemate after 7 years with his former analyst. Gender lines were tightly drawn in the client's family of origin. His father was a self-absorbed artist whose ambitions were greater than his talents. His mother had become embittered by his father's passivity and isolation and divorced him when the client was 10. He became closely aligned with his father because of his mother's hatred of all men, but even so, his father hardly saw him. Mitchell's client fantasized both he and his father to be superior, suffering, and unrecognized geniuses. Although the son was a promising artist, much more successful than his father, he had a habit of sabotaging himself, as if actively succeeding were somehow terrifying. He constantly sought leads and advice from others, including his analyst, about what he should do and how he should spend his time. He valued more than anything what someone else could bring or give to him. In sexual intercourse, he reported at times feeling confusion over whether the aroused penis was his or the woman's. He was excited by the thought of what being penetrated by a penis might feel like.

The transference in both analyses was organized around the desire and dread of what he could get from his analysts, both men. The analysts were both seen as possessing precious knowledge that they sadistically withheld. He had read some things Mitchell had written and felt that he would be more interactive than the previous analyst; he would give him more. But he was soon struck with how insightful the writings had been and how dull Mitchell seemed as an analyst in person.

What seemed not to have come out in the previous work was what a desolate image of masculinity this man had inherited from his father—an identity that condemned him to live in a depressive, heroic solitude. His longing to be penetrated—by ideas, by a penis, by scintillating analytic interpretations—represented "both a desperate hope finally to get something from his father and an escape from the masculine confinement that constituted being a man" (Mitchell, 1997, p. 251).

In the transference, Mitchell was granted superior knowledge, making the client dependent on getting the analyst to deliver or else suffering from deprivation. Early on, he had a hard time remembering anything Mitchell said but finally fixated on one of the analyst's questions. In speaking of his last analysis, he lamented that for him to change he would have to give up a sense of himself as special—which he was not sure he could ever do. Mitchell (1997) asked where he got the sense that the major factor in constructive change would entail his giving up something precious to him. The question served to define a different kind of relationship existing with Mitchell that did not demand submission.

> The first analyst seemed to be saying something like, "Your problems with assertiveness are due to your remaining your very special father's very special little girl. Cut it out; give all that up." Yet the patient experienced that injunction as implicitly claiming, "My penis/authority is bigger and better than your father's.
>
> "I want you as my little girl. To make it with me, you have to give up him." (p. 252)

Gradually in the role-reversal countertransference, Mitchell (1997) found himself implicitly or explicitly making such submissive claims himself:

> an envy of his relationship with his father ... seductive hints that he could certainly be a most loyal and rewarding devotee, if only I could convince him I had the right stuff; an intellectual toughness and competitiveness in him that made it clear that, if I was not man enough to make him want to be my little girl, he would certainly make me his; an admiration for his intellectual prowess and vast knowledge of things I was interested in that made a passive surrender to him both tempting and dangerous; and so on. (p. 252)

Using this case example, Mitchell (1997) held the opinion that, for contemporary analysts, the decisive arena for working on gender and gender identification issues is in the complex interpersonal negotiations of the analytic relationship.

> This man needed to realize that he had co-created the impasse in his first analysis ... with his horror of a surrender, which he also deeply longed for. Our joint task was to find a way for us to engage each other by which we could alternately give and receive, alternately exert power and be vitalized by the prowess of the other, and simultaneously lessen the threat of self-betrayal and humiliation. (p. 252)

Gorkin: Magical Cure by Copulation

The leading cause of malpractice suits against clinicians is sexual involvement with the client. Little has been written to alert the practicing clinician to the clinical issues that lead to erotic counter-transference experiences. The following vignette relates psychoanalyst Michael Gorkin's (1985) sexualized response to a sexualized transference and how he came to understand and work it through.

I worked with a woman in her mid-20s, K, who in the second year of her four-year treatment developed an erotized transference. Dressed most often in carefully matched and skin-tight outfits, K frequently professed a wish to seduce me. At times, it seemed as if she came to her sessions primarily to accomplish this aim. ...

At first, K's openly expressed wishes to be held, kissed, fondled, and penetrated were simply off-putting to me. Though I kept my negative reactions to myself, I eagerly wished she would renounce these demands, or better yet, be able to look at them as part of our analytic passion play. Still, they persisted in elemental force. As time went on I found myself, in turn, having sexual fantasies about her, wishing to do to her more or less what she wanted. I communicated none of this to her. I silently observed my countertransference neurosis, and what I noticed was that these sexual fantasies took on for me a deep wish to rescue her. A part of my ego accepted her demand, her argument, that if only I would have sex with her she could get better, and unless I did, she would never get better. The other part of my ego, the analyzing part, knew full well that this was folly. But the part of my ego that was locked into this fusion fantasy with her had become hooked, and it was then that I noticed another fantasy taking shape. I wished to have sex with her not simply to rescue her, but to rescue *me*. It would cure *me*. It is difficult to put this raw experience into words, but it was something of the order that I would be made whole and totally vital if only—and only if—I had sex with her. (pp. 427–428)

As Gorkin (1985) comes to understand this experience, he realizes that the client's stated desire to have sex with him was the clearest—and perhaps the only—way she knew to express her yearning for contact with him. She repeatedly had lost contact with her mother as a young child when her mother went to work and at age 11 when her mother died. By arousing his sexual interest, she was arousing his omnipotent wish to be the all-good, nonfailing mother for her—to cure her, as it were, of her abandonment dread. Likewise, the experience activated in him his desire to be omnipotently taken care of by her, thus creating a mutual sense of oneness. He comments that the strivings were full of strain on both sides and discusses Searles's 1979 work in this regard, reiterating the magical wish for curative copulation and how powerful it can be in the lives of therapists.

Gorkin: Sadistic Sexual Countertransference Fantasies

The following account illustrates how Gorkin (1987), not fully attentive to an early dream fragment and his own sadistic fantasies, left room for a number of evasions and subtle types of acting out before the client's incest history emerged. He speaks of B, who presented for treatment with occasional anxiety attacks. Early in treatment, she told of a dream at the home where she was raised with two older brothers. The family wash was hanging out to dry in the backyard. Her panties and bra were visible. She had no associations, even though he mentioned the obvious possibility of washing her dirty linen in public.

Her therapeutic style was to talk briefly of her family and work so that Gorkin (1987) would be inclined to probe for details, although he soon became uncomfortable with what felt like intrusiveness to him, and the banter shifted to mild flirtatious baiting that he reciprocated until he noticed the emergence of sadistic sexual fantasies toward her. "I wished to take her clothes off, tear them off, and grab her all over. These fantasies were attended less by warm feelings than by a sense of using her. Sadistically, I imagined how much she would like it, even though she would tell me to stop" (p. 124). Gorkin did not mention his fantasies but waited until he could draw attention to the teasing pattern they had developed. This led to her divulging incestuous involvements from ages 11 to 13 with one of her brothers. She was at first reluctant with her brother but then often teased him into it. Then came the shame of her sexual fantasies toward her analyst, involving his repeatedly forcing her to do something against her will that ended with her being humiliated.

> I feel certain that, had I been more immediately aware of my sexualized countertransference, I would not have acted provocatively with her. Still, having done so, I felt that an acknowledgement of my role was needed.

Thus stated: "You and I have become involved in a mutual teasing, which I have obviously enjoyed, and I imagine you have, too. But in so doing, I think that I have repeated with you, without actually having sex with you, some of that sexually provocative play that took place between you and your brother." This acknowledgement was fully accepted by B. (p. 124)

Gorkin (1987) reported that following these exchanges the sexual fantasies on both sides diminished, and warm nonsexualized relating continued to the end of treatment. A listener working with this woman would be wise to consider that this characterological sadomasochistic-teasing scenario likely did not begin at age 11 with her brother but can also be listened to as a screen memory—as an aspect of her original symbiotic exchange with her mother. Entertaining this listening possibility may clarify a number of the other enigmatic exchanges that also press toward a sense of mutually experienced oneness through titillating teasing.

Gorkin: Erotic Countertransference as a Clue to Gender Identity Issues

Gorkin's (1987) sexualized fantasy about M, a 10-year-old boy patient, alerted him early in the analysis to issues that were to unfold more clearly later. His account shows how a fantasy—in this case, a specifically sexual one—can contain unconscious understanding of issues that must be worked through by the patient. M was slackening in schoolwork shortly after his parents divorced. M shrugged off any disturbance, sadness, anger, or guilt about the divorce and began to draw pictures—usually of pirates and male superheroes. He often played soldiers and was an ardent baseball fan—all of which suggested age-adequate masculine gender identity. But, in spite of this, Gorkin reported that he found himself

> reacting to him in ways I might have reacted to an alluring girl: as cute, endearingly charming, and above all, seductively cuddlesome. At times I wanted to throw my arms about him, squeeze him tight, give him a kiss. I felt him to be a lovely young girl. In attempting to sort out for myself whence this reaction came, I began to pay closer attention to the subtleties of M.'s interaction with me. I then began to notice how his movements had a kind of furtive quality to them. He occasionally

would walk and almost brush up against me, cat-like. Also, some of his gestures, while not effeminate, took on a seductive cast—for example, a lingering look and slow running of his hand through his hair as he hesitated near the door at the end of the session. (p. 125)

Gorkin (1987) was alerted by his countertransference reactions and in interviews with the boy's mother discovered how envious M has been of his younger sister, who was his father's favorite. Moreover, before he started school he had frequently wanted to dress up in girl's clothes. His mother had thought at the time that there was something "vaguely homosexual" about this, but she now saw that he was "a real boy, a terrific athlete and baseball player." Gorkin described 3 years of treatment in which many gender confusions were explored, stating that they were so subtle that he might not have been sensitive to them except for his own sexual fantasies of M as a seductive young girl.

What is more, I found my countertransferential response useful throughout the therapy, particularly in gauging the progression, and at times regression, in M.'s therapeutic development. Finally, and perhaps most crucially, my awareness of the countertransference was of considerable help in preventing me from subtly acting out M.'s wish (and mine). Without this awareness it is likely that I would have unwittingly encouraged the perpetuation of, or brought about the premature renunciation of, M.'s (and my) wish for him to be a lovely young girl. (pp. 106–107)

These clinical vignettes illustrate aptly the nature of the replicating symbiotic transference and countertransference. This way of listening suggests that either or both participants become caught in an enactment that stems from an early way of being with caregiving others. When this way of being in relationships is lived out in later life, it creates interpersonal difficulties until one or the other or both begin to grasp its significance.

5

THE EMERGENT SELF

Unilaterally Dependent Relatedness

Mothers know altogether too well the point at which a child begins to develop his or her "own mind"; they call this period the "terrible twos." The bonding dance of union, merger, identity, and collusive engagement ends with "No!" "I know what you want, and I don't want to do it your way!" Freud (1926) established negation not only as the beginning of an individual's independent mental functioning but also as the beginning of imagination, language, and culture. The child begins to refuse the (m)other's ways and to experiment with and insist on his or her own ways. After the child establishes some right to autonomy, we note the beginning development of what has been called by Heinz Kohut (1971) the "cohesive self." After establishing the right to a certain emotional separateness, the child reapproaches the mother on a new basis, this time for affirmation of whom he or she is coming to be. This process of attempting to consolidate the sense of self, which is prominent in Western cultures, may be observed from birth to death, Kohut tells us, but peaks in its emphasis during the third year of life, the subphase of separation-individuation that Mahler (1968) calls "rapprochement."

The listening perspective for this process of ongoing consolidation of the self-sense describes a "self-other tension" or the need to experience the recognition of the reassuring, confirming, or inspiring other as a consolidating part of one's sense of self. Kohut used the term *narcissistic* for the mirroring, twinship, and idealizing transferences that arise in analysis and are based on self-other tensions. The other is recognized as a separate center of initiative but *used* as a cohesion-building function of the self. Self-other tensions motivate the person to address or seek out some significant other to achieve a sense of recognition, wholeness, and cohesion. Kohut and the self psychologists have studied extensively how the self-sense can be brought into focus in the analytic experience.

Précis: Listening to Unilaterally Dependent (Self-Other) Experience

Developmental Metaphor

Three-year-olds are preoccupied with using the acceptance and approval of others for developing and enhancing self-definitions, self-skills, and self-esteem. Their relatedness strivings use the admiring, confirming, and idealized responses of significant others to firm up their budding sense of self. Framing for analysis the self-other patterns used for affirming, confirming, and inspiring the self entails studying how the internalized mirroring, twinning, and idealizing patterns used in self-development in the pasts of both participants play out to enhance and limit the possibilities for mutual self-to-self-other resonance in the emerging interpersonal engagement.

Psychotherapeutic Parameters

Traditional diagnosis: narcissistic personality organization
Developmental metaphor: 24–36 months—rapprochement
Affects: dependent on empathy or optimal responsiveness of self-other
Transference: self-others (grandiose mirroring, twinship, idealizing)
Resistance: shame and embarrassment over narcissism, narcissistic rage
Listening mode: engagement with ebb and flow of experiences of self-affirmation, confirmation, and inspiration
Therapeutic modality: empathic attunement to self-experiences—self-to-self-other resonance
Countertransference: boredom, drowsiness, irritation—facilitating

Lewes: Working Through Displays of Male Bravado

Psychologist-psychoanalyst Kenneth Lewes (2002) reported on Dan, a 30-year-old gay man who began treatment at the end of his first semester of graduate school. Dan had twice previously started graduate school and dropped out and twice been in therapy. He was becoming anxious and angry with his school situation but knew the problem was his and that he needed to get it straightened out.

> He presented as a thoughtful, well-spoken literary type. He was a handsome man with regular features and a well-developed physique, the result of daily gym workouts, but he disguised it with a wardrobe that was old, rumpled, and ill fitting. He began his treatment by announcing that he had a borderline personality disorder—all of his previous therapists had concurred—and that his problems centered around issues of attachment and separation. … He had grown up on a ranch in Oklahoma, where he was up at dawn every day to do his chores. He was also the smartest kid for miles around. His parents did not know what to make of him, and his father, a short man of towering rages, openly mocked him for his fancy ways and laziness. His mother, a gentle and submissive soul, loved him, and he treasured memories of private moments with her as she cooked or played the piano in the parlor in rare free moments. (p. 181)

People in Dan's graduate school department felt sorry for him because he was not doing well and always appeared so poor and shabby. They did not know that he spent his money flying all over the country on weekends without extra clothes, going to circuit parties, taking drugs, and dancing all night, only to return Monday to his "mouselike" existence. Usually late for his appointments, he was often disagreeable and competitive with Lewes. Further, he was quite angry when his therapist disagreed with his self-diagnosis in favor of seeing him not as borderline psychotic but as psychologically well developed. Dan did not see that he was getting better in therapy (Lewes, 2002):

> But what took the cake was my suggestion that he lie down on the couch. He couldn't believe it! Were they still doing that? It was just his luck to connect with a reactionary analytic type. For more than a year we haggled, as he suggested various compromises. He would half recline, would sit up but face away from me, would recline facing me, use the couch for half the session, and so on. I offered interpretations, of course, centered around his yearning for a passive position and his simultaneous fear of assuming it, his wish for and dread of my being excited by him or my falling in love with him. Gradually the storm

subsided, and he requested that we increase the frequency of sessions to three and then to four times weekly, despite the fact, he added, that nothing was changing. (p. 183)

In fact, things *were* changing: His academic work improved, he formed relationships with other students, he won several prizes and recovered from his fear of talking up in class. He began an out-of-town relationship, assuming the passive sexual position, but when his therapist was out of town he roamed clubs for safe-sex companions with whom he could be active. "He joked, 'When the cat's away, well, you know'" (Lewes, 2002):

> Struggling with one particularly difficult woman professor, he dreamed of watching himself as a well-behaved ten-year-old boy sitting inside a cell, tied in a chair and unable to move, a spotlight trained on him. As he struggled to describe his feelings of self-imposed torture and incarceration, he began to weep, slowly at first, then more and more violently, until finally he was literally bellowing with rage. He began to curse and swear about how sick and tired he was of all those tight-assed academic types, including me. ... The next session was even more dramatic. He appeared on time, fixed me with a determined glare, removed his denim jacket, and revealed a tight tank top showing off his muscular shoulders, arms, and chest. He reclined on the couch and then proceeded to have a full-fledged anxiety attack that lasted for ten minutes. When I suggested—rather obtusely, I thought—that his anxiety came from showing me what his body looked like, he was suddenly relieved. (p. 184)

The transference interpretation led to a memory of having been humiliated in a therapy group a few years earlier for revealing his desire to be like Marlon Brando in The Wild One—wearing jeans, boots, and a tight T-shirt with a pack of unfiltered Camels tucked up in the sleeve.

> There were several sessions after this one that centered around Dan's uncertainty about whether he could openly enjoy his phallic display or would have to suppress it in fear of his father's jealous retaliation and his mother's diffidence and timidity. (p. 185)

In discussing the case, Lewes (2002) believes it would have been a grave error to have accepted Dan's self-diagnosis of borderline because it would have overlooked the depth and genuineness of his exhibitionistic phallic (self-other) impulses as well as his conflicts over expressing them. With hindsight, Lewes came to believe that his previous two therapists had attempted to provide a safe holding environment, seeing his phallic strivings as defensive to the expression of deep attachment needs.

> Instead, the treatment took a different form. The closest I can come to characterizing the transference is to call it a kind of coach-jock paradigm. It was necessary for Dan to preen, show off, and taunt his mentor, who, though sometimes irritated and provoked by all that showing off, still deeply approved and accepted his charge's developing prowess and achievements, without becoming excited by them. Dan gradually came to tolerate acute anxiety as he wrestled—metaphorically in the treatment room but literally, I think, in fantasy—with his mentor and competitor, and thereby learned to master the intrapsychic dangers of jealous retaliation by the father. (p. 186)

Lewes (2002) speculates on how the transference might have developed with a female therapist, stating that since Dan needed to work through this anxiety back to its source, it would have been important that his therapist not be offended, outraged, or frightened at his excesses or attempt to tame, refine, or domesticate him "in the name of leading him away from supposedly pointless, wasteful, and distasteful displays of male bravado" (p. 186).

Corbett: Countertransference Fear of Passivity—"The Father Censure"

For more than a decade, psychologist-psychoanalyst Ken Corbett (2002) worked on understanding the theory of masculinity and masculine sexual development in the Western culture. In speaking of the ways a gay man's gender experience may unfold in therapy, he notes widespread countertransference difficulties with male passivity that have fostered misconceptions regarding male homosexual development. He holds that the therapist's "inability to tolerate male passivity is embedded in the inability to comprehend and tolerate the gay man's experience of gender" (p. 24). Corbett feels that the lack of understanding and positive empathy that ensue leads to what he calls "the father censure"—although he hastens to add that the same censure may come from the mother, he is here highlighting the father-son dynamic.

> The analyst (as father), via an unconscious exploitation of transference wishes (the son's wish to be like the father and disavow passive longings), seeks along with the patient (as son) to subjugate and repudiate the patient's experience of gender and sexual difference. I argue that the father's censure and the son's repression rest on a distorted theory of masculine development that emphasizes the reproduction of fathering, the repudiation of passivity, the disregard of preoedipal variation in particular, [and] the boy's oedipal desire for his father. The boy's desire for his father is but one thread within the complex strand of homosexuality. I focus on the transference reenactment of the boy's wish for the father and the difficulties experienced by the gay male patient in allowing such a transference reenactment to emerge. Specifically, I contend that it is vitally important in the treatment of gay men to empathically recognize their fears of retribution for their experience of gender difference, and to assist them in clarifying their distinct gender identity. [He later added that this dynamic also holds for men who are not gay.] (pp. 24–25)

Corbett (2002) points out that passive wishes do not negate the coexistence of active wishes, and that most gay men alternate from active to passive sexual positions in their gender orientation. Sexual practices like mutual fellatio even suggest simultaneously experiencing activity and passivity, although the underlying individual fantasy is of decisive importance.

> Herein lies the heart of the mystery: gay men move between passive and active sexual aims that do not reflect the kind of binary tension falsely associated with heterosexual masculine activity and feminine passivity. Instead, homosexual activity and passivity stem, in part, from the boy's simultaneous desire for and identification with his father. Further, homosexual gender is not structured according to differences between the sexes, and the gay man's experience of gender does not rest on a binary tension modeled upon heterosexual masculinity and femininity. *The deconstruction of this binary tension not only speaks to the mystery*

of homosexuality, but to the mystery of sexuality—the ways in which all sexualities are informed by the push and pull of activity and passivity, along with the multiple threads of preoedipal and oedipal desires and identifications. (pp. 26–27, emphasis added)

Corbett (2002) points out that, for most gay men, "the experience of being anally penetrated results in phallic arousal and erection. ... For the man who is simultaneously penetrated and erect, orgasm is generally achieved following manipulation of his penis by his partner; this behavior is underscored by the wish for his partner to see and manipulate the penis (self-other recognition), not to deny it" (p. 31).

Therapists of both genders often have difficulty appreciating how truly different a gay man's gender definitions and sexuality can be because they cannot imagine a male body being simultaneously penetrated and erect or a male mind being simultaneously passive and active. The cultural load regarding phallic arousal and active phallic penetration is coded as masculine potency—leaving no room for other versions of activity and passivity or other versions of potency. The therapist who is prey to this cultural code will indeed miss the opportunity to understand the many active–passive sexuality mixtures that are to be found in most clients of all gender orientations.

Corbett: Case of Luke—Expanding Sexual Identities

Corbett's research into culturally held theories of masculinity led him to realize the importance of therapists helping their clients to expand their own definitions of gender and sexuality. He illustrated with Luke, who entered therapy for low self-esteem, anxiety, and despair over not being able to form a relationship with another man (Corbett, 2002). In treatment, Luke was wary that Corbett would judge him and find him lacking and humiliate him like so many others, including his father, had done in the past.

As treatment progressed and Luke's defenses abated, he reported a dream in which he was giving a small boy a bath. He and the boy were having a great deal of fun and Luke felt very tender toward the child. Luke became aware that the bathroom door was open, and that there were adults in the adjoining room.

Fearing that the adults would think something illicit was taking place between Luke and the boy, Luke closed the door. The scene then changed to his parents' bedroom. He was in the bedroom as a teenager with another teenage boy. The other boy began to undress, but suddenly stopped. The dream ended with Luke feeling disappointed and angry. (p. 35)

In associating to the dream, Luke felt the little boy was himself, and that he wished to be cared for by his therapist. He anxiously revealed his fantasy that Corbett (2002) would take him into the adjoining playroom for sex. With disgust, he expressed his wish to be passive, for his therapist to hold him, undress him, and suck his penis. In subsequent sessions, he produced memories of childhood experiences in which he had been humiliated for having passive wishes and for his childhood identifications with girls. He remembered his relationships with girls as "strained allegiances" and remarked laughingly, "I didn't belong in either camp! ... What's so weird is how it was known and never spoken" (p. 36).

Corbett (2002) uses Luke to illustrate how a boy's feminine identifications—especially a homosexual boy's—do not necessarily represent so much a wish to be a girl as an avenue for passive experience and passive wish fulfillment. He points out that passive longings and feminine identifications often exist side by side with active longings and masculine identifications, giving rise to confusing gender experiences for many children, particularly homosexual children.

Corbett (2002) speaks to the importance of therapists helping all their clients speak about and clarify their own unique and distinct gender experiences. Expanding one's definitions of one's own gender and gender identities allows new vantage points from which to reassess and revalue one's unique positions. Luke, for example, came to assess his wishes as variant as opposed to deviant, thus offering new possibilities for future development. Corbett proposes that as therapists we need to formulate new theories of gender and sexual development that cast a wider net. Our new theories need not be unbounded or ignore the cultural order that sexes each subject, but they need to distinguish between the normative and the natural and to create realistic representations of the wide variety of gender variations that need to be recognized and valued in the course of human development.

Coverdale: A Countertransference Reaction to Budding Exhibitionism

My Introduction

While most of the challenging countertransference situations are associated with the so-called borderline patient, other forms of relatedness may also provide the clinician with difficult moments. What follows covers only the first two dozen therapeutic hours, focusing on the 24th session of a continuing therapy.

Budding Exhibition

Contributed by Charles Coverdale,
Licensed Clinical Social Worker

The patient was a call girl in her early thirties, quite beautiful and very sexy by any standards. Movie and television stars abound in her life, some exclusively as dates and many exclusively as clients. In her first hour, she wondered if I knew one of her clients, a well-known psychiatrist. Soon, she told of a desire to come to my house and dance for me but took my interpretation well. Provocatively, she licked her lips and ran her tongue across her teeth. At times, she seemed turned on, but my own reactions told me that she was excited by her own sexiness. She drew attention to aspects of her body beneath her form-fitting clothes, asking me to look. She was delighted by my lack of comprehension of the jargon used by clients of call girls. She left cash on a small table next to the Kleenex and clock, whispering "I'll just sneak out now," on departing. She described the perfection of her breasts and nipples, caressing them through a thin blouse and announced during her 23rd session that she was going to have breast implant surgery and would return to therapy after recovering.

Several weeks passed, and she returned to therapy in her usual provocative garb but with unusually large breasts. Sitting opposite me, she told of her happiness with choosing the largest implants and excitedly described them while caressing them through her spandex top. Then, sliding her scoop neck down, she exposed them while looking at them adoringly. She continued to comment on them for some time while caressing and holding them. She looked briefly at me and asked for agreement. I looked at them warmly and said, "Well, I can see why you're so pleased. They are just beautiful." She lingered a moment more, then pulled her blouse back up.

Now that the reader is sufficiently outraged, I would ask you only to remain open-minded throughout the discussion. I did promise you that the self-other transferences can create difficult and challenging countertransference reactions, but these very reactions provide the clues essential to understanding and interpretation.

Among the difficult aspects of this case is the fact that I have a bias against implants and plastic surgery in general. I view it all as elective mutilation—unnecessary and unnatural and as buying into sexism and ageism. But, this was not my therapy or useful countertransference (and moralizing has little place in analytic understanding).

What is useful is that I did not feel very much sexually as she exhibited (and not because I do not enjoy looking at female nudity). Just moments after she covered her breasts, I added, "You know, I have the sense that you are showing me your babies." My comment was right and based mainly on the fact that I was not much titillated. Rather, as I looked on, her self-caressing reminded me of a new mother holding and stroking twin babies' heads. Thank goodness she did not ask me to hold them, as is common with new mothers in regard to their infants. (I was prepared to decline, as I sometimes do with other women's babies.)

I realize that the reader has likely formulated a belief that the therapist in this case is simply voyeuristically acting out and tacitly encouraging the patient to indulge his perversion. We return to this momentarily.

Voyeurism aside, there was a great deal that I did get from this incident. Suddenly, it was clear to me why she was in her line of work and what she got out of her job: Each client allows her the possibility to exhibit anew and receive the joy of appreciative response. This awareness (which came from her exposing herself) and my communication of this awareness put her immediately in touch with a screen memory of a mother too busy to respond to her daughter's budding exhibitionism. Further, it became apparent that her family is fundamentally religious and somewhat uptight about appreciating the body and sexual matters in general. In the several sessions since then, she has focused on unmet needs to be attended to by her mother. Thankfully, she trusted me to respond as she needed, having tested me (as I now can understand) to see if I was only self-interested.

With regard to the reader's belief in my voyeuristic acting out, I suppose that all those drawn to this profession tend toward the voyeuristic end of the continuum. Further, I admit to feeling a moment of enjoyment as she exposed herself—but as she did, it was a remarkably unsexual occasion.

Now, let us consider some alternatives. By way of contrast, one must wonder: What if I had been uncomfortable with her physical display? Had I stopped her from showing herself, surely I would have frustrated her desires to be attended to and would have retraumatized her in the same way that her mother had, all while precluding access to the very information that explained why she so hungered for response. So hungry was she that she was driven to risk subjecting herself to painfully humiliating situations. Fortunately, I did not interfere. I feel equally fortunate not to have misinterpreted. Had I seen it as a sexual ploy, it could have been interpreted as a power play or control issue. It would also have been possible to conceptualize it as an attempt for merger, a violation of boundaries, of a desire to corrupt or sabotage therapy. But, all of these formulations would have been incorrect and accompanied by different behaviors on her part. Please note that she did not look at me, except briefly, while exhibiting, and she did not glance at the front of my trousers. I realize this as I review the hour.

So, if we stay close to the evidence, we can see that, having received the desired mirroring, she was then left with a sense of completion and satisfaction. Then, following my comment about showing her babies, she responded with all the sweet intonation of a new mother giving a baby its due with the words: "My beautiful babies. I didn't realize it until you said it." With herself serving as her own narcissistic object, she wanted nothing more than to be joined in her self-adoration. At last, adoring mother and adored child were united.

Again, I was thankful for my own analysis, which helped me years ago to differentiate and understand complex and subtle feelings. I also recall having had, at one point in my own analysis, a fantasy of being seen naked by my female analyst, only to realize that it was not my grown body but that of my 3-year-old self that I had wanted seen. So, while not all exhibitionists seek mirroring, I do know of two who were. In 24 years of practice, I have been flashed only once, and I feel lucky to have depended on my countertransference reactions for guidance.

Mitchell: Maintaining an Open Clinical Position

When James moved to New York City in his early 20s, he started analysis with psychologist-psychoanalyst Stephen Mitchell (1997) after having previously been in therapy for several years in his hometown. For some time, he had struggled with issues of sexual identity and sexual dysfunction. In the few sexual experiences he had with women, his performance and satisfaction were inconsistent. He had experienced sex with a few men who had approached him, but he did not particularly care for the men involved.

> James had always been terrified that his lifelong interest in boys and his phobic dread of sexual play with girls meant that there was something terribly wrong with him. He had many good male friends and very much liked being "one of the guys." He felt humiliated by his heterosexual failings, and the prospect of life as a gay man seemed a horrifying sentence. He wanted what he regarded as a "normal" life with a wife and children. He wanted desperately to be able to form and sustain a relationship with a woman, and he wanted analytic treatment to help him. (p. 257)

His prior analyst had been warm and supportive during a time in his life that had been chaotic and frightening. His analyst had responded to James's fears that he might be gay by reassuring him that he probably was not, and James sought this same reassurance from Mitchell (1997). Surely analytic exploration would enable him to settle down into a normal heterosexual life.

> On one hand, James did have some erotic responsiveness toward women, and there were some dynamic issues that related to fears of women, which, if they were worked through, might make sex with women possible. On the other hand, throughout his whole life James clearly had had a stronger

erotic responsiveness to men. Would helping him fashion a heterosexual adjustment be collaborating in condemning him to self-betrayal? Is maximal sexual gratification the key to personal fulfillment, as so much of our contemporary culture seems to suggest? Or is his longing for a heterosexual life a legitimate wish to have things easier for himself, perhaps with fewer obstacles to fulfillment in other areas, like his career? (p. 257)

Mitchell (1997) considered the complications of attempting to maintain therapeutic neutrality under such circumstances. In the countertransference, Mitchell experienced the importance of sexual satisfaction himself but wonders if it is or should be central for everyone. He wonders if helping James come to terms with a gay life represents an avoidance of his own vestigial homophobia or a conformity to current political correctness. Would encouraging heterosexuality represent Mitchell's own preference for heterosexuality, a collusion with James's homophobia, or a respect for what James said he wanted for himself? Mitchell remembered that people often want things that are self-destructive.

> I wasn't getting very far with these considerations and was at risk of becoming as obsessively mired as he was. The following line of thought began to emerge, which, along with some of the questions I was struggling with, I shared with him. Neither he nor I knew with any certainty what his sexual identity was nor, in fact, whether he, or anyone else, had a preformed, irreversible sexual identity. I reframed the issue, therefore, from the question of which way he wanted to move to the question of whether he wanted to move at all. I suggested that his life, in many respects, had been organized around his lack of clarity about something that, because of his paucity of experience, he could not possibly be clear about. Perhaps his belief that psychoanalysis would help make him heterosexual was a device for preserving the status quo, and perhaps preserving the status quo was really his major interest. I suggested that his inaction was itself a choice and that while he was ruminating about heterosexuality and homosexuality, he was, in fact, choosing asexuality, which was itself a possible, viable life course. (p. 258)

Mitchell (1997) reported that his position was initially disturbing to James, who felt he was being less caring and supportive than his previous analyst had been. But on reflection, James could see that asexual life did seem to be the choice he was passively making, and that he did want to more actively explore his options by seeking out different kinds of sexual experiences. Therapy then became occupied with working on his anxieties regarding unconventionality, around performance, and perhaps most important, "his terror of actively seeking anything and the vulnerabilities inherent in desire itself" (p. 258). In time, James was able to establish two satisfying relationships with women who fell in love with him, but he could not imagine giving himself over to them. He felt his performance was adequate and satisfying.

> He still felt a stronger response to men and needed to discover what a romantic relationship with a man would feel like. So he sought that out and fell deeply in love for the first time. He began to make various kinds of contacts with other gay men, as well as with his straight friends, and felt at one with himself in a way he never had previously. Some years later, looking back, James noted several times that he had felt particularly happy about the relationships he had with women before he moved in a homosexual direction. That he had been able to make it sexually with women—that he had been able to have a girlfriend for some time, that he knew he could have had a reasonably satisfying conventional, heterosexual life—all this made him feel that he was making choices based not on fears or his own preferences. (p. 260)

Mitchell (1997) reported that what was important about this experience for himself was that he and James had been able to avoid "letting abstractions and beliefs get in the way of experience" (p. 260). Beliefs about pathology, the constitutional irreversibility of homosexuality, and the desirability or the dangers of conformity could have interfered with James's exploration of his own experience. It seemed helpful to both of them to be able to explore James's conflicts without assuming that they knew things they were in no position to know.

Mitchell (1997) took this opportunity to openly disagree with Isay (1990) that assuming homosexuality to be constitutional provides the most open clinical position. Mitchell acknowledged that the particular solution he and James worked out is not necessarily right for everyone in that not everyone feels the same diversity of sexual longing. Everyone also does not feel it necessary actually to experience sexual variations to know what feels right for his or her own sexuality. Mitchell added that different people need different experiences at different points in their lives. He speculated that at the time of James's prior therapy he was living in chaos and fear, and that the reassurance he extracted from his analyst at that time that he was probably heterosexual allowed James to postpone dealing with the issue of his orientation.

> It is not clear to me that he could have used his experience with me earlier. What seemed most important was that I was able to work on my own various biases and values enough to arrive at a way of working with him that we both came to feel was relatively free of a programmatic intent, except for the value placed on action and responsibility embedded in my way of working analytically. (p. 260)

Wittkin-Sasso: The Analytic Use of Desire

Psychoanalyst Gail Wittkin-Sasso (1991) highlights sensuality—information from the senses—to be an integral part of empathy. Following Kohut (1959), empathy is seen by her as involving the analyst's capacity to perceive the patient's inner life—to imagine, fantasize, and wander in, around, and through the patient's stories and affects. Empathic activity is not only satisfying to the analyst, says Wittkin-Sasso, but also shows the analyst's sensuality in its most precise, creative, and effective aspects. Sensual information is basic, primitive, visceral, and intuitive. Sensual fantasies point to meanings rooted in the relational engagements of the analysis long before conscious awareness occurs. She cites Sandler in his supposition that when sensuality is arousing—or repulsive—fantasy themes of yearning, escape, nakedness, exposure, loss of control, and seduction may appear spontaneously as "free-floating" associations (Sandler, 1976, p. 44).

> For example, I awoke one morning feeling strange and anxious. I realized that I had dreamt about a patient, a man some years older than I, whom I had been treating for about a year. In my dream, we were standing, he behind me, fully clothed. He was hugging me loosely while his face was buried deeply into the back of my neck. I felt no arousal but did diligently assess the professional propriety of this entwined stance of ours. I looked around to face him. His eyes were half closed and he had a look of transported, desirous rapture on his face. In my dream, I experienced a strange

ambivalence. On the one hand, I was my professional self. I determined that our standing together in this way was technically acceptable because I had set the limits. I was in control. My patient was like an eager adolescent and I, the analyst-woman in control, appreciated his developmental [self-other] need and could objectively sustain the intense power of his yearning. I felt gratified. I felt adored. I felt frightened. It then appeared that he wanted to take me over from the inside out. As I looked at his swooning expression I felt his urge to move into me, to become me. I felt invaded, exploited. He couldn't see me because his eyes were closed, back into his head. And here was the dialectic: He was so enraptured in his own internal ecstasy of a representational-me, that, even as we touched, I experienced him as chillingly remote, *self*-involved, uninvolved. I felt his profound lack of connection through the sensual contrasts within my dream. (Wittkin-Sasso, 1991, p. 692)

The analyst reported (Wittkin-Sasso, 1991) initially being concerned that her relational unconscious had seduced this patient, but on reflection, she realized that her erotic countertransference dream pointed toward the man's essentially narcissistic character structure—that is, he needed sensual merger to feel confirmed (recognized) in his own sense of self. His half-open eyes revealed the confirming self-other transference experience.

> I believe that the depth of my own yearning to connect more substantially with this patient, and thus feel myself truly valued, is what produced the sensual dream metaphors. Not only was I experiencing the fragility of our connection, but in doing so I was able to assess more accurately the structural limits of this patient's capacity for relatedness, a diagnostic understanding which I had not fully recognized earlier. (p. 693)

In her discussion of the erotic dream, she took the position that countertransference freedom results from the constant vigilance and self-control inherent in the structure of the analytic frame. Citing Gill (1987), Wittkin-Sasso (1991) held that the course of events in treatment is that an analyst inevitably falls into patterns induced by the patient, and that the analyst must realize this and interpret what has happened. The analyst's affects must be processed within a reflective awareness of the influences our participation inevitably have on the treatment (Ehrenberg, 1990). These considerations allow the analyst freedom to experience personal desire through countertransference imagination that integrates affects with perception.

Wittkin-Sasso (1991) quotes Freud (1915): "The love between the sexes is undoubtedly one of the first things in life, and the combination of mental and bodily satisfaction attained in the enjoyment of love is literally one of life's culminations. Apart from a few perverse fanatics, all the world knows this and conducts life accordingly; only science is too refined to confess it" (p. 693). Says Wittkin-Sasso: "While the need for relational intimacy, personal integrity, and emotional authenticity is probably much more human than gendered, the tension created from psycho-cultural gender differences contribute sensual power to both our fantasies and our experience of desire" (p. 693). Her dream had clued her in to this man's need for self-other merger that not only excluded her from his awareness but also deprived him of much-needed recognition of who he was and could be.

Hedges: Stephen, Sean, Pornography, and the Internet

I include here two brief vignettes that relate to our current interests in understanding pornography and the Internet. The formulations generated by these two men offer some alternatives for us to consider that contrast sharply with popular black-and-white thinking about Internet pornography.

Stephen

Stephen's marriage of 10 years was in danger because of what he considered his lifelong addictive use of pornography. It had taken his wife, Amy, several years to become aware of his habit, which caused her to feel devastated and violated. She wanted mutuality and intimacy in a growing relationship and experienced his porn interests as threatening to the marriage. He did not like his daily use of pornographic images and fantasies either, but they had been a part of his life since early adolescence.

After several promises and shame-filled lapses on Stephen's part, his wife experienced her needs in the relationship as severely threatened and insisted that they get help. Stephen felt that her position was justified and was actually relieved at the opportunity to take a look at something that bothered him as well. Couples work and recovery group work was begun, shortly to be followed by each seeking individual therapy. Stephen's and my early individual work was spent outlining the general patterns of his pornography use, the history of intimacy and relationship in the marriage, and many painful and humiliating memories from childhood. Stephen very much loved his wife, felt that she was justified in considering his habits a violation of their intimacy, believed she was justified in not trusting him at present as he had repeatedly lied to her regarding pornography, so he willingly cooperated in her inquiries and investigations when she became anxious and insecure. He readily grasped that while his use of pornography was a habit he brought from the past, conflictual events in the marriage clearly had an impact on him and on his masturbatory habits and fantasies.

Stephen and Amy's couples work was going well as they were learning to sense each other's daily preoccupations and withdrawals from the relationship and had instituted a number of ways of being with each other's anxieties and finding ways to meaningfully reconnect. Both admitted the road to developing a better relationship would be difficult, that they were not through the forest yet, but that the work was rich and rewarding, even if frightening and exhausting.

A year and a half into individual therapy, Stephen started his session with, "Do I have a story for you!" Our last few sessions had been good, and the last few weeks in the marriage had been good. This had enabled him to reinstitute his morning meditations, which did serve to energize him throughout the day. He had experienced four good days, but the weekend with visiting intrusive in-laws had wrecked him. Even before they arrived, he could feel Amy withdrawing as she always did in face of these stressful visits with her parents. The two of them had talked about her growing emotional unavailability as the weekend approached, but her emotional preoccupations nevertheless caused her to withdraw steadily from the relationship.

Stephen understood this and worked on cutting her some slack but still felt himself in a <u>downhill spiral of abandonment</u> that was made significantly worse by the demanding, intrusive, accusatory interactions with his mother-in-law. He understood this as her nature, but her presence always frustrated and depleted his inner resources. According to Stephen:

"That's when the sexual fantasies began and no matter what I did I could not escape the impelling images. I stayed away from the computer at home, but I kept hatching schemes to get away to the office and hit the Internet—which I succeeded all weekend in resisting. I was angry at Amy, her mom, and her dad for 'making me have' the fantasies and for throwing me into temptation when I was doing so well. I knew better than to blame them, of course, but I was feeling abandoned, frustrated, and angry—I wanted to sneak away, I wanted revenge, I wanted to get even for these assaults. A year ago I couldn't have seen all of this. I would have just felt in a major bind, and probably would have lapsed. But the worst part of the weekend was that I realized I had an extra $10 in my pocket that Amy wasn't aware of—our budget is tight so she manages the money and is usually aware of exactly how much money I have with me. I realized I could cruise right down to the dirty bookstore, find a magazine and spend a few relieving minutes in my car before trashing it and coming home. I can't tell you how many times I relished and then dismissed the fantasy. I even could identify the things at the time that were happening that would set it off, but I couldn't shake it. My 'sobriety commitment' to myself and to Amy is to be completely honest about lapses and threatened lapses—which I have been. And, as you know, there has been hell to pay in our relationship every time she thinks I have come close to a real lapse. I wasn't exactly close to a lapse but the fantasies were driving me crazy.

"And here's the worst part. We had tried to re-connect Sunday night after her parents had left but we were both so totally drained we could only acknowledge our lack of connection and exhaustion before we collapsed into bed. The thought had kept recurring that, knowing that my usual Monday morning meeting had been canceled, I had some extra time before I had to be at work. I could get to the bookstore with my extra $10, spend some time in my car, and still get to work in time. I showered early, excited to be knowing what I would be doing. Then I found myself, excited and almost involuntarily headed toward the bookstore. I pulled up in front. I shut off the motor. Only then, did I catch myself. I was horrified that it had gone this far. I started the car up again and got to the office badly shaken that I had come so close to a slip—and that it had happened almost without my awareness, like some sort of a blind drive, like a bad dream. Now doctor, *you* tell *me* what on earth this is all about!"

I said that it didn't sound like a sex story at all. Like it was about something else altogether. Stephen was puzzled. I asked him to speak about the feelings of abandonment, assault, revenge, sneaking, and getting even. Stephen's thoughts went to themes we had covered recently in therapy—his father's unrelenting hatred of everything and everybody in his life and his mother's willingness to put up with his father's repeated abuse of her and all of the family members. He again recalled the horrible sense of shame that ran throughout his childhood when his father flew into rages, blaming him for everything that made his father unhappy. Raging at him every time his mother fell into a depression as if it were his fault. He had a vivid memory of being humiliated and forced to leave the dinner table and for the first time excitedly sneaking down the hallway and into his parent's bedroom—going directly to the place under his father's side of the bed where his father kept a stash of porn magazines. How he knew they were there remains a mystery to Stephen, but somehow he knew, and in his excitement he went directly to the stash. He took a magazine to his room and soothed himself with images and fantasies. "It seems like that's how it all began," Stephen said, "I was maybe 8 or 9 years old."

As Stephen spoke, he came to understand full well what had happened over the weekend and the excited dissociative quality of the temptations. He already knew that the sneaking, revenge, and get-even fantasies had started much earlier in his life. He had recounted telling examples of experiences of humiliation by his father and failure to protect by his mother going back as far as he could remember. He now understood quite clearly how his good week with a sense of growing internal strength had been violated by the weekend and set off the dissociated fantasies and bookstore enactment.

Thus far in our relationship, I had chosen not to inquire into the exact nature of Stephen's exciting images, and he had chosen not to mention them. Now, I asked him if he thought we might learn anything by examining some of the sexual fantasies and images that had occurred over the weekend. He thought we might. It took him a few minutes free associating to actually pull up what images had been there: "It's like they exist almost in a dream world, somewhere else other than in me." He restored the fantasies of getting to a computer and finding chat rooms as he had done many times before. He would then begin a conversation with a woman. As he would express a wish—for her to unbutton her blouse, to allow him to see, to touch, or whatever—he would experience intense excitement. But, he reported, it was not exactly the specifics that were so consistently exciting as he reviewed in fantasy actual conversations he had engaged in with women. It was imagining going to meet her and her willingly and excitedly supplying him with whatever he wished. In short, he said, her eagerly and lovingly recognizing and responding to his every need as soon as it arose—a gratifying (self-other) interaction of two accommodating each other. I said, "Something you can never remember happening." Stephen responded, "Absolutely not—it was the other way around, I had to take care of her [his mother]. When I wasn't taking care of her, I was sent away. I can remember always being alone with my fantasies and then later with my Dad's porn and very early with my own sources for porn. It was a way of surviving the emotional abandonments, the humiliations, the physical assaults, the total lack of responsiveness my parents had toward me. Like self-recognition when I can't otherwise be seen or cared for. This conversation is very helpful—it's like I've always known all of this, but it has never reached the level of thought so I could take responsibility for my emotional reactions."

Sean

Sean's situation was very different. It was 14 months into therapy before he sheepishly announced that he had another problem he was ashamed to talk about. He frequented Internet porn sites. He enjoyed his experiences—sometimes several times a day, sometimes several weeks apart—but he knew it was wrong somehow. He had never told his wife of 5 years. And, their sexual relationship and emotional intimacy had always been good, so she had no reason to suspect that "a lot of my potential love for her drains off this way." He knew with his head that masturbation is normal, but nevertheless he felt guilty and knew that "something isn't quite right."

It took working through some shame for him to admit his porn interests. Much of our work centered on his being a gifted child imprisoned in a family that had no idea how to respond to him or to challenge his curiosity and intelligence. Striving for self-other recognition, he remembered childhood competition for grades, in sports, and in motorcycle and car racing. He now owned a small fleet of racing cars and flew about the world frequenting car meets, at times doing some of the actual driving himself.

In his work, he had started several successful companies that he had passed on to others to run. But, there had been a series of interpersonal disasters in which others that he had trusted (idealized self-others) had let him down and even betrayed his interests in favor of theirs. Needless to say, many of our hours had been filled with memories from his growing-up years in which parents and loved friends failed to see him, to recognize his creative ingenuity, to support his far-reaching endeavors, and to appreciate his integrity and good intentions. We worked a while on how others envied his gifts and success and how he had frequently "put himself on a cross" to rescue others—without appropriate gratitude.

He would be working in his office when temptation would arise, and he would find himself searching porn sites or reviewing his bank of stored video images. He was clear that he was interested in primarily one thing—"a fabulous blonde with big breasts and a figure to die for—the Marilyn Monroe type." She had to be very interested in him—in his body, his penis, his good looks, his business successes, his brilliant mind, and his wonderful personality. He was, of course, very ashamed to admit all of this to me—not really believing any of it was true and clearly seeing through the unrealistic image he sought and the admiration and excitement that she would necessarily have for him and how wonderful he was. He was disgusted at how "narcissistic" this all was, how stupid it was, and what a waste of time and energy it was—he had to stop it. He had made many resolutions, but in "unguarded moments of weakness," he succumbed to temptation. That he was not the only one to be suffering from an Internet addiction these days did not seem to help. He acknowledged that realistically it was going to continue for now and agreed to try to hold back self-blame in the name of trying to see what was going on for him. We reviewed a number of episodes over about a 6-month period, each time "putting things in slow motion" to examine his general mood that week, what had happened "the day of the crime" and the day before. He could readily appreciate that not becoming preoccupied in shame and self-blame allowed him to see an entire sequence of events in which the frantic porn search was embedded as an effort to shore up a faltering sense of self.

Not unexpectedly, the day came on which he announced that he had had "the shittiest week possible" and "had to rely on porn to get me through." A series of bitter personal and professional circumstances had hit him all at once, and the beautiful, reassuring, soothing, validating blonde had come to the rescue again—he saw it all so clearly now and did not fault himself for it. He could see how throughout his early childhood the idealization of his father (who he could later see did not deserve to be idealized) had often been called on to shore up a failing sense of self-esteem. The exciting, self-confirming, idealized blonde of his fantasy life was his adolescent answer to all of the failed attempts at relating to girls and trying to "score."

Why had he not picked this kind of person for a wife? He was sure his sex life would be even better, and he would not have to resort to fantasy. The answer slowly became clear. He longed to have a *real* relationship with his wife that was mutually confirming—not a hollow fantasy. But, he was also discovering that a real relationship with his wife was bound to be mutually disappointing and require working together toward repairing the ruptures. They were both in therapy and both doing well, and they were both committed to supporting each other through disappointments, misunderstandings, and disagreements between them.

After these insights, Sean could focus on the kinds of blows from the world that would set off "Internet regressions" and learned to process them with the person involved or with his wife. Over the succeeding weeks, he reported that the frequency of powerful sexual experiences increased with his wife, and that Internet temptations were subsiding. Sometime later, he had a sudden setback, felt the need, considered it, hit the stored blonde, allowed himself the luxury of having her help him momentarily—but never lost sight of what was going on for him. The blow had hit his self-esteem in momentarily devastating ways, the fragmented self craved to regain body–mind cohesion, so he turned to reassuring fantasies and the chemistry of excited masturbation to regain his balance. He reported, "I didn't feel guilty. I knew what had happened and that it would affect the rest of the day, including an important meeting that afternoon. My blonde doesn't do the trick for me much anymore but under the circumstances she did. I'm glad I have her for emergencies, but I'm also glad that she's really no longer a part of my life and relationships. Our work has helped me see how fragile my self-esteem can be and helped me develop ways of addressing narcissistic wounds in realistic ways so that I don't have to resort to fantasy—because that's what it is, something that isn't real and doesn't really address what I'm feeling or needing at the time. It's so hard to break childhood patterns."

The vignettes offered in this section have illustrated a variety of ways that sex serves to shore up a fragmenting sense of self or a failing sense of self-esteem. When self-other empathic recognition fails, sexual stimulation often serves to restore, at least momentarily, a sense of safety and well-being.

6

Self and Other Constancy

Independent Relatedness

Freud first intuited that it was during the third through seventh years that the problems of independent psychic life (selfhood) were faced and worked through by children. Borrowing the mythic themes of Sophocles' *Oedipus Rex* and Shakespeare's *Hamlet*, Freud discovered in his own self-analysis (in 1897) the power of emotional triangulation among independently functioning selves. Carl Jung pointed to Electra as the mythic model for triangulating selves in girls. It is one thing to search for nurturance and intelligibility in the world (the organizing experience). It is yet another thing to seek to establish dyadic reliability (symbiotic experience). And, it is yet another experience to look to the other for consolidation of a sense of self (the self-other experience). But, the most complicated aspects of human life develop when a full emotional awareness of third parties, of *contingent emotional relationships among interacting selves*, is integrated into psychic functioning. That is, the impact of the mythic Oedipus/Electra triangulation experience relies on the child's growing realization that each relationship exists within a broader set of contingencies determined by third parties. Symbolically and historically, the third party is represented as Father or The Fathers, but in actual human experience, the third party appears along with language and cultural awareness as that which comes between the symbiotic Mommy and me, as that which intervenes in our private dyadic relationships and catapults our relatedness into the broader human community of thirds.

Full emotional third-party awareness elevates us to the level of symbolic understanding, gives us an outside perspective (expressed in symbols) on every dyadic relationship we establish, simultaneously robbing us of exclusive emotional ownership of the one we most wish to love and to be loved by. The researches a child conducts and the conclusions he or she draws about how triangles work in relationships form a strong emotional web that Freud first understood and referred to as the Oedipus/Electra complex. In this reading, what has been called "castration anxiety" can only refer to the anticipated loss of the personal power once experienced in dyadic relationships and is by no means peculiar to boys. It is the social order (the language system, cultural restraint, The Fathers) that intervenes to cut off this personal power we once experienced in primordial dyadic (symbiotic) relating.

The assumptions about third-party contingencies and dangers developed during this period are often conflictual and undergo repression. These repressed patterns tend to govern subsequent relationships to such an extent that Freud labeled them "neurotic." The Freudian or self-and-other constancy listening perspective operates on an entirely different plane (the cultural verbal–symbolic) than the three that precede it and can be thought of as leading toward independent relatedness. Loewald (1979) pointed out that Freud's notion of the power of unconscious psychic constellations *waning* throughout a lifetime contrasts sharply with his translator's term "resolution of the Oedipus complex." Thus, striving for the independence experience in contingent relationships is a lifelong task.

Précis: Listening to the Independent Relatedness Experience

Developmental Metaphor

Four- and 5-year-olds are dealing with triangular love-hate relationships and are moving toward more complex social relationships. In their relatedness, they experience others as separate centers of initiative and themselves as independent agents in a socially competitive environment. Framing the internalized patterns of independently interacting selves in both cooperative and competitive triangulations with real and fantasized third parties entails studying the emerging interaction patterns for evidence of repressive forces operating within each participant and between the analytic couple that work to limit or spoil the full interactive potential.

Psychotherapeutic Parameters

Traditional diagnosis: neurotic personality organization

Developmental metaphor: 36+ months—(oedipal) contingent triangulation, competitive and cooperative

Affects: ambivalence; overstimulating affects and repressed drives

Transference: constant, ambivalently held self and others

Resistance: to the return of the repressed

Listening mode: evenly hovering attention/free association/ equidistance

Therapeutic modality: verbal–symbolic interpretation—interpretive reflection

Countertransference: overstimulation—generally an impediment or detraction

Kernberg: Love in the Analytic Setting

Otto Kernberg (1994) begins his discussion of love in the analytic setting by declaring

> The analyst who feels free to explore in detail, in his own mind, his sexual feelings toward the patient will be able to assess the nature of transference developments and thus avoid a defensive denial of his own erotic response to the patient; he must at the same time be able to explore transference love without acting out his countertransference in a seductive approach to the exploration of the transference. (p. 1145)

Kernberg (1994) believes that exploring the sexual experience of patients of both sexes offers an opportunity for the analyst to resonate with his or her own bisexuality, as well as an opportunity to cross a

> boundary of intimacy and communication that is only reached in culminating moments of intimacy of a sexual couple. ... This is an experience unique to the psychoanalytic situation, an activation of an intensity and complexity of countertransference that probably can be tolerated and used for work only because of the protection offered by the boundaries of the psychoanalytic relationship. (p. 1146)

Kernberg (1994) illustrates his thesis by reporting on Miss A, a 32-year-old single woman referred for depression, polysubstance abuse, and a chaotic lifestyle in her work and in her relationships with men. Although intelligent, warm, and attractive, at first Kernberg saw her as somewhat plain and neglectful of her appearance and attire. Despite successful graduate school experience, she had a history of frequent job changes due to affairs with fellow employees. Typically, she would fall in love, become clingy and dependent, and then be cast aside by the men she dated. She would then become depressed and resort to alcohol and drugs. Kernberg reported on events that took place during the third and fourth years of her psychoanalytic treatment.

Miss A had been involved in a long, turbulent relationship with a married man who was unwilling to leave his wife for her but with whom she was considering having a child. In treatment, she complained bitterly about his being sadistic, deceitful, and unreliable. When Kernberg (1994) questioned her about the relationship, she accused him of attempting to destroy the most meaningful relationship of her life and of being impatient, domineering, and moralizing. It seemed that she was experiencing her therapist as an unhelpful, critical, unsympathetic father figure, while repeating her masochistic relationship pattern in the transference.

Kernberg (1994) noted in the countertransference that he had been reluctant to explore with her the positive aspects of her sexual relationship with her lover for fear of seeming invasive and seductive. It seemed that she had heard his earlier interpretations as an invitation for erotic submission. "I interpreted her fear to share with me the details of her sexual life as related to her fantasy that I wanted to exploit her sexually, and seduce her into developing sexual feelings toward me" (p. 1152).

What was then revealed was that she was having trouble having orgasm with this man, not unlike with previous men. She could only achieve full sexual excitement and orgasm when a man would become enraged at her and hit her. This clarified both her unconscious efforts to provoke men to hit her and her drug behavior, which led to her being impulsive, uncontrolled, demanding, and complaining. Her explorations of this material led to the end of the current relationship, and in the grief that followed, she experienced conscious erotic feelings in the transference. Her new image of her therapist was that of an idealized, protective, loving, and sexually responsive man. "I, in turn, having experienced her previously as a somewhat plain and sexually not particularly attractive woman, now developed erotic countertransference fantasies during the hours, together with the thought that it was really remarkable that such an attractive woman should not have been able to maintain any permanent relationship with a man" (Kernberg, 1994, pp. 1153–1154). But, Miss A soon began to become frustrated and humiliated by Kernberg's lack of responsiveness to her sadomasochistic wishes and came to consider him cold, callous, and sadistically seductive.

> The intense affect of these recriminations, her accusatory, self-depreciatory, and resentful attitude … led to a shift in my countertransference. Paradoxically, I felt freer to explore my countertransference fantasies, which ranged from sexual interactions replaying her sadomasochistic fantasies to what it would be like to live with a woman like Miss A. My fantasies about sadomasochistic sexual interactions with Miss A also replicated men's aggressive behavior toward her that she had unconsciously tended to induce in them in the past. My fantasies culminated in the clear recognition that she would *relentlessly provoke* situations of frustration of her dependency needs, angry recriminations, escalating to violent interactions, and public display of depression and rage. She would present herself as my victim, which would unfailingly destroy our relationship.
>
> As I utilized this countertransference material in my interpretation of the developments in the transference, Miss A's profound feelings of guilt over the sexualized aspects of the relationship with me became apparent. In contrast to earlier complaints about feeling rejected and humiliated because of my lack of a loving response to her, she now felt anxious, guilty, and upset over her wishes to seduce me, and evoked an idealized image of my wife (about whom she had no information or awareness). I realized in retrospect that my resistance to exploring countertransference fantasies earlier had prevented me from following them in a direction that would have made the masochistic self-destructiveness of the patient's erotic wishes toward me much clearer. (p. 1155)

Kernberg (1994) believes that this story illustrates triangular transference love as it develops in neurotic personality organization and the usefulness of exploring transference as well as countertransference feelings. He concluded: "The analyst's freedom to explore fully his feelings and fantasies evoked by the patient's transference is basic to his understanding of his countertransference, enabling him to formulate transference interpretations in terms of the patient's unconscious conflicts" (p. 1156). Despite the current trend toward more relational countertransference disclosure when listening in perspectives I, II, and III, most analysts, including Kernberg, still apply Freud's recommended restraints when listening to "neurotic" layers of personality since disclosure runs the risk of being gratuitous or distracting to the gradual unfolding of transference concerns.

McDougall: Homoerotic Stimulation in the Countertransference

Joyce McDougall (1995), in an extended case study, reported on the analysis of Marie-Josée, a 35-year-old woman suffering from extreme neurotic anxiety, as well as insomnia, claustrophobia, and agoraphobia, which she regularly medicated. In the brief account that follows, two dreams illustrate the workings of sexual themes in the transference and countertransference.

The phobia that caused Marie-Josée the greatest suffering occurred when she was alone at night because of her husband's frequent out-of-town business trips. In preparing for bed, she would become overwhelmed by a sense of impending danger and then be unable to sleep or would awake in the night with a frequent need to urinate, which she attributed to having small (child-size) kidneys. Often, her fears would be so great that she would go to her parents' house until her husband returned. As the analysis deepened, McDougall (1995) had the distinct conviction that Marie-Josée's mother colluded in her fears by being seductive and engulfing. The analytic work soon pointed toward the probability that her phobia of being alone at night and her symptom of urinary frequency both related to infantile longings and primitive erotic fantasies related to the theme of unconscious homosexuality.

Marie-Josée revealed her recurring bedtime fantasy to be that someone (at first a man, but later in the analysis a bisexual figure) will enter through her bedroom window and rape or kill her. While this nightmarish fantasy at first is loaded with terror, as it became interpreted as an infantile wish she began to appreciate the excitement inherent in it. Erotic elements became added to the fantasy, which became accompanied by compulsive masturbation that gradually replaced the sleeping medications. At this time, Marie-Josée increased her complaints regarding her mother's intrusiveness and soon had the following dream:

> I was swimming around in a tumultuous sea and I feared I might drown, although I noticed that the water and the scenery were rather pretty. I had a feeling I'd been there before. The waves got larger and I said to myself, *I'll have to find something to cling to or I shall die in this water.* At that moment I noticed one of those—I forget what they're called— sort of hitching posts that are used to attach boats. I reached out to grasp it. It was made of stone. Anyway, I woke up in a state of panic. (McDougall, 1995, p. 21)

In her associations to the dream (McDougall, 1995), Marie-Josée's fear of dying in the engulfing ocean was given special meaning since in French the words for *mother* and *sea* sound identical.[1] The detail of the hitching post "made of stone," which in French is *pierre*, used the same word as her father's name, Pierre-Jose, and the source of part of her own name. The exact name for the hitching post, which escaped her momentarily, turns out to be *une bitte d'amarrage*, the difference in French between *bitte* and *bite* being "mooring post" and "cock." Marie-Josée commented:

> It's just the panic I always feel when I have to go outside, and it's all got to do with my mother. She's everywhere, threatening to possess me. ... [T]his has something to do with my father and my memory of seeing his penis that day in the bathroom, when I was about four. I was afraid my mother would be angry with me for having spied on him with such excitement. Perhaps that's why I woke up with a feeling of panic? (p. 22)

McDougall (1995) reported that, in her attempt to flee from the import of the dream, Marie-Josée turned her attention to what she saw as lack of progress in the analysis. In transference, McDougall said that she "had now become the bad mother who was neither helping her to

---

[1] The analysis occurred in Paris and was conducted in French.

find her way out of this maze of frightening fantasy, nor teaching her to swim in tumultuous seas, nor indicating the means by which she might turn to her father in a protective and erotic fantasy wish" (p. 22).

In time, Marie-Josée's night terrors subsided, but her daytime panics persisted. She developed a clear understanding that she continues to endow mother with environmental omnipotence, a desire to possess her body and soul and to prevent her from having a closer relationship with her father. Further, she grasped that she must have some psychological investment in keeping this scenario alive. At this time, McDougall (1995) had her own dream:

> I am supposed to meet someone in a *quartier* of Paris (which is little known to me) that has the reputation of being dangerous at night, particularly the underground railway in that area. I am permeated with a sense of something uncanny yet vaguely familiar at the same time. Several people get in my way and I hurry on, pushing them aside. Suddenly I am inside a house and find myself in the presence of an attractive Asian woman, dressed in a provocative, sexy manner. She looks at her watch and then remarks, *You're rather late, you know.* I stammer out some sort of excuse and reach forward to caress the silken fabric of her dress as though to seek forgiveness by being seductive. At that moment it becomes evident that I am supposed to have some erotic contact with this mysterious stranger. I feel embarrassed because I am not sure what is expected of me. I decide that I have no choice: I must renounce all will-power and passively submit to whatever this exotic creature wants. The anxiety, probably mingled with excitement aroused by the disquieting erotic scene, woke me up with the jolting conviction that my life was in danger. (pp. 24–25)

Unable to return to sleep, McDougall (1995) analyzed the many detailed elements of her own dream that were filled with implications for Marie-Josée's analysis. For present purposes, several aspects are important. McDougall saw that her own repressed homoerotic desires for her own mother had been blocking her from helping Marie-Josée from realizing how important her mother's love had been for her. The Chinese silk element links to a former Asian patient and to an envy McDougall felt for that woman's relationship with her mother.

I began to search for clues of evidence that I had *denied* my childhood erotic feelings for my mother. I recalled an evening when I was eight or nine years of age. She had come in to say goodnight to my sister and me because she and my father were going to a party. She was wearing a dress of shimmering apricot material that seemed to change color as she walked. I asked her what kind of material the dress was made of and she said, "It's shot-silk." I thought I had never seen anything so beautiful!

My first response to this memory was that I must have been jealous because my father was taking *her* out instead of me. But that supposition did not necessarily exclude the other possible wish: that *my mother would choose me*, rather than my father, to go to the party, and that I, too, would be dressed in apricot shot-silk. ...

I began to feel a nostalgic longing for a barely remembered past, redolent with primitive and erotically-toned feelings of love and hate. Long-forgotten fantasies of the fear of death—my own or my mother's—also returned. As for my father, the little girl in me believed him to be immortal. Only he could save my mother and me from some kind of erotic, fusional death! (p. 26)

McDougall's (1995) associations to her dream let her realize how envious she was of the care and attentiveness shown to Marie-Josée by her mother. She had analyzed so carefully the hostile feelings in her patient and in herself but had overlooked the positive feelings and the disavowed homoerotic ties to mother. This oversight, McDougall believes, was due to her own investment in maintaining the repression of her own infantile wishes to be the chosen object of her own mother's love life. Further, she seems to have overlooked Marie-Josée's disavowed pleasure in having a homosexually desirous mother.

My countertransference deafness, together with my repressed fantasies, had functioned like an opaque screen, preventing the analytic "light" from clarifying not only Marie-Josée's unsatisfactory adult sex life, but also a dominant fantasy element in her partial frigidity: namely, her unacknowledged homosexual wishes.

These could now be verbalized and thus allow insight into Marie-Josée's previously unrecognized envy of her mother and her mother's sex and her childhood longing to take possession of her mother in order to be a woman and a mother in her own right. These new insights eventually gave access to the significance of her rejection of the wish for a child of her own. She was still the child, with a little girl's genitals and a little girl's bladder. (pp. 24–30)

McDougall (1995) points out that the route from girlhood to adult femininity is full of pitfalls. The roots of feminine eroticism are germinated in the early mother–child sensuous relationship of infancy and potentially give rise to a number of erotic zonal confusions. Even when the orientation to heterosexuality appears to have successfully arrived, says McDougall, there is likely with women clients to be a continuous struggle to integrate the earliest homoerotic sensual relations that occurred with the mother of infancy. The two dreams and their analysis illustrate the continuous search for solutions to long-buried erotic wishes of childhood and how their conscious consideration or verbalization can open the way to their integration into a more harmonious adult sexual self. Note again, as in the previous case of neurosis reported by Kernberg (1994), that McDougall interpreted *from* the countertransference without feeling the need to speak *of* the countertransference.

Précis: The Listening Perspective Approach

The listening perspective approach has emerged out of myriad considerations that have evolved over a century of psychoanalytic study (Hedges, 1983/2003, 2005). It is formulated in terms of a major self and other relatedness paradigm shift that highlights (a) consciousness raising, (b) systematic subjectivity, (c) a search for narrational truth, (d) acknowledgment of the uncertainties of the participatory universe, (e) the systematic establishment of vantage points from which to listen, and (f) a variable responsiveness listening technique (Hedges, 1992). The conceptual advance that the paradigm shift of listening to and interaction with self and other representations makes possible is an approach to psychotherapy based on differential listening to developmental relational issues and differential techniques utilizing strategic emotional involvement (Hedges, 1996).

PART 3

THREE EXTENDED CASE STUDIES ILLUSTRATING SEX AND SEXUALITY IN THE TRANSFERENCE, RESISTANCE, AND COUNTER-TRANSFERENCE OF PSYCHOTHERAPY

$$7$$

THREE EXTENDED
CASE STUDIES

Dora: Eros in the Transference

In my book *Interpreting the Countertransference* (Hedges, 1992), I report on my failed engagement with a woman who, over a 3-year period, developed an erotic transference. When I have presented this case to professional audiences, listeners regularly protest that the treatment was not a failure, that Dora was very connected to me, and that she benefited considerably from our work together. True as this may be, it was the countertransference work that failed because at that time I did not know how to understand and work with the intense feelings aroused in the erotic transference.

At the beginning of the session, Dora would sit up and look deeply into my blue eyes, stare at my chest, and enjoy the little hairs that "peeped up" from my open shirt collar. She would dutifully use the couch for her thrice-weekly therapy, but at the end of sessions she would again want to breathe deeply and take me in visually. I was "her type," she said. As the mutual therapeutic seductions progressed, there were many elements of mutual enjoyment, but Dora continued to fear that I did not like her, that I would see her as a weepy, depressed, housewife or find her a pathetic, struggling student or some other kind of demeaned creature.

Therapists who have heard or read about our work together usually register sympathy with my plight as all efforts on my part to bring to light the possible meanings of what I experienced as her erotic intrusiveness were impatiently or angrily deflected. Midway in treatment, I "flinched" one day when she was adoring me, and she went into an immediate angry and anguished tailspin, wildly declaring that I had never loved her, that I truly did think all the negative things about her that she feared I did, that she could never trust me again, that she must stop her therapy at once. I recovered momentarily and convinced her to keep working, which we did for another year before a similar incident occurred, and she abruptly terminated—a painful experience for both of us.

Almost from the outset, I had been struggling with feeling intruded on by her ongoing erotic interest in me and had sought consultation, which did put me in touch with childhood material of my own that related to my experience of a sexually intrusive adopted sister and a highly intrusive seductive mother. Sexualization of the therapeutic relationship is not uncommon, and it may take various forms and be attributed to different causes, but a few common themes often emerge.

One frequent determinant for the sexualization of the dyadic experience is the fusion or confusion between affection and sexuality. That is, certain kinds of sensual or affectionate attachments from early childhood are retained in the personality through puberty, when they become enmeshed in an individual's sexuality. The sexualized affection can then be transferred to subsequent relationships, including the therapeutic one.

Another cause for sexualization of replicated interactions arises from the ways in which mind–body boundaries form or fail to form fully in early childhood relationships. In various ways, mind–body boundaries may remain defined idiosyncratically and, to a greater or lesser extent, imbued with erotic or incestuous overtones. Early ego functions surrounding issues of interpersonal boundary definition may have been limited or peculiar for a variety of reasons. The result is that later sexual development does not become integrated smoothly into conventional definitions of interpersonal boundaries, and certain merger experiences may remain erotized.

In the present vignette, a third possibility to account for the sexualization of the replication arises that is different from those ordinarily encountered. Here, the sexualized replicated transference shows up as a function of the *therapist's personal vulnerabilities or sensitivities* that would not necessarily need to be at all sexual in nature. That is, when a symbiotic or separating dyadic exchange is replicated in the analytic relationship, it is the *affective mode of relatedness* that is reestablished on a pre- or nonverbal basis. The content of the interaction is often not of particular interest in itself, but what is of crucial importance is the affective nature of the emotional interchange to be replicated. What had to be replicated with Dora was a particular style, pattern, or model of early mother–child relatedness in which the child felt that whole sectors of her spontaneous and creative potentials had to be suppressed to support the mother's vulnerable personality functioning. The mother's dependency hung heavily on this child as the mother demanded incessant reassurances in a variety of ways, leaving the girl feeling elated that her mother loved her and simultaneously helpless and stifled by her mother's intrusive attention, which was totally fixed on her to maintain the mother's cohesiveness and functioning in the world. So, Dora had derived much enjoyment and satisfaction from what she experienced as my permission to let her gaze at me and to feel consolidated as a result of her erotically tinged scrutiny of my eyes, my hair, my chest, and other parts of my body. As far as I could determine, there was no history of overt incest in her family, although her older brother was frequently obnoxious, using double entendres with off-color implications. I have to surmise that Dora was skillful in ferreting out an aspect of my personality that was vulnerable to a similar quality of emotional threat that her early relationship with her mother and possibly also an insinuating brother contained.

My assuming that the problem was created by a series of episodes in *my* preadolescence or a personal vulnerability in my personality dating to my own symbiosis ignored completely the possibility that this vulnerability was being actively stimulated by her at a level not conscious to either of us for the purposes of recreating a certain stylized and highly charged emotional atmosphere. In considering the countertransference material in the narrow sense and acknowledging a specific vulnerability in my historical past, I failed to appreciate the transference replication involved. I thereby lost the opportunity to move the consideration of the transference replication of uneasiness, fear, hatred, confinement, and strangulated creativity that I was feeling onto the plane of the therapy. It was not until several years later that I came to understand where I had gone wrong.

The process of countertransference interpretation is subject to considerable "give-and-take" creative interaction between two people and often takes months of collaborative work to accomplish. In replication, the unique personality features of the therapist are often utilized for expressive purposes by the client. The relevant dimensions can be expected to become embedded in or entangled with the personal images and idioms peculiar to the therapist's personality or character.

Christopher Bollas (1983) speaks of "countertransference readiness" as a cultivated state of "freely roused emotional sensibility" that is available to the therapist through hunches, feeling states, passing images, fantasies, and imagined interpretive interventions. Like many clinicians, Bollas entertains the possibility that, for differing reasons and in varied ways, clients re-create their infantile life in the transference and countertransference of the analytic relationship. Clients may enact fragments of a parent, thus inviting us unconsciously to learn through experience how it felt to be the child, or they may hyperbolize the child to see if we become the crazy or abusive parent. Bollas holds that preoedipal clients tend to create idiomatic environments in which the therapist is invited to fill the differing and changing self and other roles. Bollas emphasizes that we must sustain long periods of not knowing where, what, who, and how we are meant to function while the person manipulates us through "transference usage" into "object identity." More often than not, Bollas says, we are made use of through our affects much as baby "speaks" to mother by evoking a feeling-perception in the mother that inspires some action on the baby's behalf or leads the mother to put the object use into language, thereby "engaging the infant in the journey toward verbal representation of internal psychic states" (p. 204).

Bollas's (1983) working technique follows Winnicott's (1947) attitude in regard to the therapist's thoughts as subjective objects to be put into the potential space between, objects with which two can play. As examples, Bollas might preface a feeling or subjective statement with, "You know, I really don't know whether what I'm going to say is true, but … "; "Now. I don't think you are going to like what occurs to me, but … "; or "This may sound quite crazy to you, but … , "and then proceed to say what he thinks or feels.

Bollas (1983) points out that, not unlike the early situation with mother, the therapist seeks out and relates to the unconscious gestures of the client. That is, the analyst is "finding and supporting the infant speech in the analysand and doing so, ironically, by speaking up for his own nonverbal sensations" (p. 210). Bollas believes that responsible and comfortable rootedness in subjective experience that can be shared by two leads toward a mutual "sense of appropriate conviction that the client's true self has been found and registered" (p. 210).

I have developed several suggestions regarding interpretations of countertransference arising in response to a symbiotic replication.

1. At this level, the best interpretation is often action—simply being there in some important way (rather than the abandonment previously experienced in early childhood that is often replicated with verbal interpretations).

2. A format for presenting countertransference interpretation is a tentative and slow, head-scratching, yawning attitude, such as, "I've had some thoughts I can't account for. Perhaps they are relevant to *our* experience." The first-person plural pronoun reflects empathy with the symbiotic experience. The sense of the symbiotic "we" always needs to be present.

3. It is often valuable to discuss the "two levels" of "our" relationship:
   a. The "real" level: "All is going well between us as part of the analytic hours."
   b. The fantasy or countertransference work level: "You have fantasies and dreams about me or us that are helpful for us to examine sometimes, and perhaps we can also learn by examining sensations, feelings, or dreams of mine—since we are in this together."

4. I define two rules of thumb regarding interpretation when I am not certain:
   a. Contentwise: Try interpreting at the lowest level first, that is, at the level of symbiotic need and deficit rather than the higher developmental level of conflict of thoughts, desires, and inhibitions. If one is wrong, the effect is harmless, and the client will make the correction, whereas interpreting at the highest (oedipal conflict) level may represent a major misunderstanding of relational needs and therefore a break of empathy.

b. Formwise: Interpret or respond at the highest level of abstraction first, that is, at the verbal–symbolic level rather than the self-other or merger–interaction level. If you are wrong, you simply will not be heard, whereas interactive interpreting may not maximize the symbolic possibilities of the moment.

Three Common Treatment Errors

In attempting to analyze replicated symbiotic or merger scenarios, three technical errors commonly arise in regard to handling the countertransference.

The first and perhaps most widely noted error is the therapist's simply ignoring disturbing countertransference feelings because he or she knows them to be related to recurring personal issues or sensitivities.

The second widespread technical error is the therapist's disregard of probable countertransference distortions or idiomatic biases in favor of getting some "fix" on what is "really happening"—perhaps in the form of some theoretical notion borrowed from or confirmed by a well-known authority regarding "defensiveness," "splitting," "narcissistic rage," "incestuous entanglements," "empathic failure," "emerging archetypes," or whatever.

The report I have offered of my countertransference entanglement with Dora illustrates yet a third variety of technical error: a readiness on the therapist's part to assume personal responsibility for the emerging disruption or untoward feelings, thereby sidestepping completely the more important interactional/communicational component, which may contain the crucial processes and imagos required for the psychotherapy, the emergence of which the two people involved are resisting. The collaborative narrational work required is always long and difficult and frequently touchy to one or the other or both of the participants.

Having by now had the opportunity as a supervisor as well as in subsequent consulting work of my own to learn how to identify broadly and to launch into collaborative work on specifics of this kind of countertransference entanglement, I have been able when reviewing the present case to have a confident sense of the right general direction the work might have taken and did not. I am sure if I had understood what we were dealing with that I could have found some tactful way to tell Dora that I did not like the (apparently) erotic interest she was taking in me—first, because it stimulated uncomfortable feelings from my own past but more importantly because it seemed to me that she was needing to put me in the same untenable position she felt as a child with her mother's intrusiveness and we were not really looking at what was important. The Dora case stands as a clear example for which sex in the transference has little or nothing to do with sex but points to issues of symbiotic intrusiveness dissociated and enacted by both participants.

Ted: Eros in the Resistance

Ted wheeled into the parking lot of my office building in a late-model BMW. Sharply and expensively dressed and offering a quick step, a ready handshake, and a winning smile, Ted explained that for months he has had to hide his Internet activities from his wife because she thought his fetishes were disgusting and sick. During their courtship some 10 years prior to this, Lisa was clearly excited when Ted would pick her up and discretely slip a handcuff on her wrist in the car on the way to and from the opera or the theater. She would giggle, and her eyes would light up with a clear excitement, which would win the evening for him. For several years, she participated willingly and seemingly excitedly as they played with soft ropes, thumb cuffs, butt slaps, and other restraining and discipline toys that they would buy during their periodic visits to the Pleasure Chest in West Hollywood. But, over the years Lisa began to lose interest, was not in the mood, would turn away, eventually showing loathing and disdain for what she viewed as Ted's "sick and perverse interests and fantasies." Lisa now claims that she never had the slightest interest in any of these things, that they had always disgusted her, and that she had simply gone along with Ted's fetishes and silly games to satisfy him. He was absolutely certain that this simply was not the case. Ted declares that Lisa was engaged and excited by bondage and discipline fantasies and play early in their relationship and has since gone into defensive denial.

Lisa now wants to know what would people think of him, of her, of them if they only knew about how they had carried on? What about her parents and her three grown sons and their wives and her grandchildren, all of whom have a great relationship with Ted—what sort of opinion would they have of him if they knew what his sex thing was? Would he please get rid of those disgusting porno flicks and magazines that he had forced on her all these years and throw away all the black leather and tight silk fetishes he had bought for her?

Needless to say, sex has grown less and less frequent between Ted and Lisa. Ted has resorted to private bondage fantasies while having sex with Lisa. His clandestine masturbation with the few remaining fetishes and with the ever-expanding range of pornography available over the Internet has increased of late. Ted has read a lot of psychology books and had some prior limited therapy. He sees himself as an anal-retentive, obsessive-compulsive personality type—neat, tidy, organized, and frugal in business and finances. My fee was much too high for him, he said; he has large retirement deposits to pay regularly, but he would check to see what his insurance would pay. Also, he could come to sessions only during lunch hours because he did not want anyone to miss him at work or home or to know that he was in therapy again. Lisa had been in therapy before, and they had tried some couples work, but she felt each of the therapists had supported him somehow and now did not want any more therapy.

Ted loves his wife; he has remained faithful to her and could not imagine leaving her. They have built up a good life of love and respect together—even if it has become somewhat superficial and necessarily dishonest over time. They live in a big house, and both drive luxury cars. Ted and Lisa have built up a sizable retirement fund. The two like traveling together and have found some great bargain travel packages over the Internet. They love fine wines and enjoy cooking gourmet meals for each other. But, Ted had to be honest with me: A sexually frustrated man is naturally aware of life's many temptations. He had bought a few new pieces of paraphernalia lately, concealing them from Lisa. He just wanted to be himself, that was all. Why would she not accept him?

Meanwhile, some of Lisa's girlfriends had started attending the Crystal Cathedral, and Lisa wanted Ted to start going to church with her. There was a couples' retreat coming up soon. Ted said he was not opposed to religion or even to attending church with Lisa occasionally; but since neither he nor Lisa had ever been particularly religious people, Lisa's sudden and inexplicable interest in church had come as a complete shock to him. Out of deference to Lisa's changes in attitude, Ted has gotten rid of most of the fetishes and pornography, although he still kept a few of his favorites locked up at the office and in a briefcase in the trunk of his car. He has consented to go with her to the couples' retreat, but he is not sure why. Ted feared that Lisa wants to expose, shame, or publicly humiliate him at the church retreat.

Ted reported to me that he has lived in deep shame over his secret sexual interests and pursuits ever since he could remember. He had been so happy and relieved when Lisa had been able to share an interest in his games, toys, fantasies, and fetish excitements. He likes B&D (bondage and discipline) stories, fetishes, and games, but hastens to emphasize only "between consenting adults." He is turned off by S&M (sadism and masochism) activities and fetishes because he really is not into pain. Cross-dressing, rubber, hardhat, cowboy paraphernalia, bestiality, or diapering fetishes hold no interest for him whatsoever. There seems to be something about the suspense and fear of captivity and control that excites him; pictures of men with erect penises somehow dominating women lure him. His wife thought that he must unconsciously hate women, but he does not think that is what B&D is about: It is about making love to a woman and playing with control. Ted has at times worried that maybe he is a homosexual, but he is not really drawn to men. Ted does identify with and have a lot of empathy for the secrecy, shame, isolation, and persecution which many homosexuals have had to endure while growing up.

On the Internet, Ted had discovered a whole new world—wonderful people everywhere who were very much like himself. It seems that the world is filled with decent, upstanding, law-abiding, self-respecting human beings of high character who are well educated, morally upright, and culturally rich and diverse and who share his fetishistic interests. Ted now talked often in chat rooms with people who have always felt isolated, lonely, ashamed, persecuted, perverted, and "sick" because of "sexual preferences they were born with—or at least interests and preoccupations they have always known about and were told to be ashamed of." As a result of Internet contacts, Ted is now certain that there is nothing wrong with his fetishes—it is just that they are not mainstream.

Beyond the chat rooms, Ted told me that there are numerous informative articles, published forums, book reviews, philosophical tracts, and religious commentaries that appear daily to offer fresh perspectives on sexuality. The deluge of new and exciting information makes it clear to Ted that not only are fetishistic interests of all types widespread and enjoyed by many, but that they are not at all as unwholesome, corrupt, perverse, or sick as mainstream culture portrays them. "These people are mostly serious individuals struggling to make sense of who they are and to share common problems and dilemmas with others like themselves. Oh, to be sure, there's some sickos among the lot, but sickos are everywhere anyway, so it really doesn't matter. They have problems to work out, too."

Ted wanted somehow to come out of the closet, he said—not to shout his fetishes from the rooftops but to be comfortable discussing them whenever and wherever they naturally come up without fear of social censorship and without fear of an explosion of rage or humiliating shaming from his wife. He sees that he is agonizing like he had always agonized. But, with the help of his Internet contacts, Ted now realizes that there is no need to hide in shame and no need to feel guilty, sick, perverse, or dirty anymore, but he does not know where to go with it all, how to convince his wife, how to "go public" as it were. "I just need to find peace with my sexuality. And I have no idea what that would look like."

Neurosis and Perversion

As early as 1905, Freud (1905/1975) had begun his formulation of neurosis as the excessive inhibition of sexuality and aggression, while he formulated perversion as the compulsive acting out of sexuality and aggression. Mental health was somewhere in between. For more than a century, our clinical research, our therapeutic skills, and our cultural awareness of sexuality have all revolved in one way or another around this distinction between extremes in inhibition and excitation.

Our earliest caregivers teach us to regulate, balance, and integrate these basic tendencies in our personalities and brain functioning—something parents and developmental specialists have been telling us all along.

It has been no secret to us therapists that people are fundamentally polymorphously perverse, that fetishes of all types are ubiquitous, and that the joy of sex involves delectable appetizers, rich and full main courses, and delicate sweet desserts. As the old Latinate goes, "There is no arguing about taste." But, the Teds and Lisas of the world are only now, due to the Internet, awakening to the numerous and complex dilemmas that human sexuality affords them, and they are confused and frightened.

Aside: Let's Talk a Little Freud, Yes?

I must include Freud here for it was he who first started me thinking about the nature of fetishes, how they develop, and how universal they are. His first cases were of men with shoe and ankle fetishes—fitting for the Victorian era, during which the only errant female flesh to be pursued might be a quick ankle flash beneath one of those alluring full-length skirts. The fetish was traced psychoanalytically by Freud (1927), until it was understood at last as a symbolic substitute for the mother's elusive excitatory center, her clitoris. Outlandish? Let us follow Freud's thinking.

Each young child is in close body–affect connection and communication with his mother during the child's earliest years. The child follows with excitement the mother's every move, her every intonation and glance, her every rise and fall in temperature—in short, her every arousal, however subtle or disguised. Like all roller-coaster rides of love, the young child's arousal seeking and inhibitory centers are always spiraling up and then crashing—sometimes under his or her control but often at the helpless or scary mercy of mother, of others, or of events. The child naturally wants to know what regulates the mother's arousal and interests to be certain of triumphing over competitors and getting enough of mother when needed. "There must be some unknown or hidden mechanism of her arousal," says intuition, "some locale of her excitability, some place in her that, if I could but touch it, I could control her interests and excitement. Then I could gain priority and control over her other interests. I must find a way to penetrate to the core of this mystery—to capture, to captivate, to control, to have, to manipulate, to enchant, to ensure my well-being, to have my mother all to myself forever!"

But, the deepest any Victorian child in Freud's social class could penetrate the mother was the hem of her skirt—to get a glimpse or perhaps a quick feel of her ankle or her shoe. "If I can control that, I shall never be without her, I shall never want" and so the birth of desire and the particular symbol of that longed-for sense of safety and control over love, the symbolic fetish in this case being a shoe. Female fetishes, largely unobserved by Freud, were thought to be rare; then again, there was no Internet in Freud's time.

Chat-room fetishes in their current forms are the offspring of decades of marketing strategy by a highly sophisticated international pornography industry. As we know, mass-marketed products are supported by saleable images that are known to have a wide subliminal appeal. The images are then arranged in enticing commercial narratives designed to enhance the product's appeal and to expand its market. For example, bondage, discipline, sadism, masochism, feeding and toileting concerns, and parent–child motifs are all part of the current cultural load and part of everyone's strained early childhood experience in one way or another. The enticements known in Victorian times of ankles and shoes, on the other hand, have largely slipped into the annals of sexual history.

People who have felt exploited, victimized, isolated, and shamed for the imaginary routes that their personal sense of arousal and sexual excitement have historically taken quite understandably search for ways of "validating" themselves, of honoring "the way that I am." One way of removing the persecutory sting of social stigma is to huddle in safe groups of like minds: "See, I'm not so strange, sick, or unworthy after all; there are other high-minded souls who share my fate." But, whatever personal ways one uses, attempting to recover from the painful feelings of being a victim in childhood and later working to build new kinds of self-esteem, naming one's childhood abuses and coming out of the closet seems to be in vogue these days. "I am what I am, and people have to accept me for it" clearly rides on a vanguard wave of the civil rights movement, and personal confession has proven popular and effective to many.

Doing Psychotherapy With "I Am What I Am"

Whatever the sociocultural status of one's sexual fantasies, fetishes, and enactments, responsible psychotherapy continues to focus on the *internal* status of our psychological life. If, as we tend to believe, the foundation of our character, our basic nature—the "I am what I am"—is laid down in our genes and in our earliest family relationships, then psychotherapeutic inquiry seeks to discover the personal and the idiosyncratic, the unique and the special in us that lies beneath the archetypal fetish images produced in the pornography marketplace. But, what happens when we lift the veil of commercialized forms to discover how on a daily basis we live out, in all of our relationships, the unconscious themes represented in our addictions, compulsions, fantasies, and sexual enactments?

Late in the course of long-term, intensive psychotherapy, when one has painfully noticed one's various passions for destruction and self-destruction in relationships, comes an awareness of that subtle and dark, yet unexplored, vortex of masturbation and orgasm fantasies. The interest and curiosity about one's nature has by this time reached a compelling pitch. One begins to notice the images and narratives that silently impel one toward and into orgiastic release. Then, one notices that just as quickly as these images emerge from the dark sea of the unconscious to produce or accompany orgasm, like dreams they slip quickly away into the dark unthought known again. One struggles to capture them, to catch an inkling, a glimpse of the elusive Aphrodite, before the veil is again dropped and desire re-begins its ineluctable cyclical course.

By this point in psychotherapeutic self-study, one is no longer so shocked when standing naked before the mirror of one's clearly asocial, immoral, bizarre, destructive, and self-destructive compulsive, addictive, and perverse "otherness" fantasies and enactments. One day, a dream image or orgasm fantasy arrives that penetrates the veil and leaves a clear erotic path through the mists. *This is who I am* and how I unconsciously but passionately structure all relationships in my life. One at last grasps one of the epicenters of one's sexuality—not entirely unknown before, but dissociated and unformulated—the ever-fleeing desire of one's soul and how that desire structures one's personality and all significant and intimate relationships.

As speaker and listener in psychotherapy move into the earliest of preverbal symbiotic or character scenarios, one's most personal relational and sexual motifs can be spoken. The psychological structure built during (the preverbal symbiotic) era may be regarded as retained relatedness modes from the early mutual cuing processes, overlearned ways for two to interact. The subtleties and peculiarities of each symbiotic dance are what interest us most in analytic study.

> The search to define one's symbiotic modes is always unique for they are always highly idiosyncratic, strange, and usually shocking to our higher sensibilities. One man was finally able to state with conviction, "My deepest passion is to be beaten, raped, robbed, and left for dead." Another said, "I have a hard dick for women who can't be there for me." Or another stated, "I wish to be passive until I am finally abandoned altogether." Another said, "My deepest longing is for an empty teat." These statements of a person's scenario reflect years of psychoanalytic work and in each case are radically condensed into an almost bizarre bottom line that captures the deepest and worst of one's perverted relatedness desires and potentials based on some of the earliest relatedness strivings. This kind of deep realization about one's passionate involvements with others is usually reflected in unconscious sexual longings of a perverse, masochistic nature. Unconscious masturbation or orgasm fantasies, as they come to light in analytic work, always strike one as perverse or self-destructive in one way or another but regularly point toward one's deepest relational strivings. (Hedges, 1992, p. 122)

Searching for the Meanings of Past Satisfactions in Therapy

Whatever else can be said about our many and varied sexual proclivities, it is clear that they are derived from a past that is deeply embedded in our personalities and colors the ways that we choose to view and relate to our world on a daily basis. From the standpoint of clinical listening, it seems useful to consider most compulsions, addictions, perversions, and fetishes as the search for body–mind states that were once deeply satisfying and that have become somehow lost in our adult lives. All of our compulsions, addictions, perversions, and fetishes symbolically mark important experiences of deep satisfaction or frustration in our earliest relationships. Like symbols in dreams, our repetitive sexual fantasies and enactments stand as psychological representations of truly important parts of ourselves that deserve to be cherished, understood, and lived in the most fulfilling ways possible. Knowing about and respecting our personal symbols and representations and how they arise from our bodies and persist in our personalities, relationships, and sexuality is a vital part of the self-realization of psychotherapy. But, simply surrendering to powerful compulsions, addictions, and fetishes—Internet or not—does little more than to repeat the ways our first loves satisfied or frustrated us.

The real problem with "acting out" is that it is living in past relationships rather than present ones. Finding others who share our fetishistic interests may do much to spice up our sexual encounters, to relieve our sense of isolation and shame, or to make us feel less deviant; but channeling our energies and investments toward ever more exciting, perverse, and addictive fetishistic enactments leaves us progressively more removed from real relationships and from the frustrations and fulfillments offered by living life in the present in a real world of relating people. Persistently living out repetitive sexual fantasies and enactments denies our human capacity to achieve growth and transformation through real and novel kinds of personal relationships in which a mutual investment in, understanding of, and caring for the emotional well-being of the other is paramount.

Whatever approach a therapist chooses, let us hope that it honors and calls for elucidation of the client's various personal meanings implicit in or represented by his particular sexual preferences, fetishes, fantasies, or enactments. The psychotherapeutic balancing act is ideally carried on between recognizing the past loves and past love frustrations as represented in a person's sexual preferences and enactments and then encouraging participation in real, exciting, and novel relationships that have the power to generate many kinds of human inspiration, growth, and transformation.

Back to Ted

Toward the end of my first session with Ted, I tested his mental flexibility in several ways. First, I suggested that while he had described how being the captor, the one in control, excited him, he had not yet described for me how it felt being held captive, in bondage, and being disciplined. I thought he was going to jump out of his chair for joy that I had brought up the matter. Ted proceeded with relish to fill me in on the details of that side of his fetish life—the role-reversal effect that we have learned to expect in one way or another in all character/symbiotic scenarios.

Next, I tried suggesting that such powerful sexual fetishes usually had emotional correlates elsewhere in life and relationships. Again, Ted responded with elation that I seemed to understand that bondage and discipline were indeed embedded in his character and reflected in many aspects of his total life situation, and he readily provided a series of examples.

Finally, I suggested that what he had been describing for me with his wife is a *marriage* based on bondage and discipline in the truest psychological sense. Bingo again. He loved me, but our time was running out, so I made it his homework assignment to think about all of the ways that he and his wife kept each other in bondage and meted out punishment to each other on an ongoing basis. He liked the assignment and wrote a check.

Being a good compulsive organizer, Ted brought a list to the second session of all of the ways he kept his wife in bondage and punished her emotionally and a list of all the ways she had him in bondage and punished him emotionally—concluding with, "but it isn't fun with Lisa anymore." I said that we would have to work on understanding all that was going on between them, and that fetishes and sex fantasies that exist outside real relationships are always "more fun" when our own mind and pleasure sense are in near-total control. Real ongoing relationships pose more of a problem for us and do require considerable mutual understanding and ongoing processing—which it sounds like he and his wife had not kept up over the years. He agreed.

Ted had found that his insurance would pay little and told me all that he felt he could pay a month—a shockingly low amount for a man so well placed in the world. I told him that I did want to work with him because I was interested in what he was working on (which was quite true), so I offered a generously discounted fee. He agreed to think it over and to try to negotiate a compromise financial arrangement next week. Turning money loose was clearly a difficult dynamic issue for Ted, but I would only negotiate so far. He and I had connected well and had both immensely enjoyed the sessions together.

Ted began the third session by telling me how much he had gotten from our time together. Then, he announced that he could not go along with the financial arrangement I had proposed, but that he did want to go ahead with the current session anyway. I felt the torture rack slide open—the cold, pecuniary sadism, and the threatened punishment for my not agreeing to play his game according to his rules. The way he approached the subject invited me to "talk him into it" or "to give in more," both of which I chose not to do. I am not generally a control freak in such circumstances—in fact, I tend toward compliance and oversolicitousness. But, since the man was so bright and articulate, and because I had already offered him a good deal and he knew it, I chose to wait him out and to say my regrets and goodbye at the end of the hour. At the close of the session, Ted did reveal that he did not see how he could possibly be the person he needed to be for himself and stay in his marriage. Clearly, my implying that therapy would entail working on his relationship rather than continuing his nonrelated Internet fetish activities was not a route that appealed to him.

Did Ted's resistance to therapeutic explanation manifest in his attempt to dominate me? Or, was my refusal to allow myself to be dominated more of a counterresistance to work with Ted? The "Ted-and-Lisa" vignette poses many questions that can hardly be answered here. But, we do know that a whole new population of sexually confused and frightened people is being created for us by Internet chat rooms and porn marketing. We can expect that more refugees from all kinds of Internet chat rooms and romances will be surfing toward our offices soon. How many of them will be ready for therapy? How many will be ready to involve themselves in realistic relationships with a therapist or with others whom they can truly love and be loved by? And, how many therapists will be ready to empathize both with the addictive fetishistic lures that are so easy to fall prey to and with the frightening and disorganizing ordeal it can be to relinquish idealized fantasy relationships in favor of problematic and challenging real relationships?

The psychotherapeutic task for all of us is to learn how to honor and live with the past patterns of love and frustration that have long been established within ourselves—and with their symbolic fetishistic representations—at the same time learning how to reach out into unexplored emotional territory toward new and potentially liberating and transformative experiences in present and future real love relationships.

Charles: Eros in the Countertransference

My last sleeping thought was, "I have to suck his balls to calm him down." My first waking thought was, "What the fuck?!" It was immediately clear that the dream thought, as well as the waking expletive, referred to the rageful encounter I had experienced with my client Charles the previous night. Some of the old British case studies with nannies being caught pacifying intractable infants by massaging their balls came to mind. The infant needed some kind of relating to that was not forthcoming from mother and nanny and so was protesting vigorously. The way to quell the protest was to invade the infant with overwhelming penetrative stimulation, driving him into somatopsychic oblivion.

I have always felt Charles to be an attractive man with whom I have enjoyed interacting, regardless of the momentary qualities of our interaction. We have had several previous occasions during which it was helpful to label certain dynamics that had come up in our relationship, as well as with other people, as somehow "sexual" in nature—whether in an active–passive, voyeuristic–exhibitionistic, or sadomasochistic dimension.

I had from time to time been aware of moments of being sexually stimulated while in sessions with Charles, but I had not yet been able to tie that stimulation to what was actually happening between us at the time. I cannot say that I am "attracted" to him in the usual meaning of the phrase. I have not been "tortured" or felt frightened or ashamed by erotic feelings that have appeared in the countertransference (as we know sometimes happens). But, as with most clients, it seems that there are undoubtedly erotic dynamics between us, and that this dream may have been my first clear clue regarding what they might be about. I report three brief episodes that occurred over a 6-month period that illustrate several aspects of the working-through process of the erotic transference–countertransference encounter.

What I do know of Charles based on thrice-weekly contact over a 7-year period is that the terrified, desperate, rageful reactions I get on occasions when I am calling for more relatedness appear to originate from experiences of a passive, ineffective, and terrified mother who found that rage or outrage served to startle the baby or get him to back off from needing to relate to her. The conscious images and ongoing dialogue Charles produces, however, more often relate to a father who is capable and present in many ways but shuns interpersonal connections with a sarcastic, critical, hostile "put-down" demeanor that has always served to keep his child's relatedness needs at bay. It seems that Father wishes to provide Charles with something that his wife had failed at but cannot. Charles rages at his father's failures to be an adequate parent or person and searches seemingly endlessly until he finds a small glimmer or niche of possible relatedness with him that he attempts to work vigorously. But, as Charles has slowly and reluctantly discovered over the years he has been with me, just as soon as the glimmer of hoped-for relatedness appears and Charles believes he has at last achieved a meaningful hold on Father, it quickly disappears.

On the evening before my dream image of "sucking his balls to calm him down," Charles had arrived with a sullenness and apparent anger that took most of the session to bring out—and it then was finally, fully, and outrageously directed at me. We attempted to get a discussion going around a half-dozen topics before the content settled on his friend and colleague Jules.

A way of working that has evolved between Charles and myself over time focuses on some relationship that is foundering in some way. I am then in a position to show Charles that the way he is experiencing the relationship is leading him to exacerbate the situation by withdrawing, becoming inert, or radiating disgust and irritation, which increasingly turns the other person away. While these kinds of interventions on my part might have the outward appearance of supportive work, when I do persist in a particular point of view regarding one of his relationships, it is because some aspect of his inner life that is engaged in the therapy transference is coming into clear view in the parallel transference relationship.

Charles has a number of long-term perennially turbulent relationships in which he is aware that people have to strain to tolerate relating with him—despite the fact that he is basically a likeable fellow whose fundamentally good nature is evident to everyone who encounters him. Over time, as I have gotten thoroughly familiar with each of his cast of characters, I have been able to help him formulate what characteristic or interpersonal dynamic in them on the one hand allows them to stay attached to him and on the other hand causes them to misperceive, misunderstand, or mistreat him. Our best work usually gets done in a format when I am able to say, "Yes, we know Jules is such and such a way, and that he has demonstrated the same thing on numerous occasions, but the question for *you* is … ." We both feel triumphant when, through our discussions, we arrive at the place at which it is not necessary for Charles automatically to go into what he calls his paranoid-withdrawing pattern in response to a perceived rebuff. Charles wants to be able to have a clear vision of what is going on in a relationship, to be able to understand how the other person's limitations are contributing significantly to the impasse. He knows that he can easily be drawn into negative counterresponsiveness but that he also has the ability to show understanding and to take some creative initiative that upgrades the quality of the relating.

In the session reported (the evening before my dream thought), I persisted in not letting Charles weasel out of his ongoing difficulties with Jules and Jules's desperate attempts to curtail and limit contact with Charles because he is so difficult to get along with—given Jules's narcissistic predilections and limitations. Charles's rage at me slowly escalated. At first, his protests were that I was not being fair to him. Then, he declared that it was true that I saw him as a pathetic character, that I blamed all of his problems with Jules on him. He protested that he was not trying to block either the relatedness with Jules or with me, and that I was making him furious. It seemed I had again forgotten the good qualities he possesses, that I had carelessly lost sight of the bigger picture in which he does well in the world, has many friends, knows how to get along; that again I was taking him at face value in what he said about his relationships and then was cruelly, viciously, and antagonistically berating him, tearing him down, denigrating him. He said, "If you can't keep the whole picture in mind, if you start criticizing me on your slightest whim because of your own limitations in vision, then what's the point of continuing therapy?"

During the last 10 minutes of the session, I persisted in my efforts to show Charles his responsibility in the ways that he was interacting with Jules and with me. I parried all accusations that I was not on his side or had tunnel vision and basically wanted him dead like his parents. He began to rock forward in his chair in despair, rage, and agony that I could not see him, that I had to stop this attack, that this proved I was worthless to him, that he was going to have to stop seeing me. At one point, he actually shouted in agonized rage, "That's it! I quit! There's no way you're ever going to understand me." When our time was up, he shouted, "You're *doing* this to me"—meaning deliberately driving him into rage so that he will never want to speak to me again. During this dramatic end to the session, I repeated several times, "I hope [i.e., expect] to see you on Wednesday." On the way out the door, he threw out in disdain, "Why? You hate me anyway?"

There was nothing fundamentally new in this scenario, except that I persisted longer, causing him to rise to a higher, more sustained frantic and angry pitch in an attempt to get me to back off. I had the courage this time to let it escalate. I had already known all of the pieces of this scenario, but we were now living it out in spades. "Mutual enactment" certainly describes the situation. I was able to refrain from defensiveness as he shouted a series of accusations (each of which on previous occasions I had refused or protested as not true). I let the accusations fly along with the demand that I immediately rectify the escalating situation—which I made no effort to do. I felt I was experiencing in the countertransference role reversal his father or mother raging at him from the perspective of the young child who in all innocence wants to relate in a situation for which a plea for relatedness is experienced by the parent as an attack or an abandonment. The parent maintains innocent and enraged superiority in the face of the child's relational need and then blames the child for "doing this to me," for driving the parent away (or driving the parent crazy with relatedness needs). My dream thoughts registered my plight: I must suck his balls to assuage him, to sedate him, to traumatize him with sexual intrusiveness into oblivion to maintain some modicum of relatedness or sense of control over the relatedness. As I awakened, I tried to imagine all the ways my countertransference plight represented his position vis-à-vis each of his internalized parents of early childhood.

In the session, I felt from Charles his parents' desperation to be assured and affirmed in their rightness by the child relinquishing his plea, his legitimate childhood needs, for relatedness and recognition— and the escalating desperation and rage they each must have felt when such reassurance was not forthcoming from the child. I could barely stand the pressure—so how could an infant or young child possibly do other than to capitulate and believe that his parents' distress was indeed his fault? At the moment of greatest intensity, I saw in Charles the terror of his mother that the baby was abandoning her by his intense expression of need for relatedness to which she had not the slightest idea how to respond. When the inner love object of infancy is unleashed to be reexperienced by two in the transference–countertransference encounter, whose pain is greater, the parent's or the child's, the client's or the therapist's? We were both suffering.

My dream representation was that *something* must be done in desperation to quell the rage. Is this the desperate parent/nanny who feels chastised by the infant's cries to Heaven? Or, is this the infant knowing that sucking quells anxiety and terror—if I could just suck on him then a sense of safety and comfort could be restored. And, in all of this, who is the violator and who the violated?

I wrote a summary of our interaction, including the sexual dream thoughts and my ideas about what was going on between us and gave a copy to Charles the next session. He and I discussed it together, and he made further comments that added to our understanding.

I realize that many therapists who support a more conservative technique will be scandalized initially by the way the session went and then by the fact that I chose to "disclose" my view of the session and my countertransference responses to Charles. I chose to do so for several reasons. First, on several previous occasions we had seen metaphoric sexual aspects in our relating, so I had no reason to expect that Charles would be particularly upset by my dream image, especially since it was verbal rather than visual. Second, because even as Charles is struggling to give up old relatedness modes and patterns, old identities, in his relationship with me and with others, he is also struggling to understand how they continue to operate for him and relies heavily on our dialogues to help expand his understanding. Most important, by holding firmly (as I did during the session) and by then inviting dialogue about our interaction, I was confronting or "standing against" the internalized scenario as we had been enacting it, thus interpreting through actions and words the relational demands that continue to limit Charles—those he has been working hard to relinquish through his analytic work.

In the months following my erotic dream thought, Charles took a number of new risks in several of his most important relationships. One day, as he related two episodes with Jules, he became very emotional in the telling, voice quaking and fighting off tears, just as he had during the two actual encounters with Jules he was relating. It seems that Jules in his own way *did* hear Charles's pleas for better relating, and that he was attempting to be emotionally responsive—even if his style was impatient and irritable. Jules basically told Charles that Charles was expecting too much from the relationship, that the slights and affronts he had given Charles recently were just the way he interacts with people, that the anger and impatience he shows Charles are on the one hand because Charles does things to piss him off and on the other hand not personal and not intended to be cruel or rejecting. Charles needs to give him his space, Jules says, to accept him for the way that he is with people, not to take his blowups so personally. My comments highlighted that Jules was demonstrating a clear investment in connecting and communicating with Charles about their relationship.

Charles had been struggling to relate all of this to me and felt rejected and devastated again even in the telling. He was in an emotional turmoil not being able to get a perspective on the whole set of events. Charles had never expressed himself so honestly and forthrightly to anyone in his life as he did to Jules, and he had never allowed such personal vulnerability or been willing to tolerate such pain. My heart nearly broke listening to him realizing how deeply his caring and affection for Jules is and how devastating the emotional rejection and hurt he was experiencing at the hands of Jules were.

My interpretive discussion focused in a congratulatory way on Charles's allowing this personal vulnerability in his relationship with Jules. I said that I understood that he was for the moment badly shaken and lost because he has never allowed himself to be misunderstood and hurt by someone for whom he has so much love and respect. That Jules does not respond the way he wishes is a horrible sadness to face. Jules's style of responding—impatiently and somewhat gruffly—is disappointing in that it is not what Charles had hoped for, but Jules's speech certainly gave evidence of hearing and responding to Charles's hurt. We talked about how Charles tries repeatedly to convert people—here, Jules—into parents who basically hate him, want him dead, and trick and seduce him into playing the sick and pathetic character so that all he can do is to be caught in angry protest. I said the following:

> For the first time in your life, Charles, you have dared to step outside of their defensive-rageful nonrelational setup and to relate to Jules from a position of caring and personal vulnerability. You risked a great deal. I know how hurt you are because Jules doesn't respond the ways you want him to, but we have seen repeatedly that he—like all other people—has personality qualities and limitations that only allow him to respond in his own knee-jerk ways, and that he is often not able to consider the impact of his comments and behaviors on you. But when you dared on these two very clear occasions (and in a few other less-clear attempts recently) to actually put your heart out on the line and to tell Jules where you were coming from and, in your own manner (quaking voice and choking back tears), to convey to him your personal emotional truth, he did respond directly and compassionately to you—whether you like his personal style or not. You have never allowed such openness to be a part of the way you relate to people. Congratulations, and welcome to the real world of relationships, in which the capacity to tolerate disappointment, sadness, and pain is a vital prerequisite.

Interpreting the Countertransference

Freud conceived of a complete psychoanalytic interpretation as a statement that is simultaneously true for the transference–love experience, for the extraanalytic love relationship, and for the love relation brought from the client's infantile past. I have considered countertransference responsiveness the "royal road" to the merger experience and to the relational unconscious (Hedges, 1983/2003, 1992). I have formulated that a countertransference interpretation is a statement (or set of statements) made in an ongoing interpersonal process regarding the therapist's subjective experiences within the relationship that speaks to or points toward the preverbal or nonconscious emotional relatedness experience from the client's (and often the therapist's) infantile past that has become enacted or replicated in the ongoing therapeutic relationship (Hedges, 1983/2003, 1992, 1996).

The emotional-relatedness scenario being enacted in the transference–countertransference relational matrix that is subject to this kind of interpretation is thought to stem from that area of prereflective, nonreflective, or nonconscious experiencing that Bollas (1987) formulated as the "unthought known" and D. B. Stern (1997, 2010) referred to as "unformulated experience." We understand that through primary identification with the early love object the relational scenario often becomes emotionally role reversed in the analytic relational encounter due to the child's early attempts to identify with the aggressor or to turn passive trauma into active victory. The internalized relational dynamic is then projected onto or into the therapist and the therapeutic relationship through various enactments or emotional reenactment scenarios (e.g., projective identification). The countertransference interpretive process focuses on the active or role-reversed (identificatory or complementary) object relations scenario, which brings the client's internalized version of the parent into full emotional play in the analytic relationship, with the client in the parent role projecting his or her child role into the therapist. In contrast, the more straightforward or passive replication of a concordant object-relations position generally informs transference experiencing and transference interpretation.[1] Restated, in the passive (concordant) replication, the therapist is experienced by the client as being in the client's internalized parent role, while in the active (complementary, role-reversal) replication, the child's role becomes experienced by the therapist vis-à-vis the client, who assumes the internalized parent role. This was the emotional situation between Charles and myself in the vignettes reported.

Countertransference Disclosure versus Countertransference Interpretation

In ordinary life, we speak of making personal disclosures in the context of developing intimacy of various kinds in relationships. We know that

---

[1] Complementary and concordant are terms introduced by Racker (1968).

making a personal disclosure invites a counterdisclosure from the other, thus eliciting a mutual sense of increasing personal closeness, with the slippery slope to sexual intimacy often thought to be not far behind. In therapy, the client arrives intent on finding a trust relationship that can allow personal disclosures for the purpose of personal insight or growth. But, as we know, disclosures in the context of a relationship perceived to be safe and trusting can easily become quite stimulating for both participants. When the disclosing process becomes mutual and mutually stimulating, we encounter again the dreaded horizon of the slippery slope toward sexual ecstasy.

Tansey (1994) and Hirsch (1994) delineate the history of erotic encounters, threats, and dreads in psychoanalytic therapy from the time of Freud, Jung, and Ferenczi through a series of other scandals that have plagued analytic societies and training institutes to the point that sexual encounters with clients are rapidly becoming harshly stigmatized and criminalized in most locales. The therapist–client trust relationship is often compared to the parent–child relationship in its potential for abuse of perceived power relations and its potential for violation of socially sanctioned barriers against violence and incest. When the analytic fathers began speaking prohibitively regarding the potentially deleterious effects of "personal disclosures" on the part of the therapist, it was clearly the dread of the movement toward the slippery slope that motivated them.

In complete counterpoint to the dread of countertransference disclosures and involvements, however, systematic studies of countertransference responsiveness began in the mid-20th century making clear what a valuable tool countertransference sensitivity in the analytic situation can be. Inevitably came the issue of whether such countertransference experiencing could safely and profitably be "disclosed" to the client and, if so, in what contexts and in what ways might this be possible and advantageous. However, the concept of "disclosure" is unfortunate in that it subtly implies a potential motive to increase mutually generated intimacy in the direction of the slippery slope. It is for this reason that I believe that our discussions of countertransference as a form of analytic sensibility and using countertransference experience as a working or interpretive tool need to abandon entirely the concept of disclosure unless we clearly discern a motive on the part of the therapist to move toward the slippery slope of erotic entanglement.

I believe it is possible to distinguish clearly between "speaking countertransference experience with a motive toward enhancing an ongoing interpretive process" from "disclosing personal countertransference feelings with a motive toward increasing an intimacy that heralds the slippery slope." I define

> a countertransference interpretation as a statement (or set of statements) regarding the therapist's subjective experiences within the relationship that interpretively speaks to or points toward the preverbal or non-conscious emotional relatedness experience from the client's infantile past that has become enacted or replicated in the therapeutic relationship.

Such definition gives us a criterion for distinguishing the motive of countertransference interpretation from other motives more related to personal disclosures and slippery slopes.

Maroda (1999) distinguishes speaking emotional honesty about whatever she is experiencing as a part of the therapeutic relationship from personal disclosures about herself or facts of her life that are gratuitous and potentially distracting. I also include in speaking or interpreting the countertransference the judicious speaking about erotic images and experiences that are a ubiquitous part of human (and therefore countertransference) experiencing—regardless of the gender constellation of the therapist–client dyad.

There is a vast difference between sexual or erotic images, experiences, and dynamics that occur regularly in various ways in all forms of relatedness and sexualized images, experiences, and enactments that point the way toward overt or covert sexual engagements. There is a difference between "an erotic" as a dynamic that can be said to characterize many mutually constructed modes of interpersonal relatedness and "the erotic" or seductive as a form of sexualized energy, imagery, or experience. The therapist who cannot discern these differences clearly or has momentarily lost sight of the differences is in need of a consultative relationship or perhaps should not be doing this type of work.

Virginia Wink Hilton (1993), from her depth of experience during many years of studying ethical complaints of boundary violations in psychotherapy, believes that anytime a therapist looks a client in the eye and says, "I am attracted to you" in a way that places a burden for response on the client, there is a violation of trust and of the socially sanctioned boundaries of psychotherapy. "I am attracted to you" as a statement made by a therapist to a client invariably has the force of an inappropriate or unwarranted expectation or demand. "There is love here" or "In so many ways, I have come to appreciate and to love you in this relationship" are a far cry from "I am attracted to you." Likewise, "You are certainly a very sexually attractive person," "How can I be anything but aware of your various attractions as a person and as a sexual being," or "Of course, I have flashes of sexual imagery or fantasy regarding you or us from time to time" are the kinds of phrases that might well occur in a relationally sensitive interpretive process and have nothing whatsoever to do with the boundary violation or slippery slope implied in "I am attracted to you."

We have all struggled many times in our lives in personal relationships, as well as in professional relationships, with how exactly to express our honest experiences and feelings of personal warmth and attraction—which may well be associated with mental content involving sensual or sexual images—so that our expressions do not invite sexual misunderstandings or distortions, do not become sexualized in the relationship, and are not expressions of a motive or a movement toward the slippery slope. In relational psychotherapy, the struggle for correct, clear, and spontaneous expression remains the same. Needless to say, tact, timing, and judicious expression are always important considerations.

The Erotic Function of Boundaries

Another issue in the possible sexualization of the therapeutic encounter stems from the fact that the sociolegal context of psychotherapy, with its ethical concerns about inappropriate expressions of violence and sexuality, draws for us a special outline or boundary that separates our professional relationships from our other relationships. When violent, sexual, or erotic considerations come into play in the therapeutic relationship, this imaginary outline or forbidden boundary may function in a variety of tantalizing ways, such as the thought of "doing it in the road," engaging in an illicit encounter in the bedroom of a spouse or parent with the imminent danger of discovery, or any of the countless illicit, forbidden, or outrageous scenarios capitalized on by pornographic artists. Thus, the erotizing effects of privacy, trust, and danger in personal intimate relatedness have the high potential of lacing the therapeutic relationship with a tantalizing sexualized coloring from time to time—especially when the goal of relational psychotherapy often involves various kinds of "seductions" into the intimacy of the relatedness dimension so that inhibiting and limiting relational structures from the past can be seen and worked through in the relationship (Maroda, 1999). Awareness of and clear communication about seduction and boundaries are often a challenge. Needless to say, many people at times confuse deep longings for emotional and sensual contact that have remained unresponded to since infancy with their adult body (post-puberty) sexualized longings.

It is crucial in our psychoanalytic theory and technique to acknowledge that sexual images, themes, and interactions are ubiquitous in human life and need to be a regular part of the therapeutic encounter and dialogue, and that the dynamic mutual engagements and enactments studied in relational psychoanalytic therapy and dynamic psychotherapy frequently constitute an erotic. The mutually arousing and stimulating forms of essentially erotic interaction may or may not become sexualized or ever threaten to become acted out sexually. Many internalized object relations scenarios that are brought by both participants of the analytic dyad were first experienced in an aroused sensual or erotic dimension—whether those scenarios were overtly or covertly sexualized in childhood or not. These will inevitably be re-created or mutually reenacted in the relational engagement of psychoanalytic therapy—often in conjunction with other strong affects such as rage and shame. Relational psychotherapists are actively studying the problem of how our theories and working techniques can more accurately reflect these human realities. Clearly documenting our thoughts, interactions, and therapeutic intentions as well as seeking out professional consultation from colleagues go a long way toward protecting ourselves, our clients, and the therapeutic process from misunderstandings and derailments.

An Erotic Encounter With Charles 6 Months Later

Despite the notable advances Charles was making in distancing himself from the emotionally demanding external or real relationships with his parents and in relating more vulnerably and effectively to Jules, to myself, and to several other friends and close work associates, from time to time he retreated to his long-internalized characteristic ways of devaluing himself and his progress. When he would persist, I would become perturbed and confrontational about how he knows what he is saying is not true. I would feel seduced into a similar emotional trap that he gets caught in with his parents in trying to bring them around into some semblance of a relationship when they cannot tolerate relating.

In the session to be reported, we were again caught in this irritated, confrontational mode, with my insisting that he is a strong, worthwhile person who is relating better than ever to everyone he knows, and with Charles angrily challenging me on every point. *I* wanted *my* view of him and of our relationship to be heard and recognized. Partly, my desire to be heard and responded to can be understood as my wish to be acknowledged as present in the relationship. But by now, there was more at stake. My insistence stood as an interpretive move to indicate his need to control his experience of our relationship rather than to risk surrendering to our relatedness process. However, Charles was just as intent on a rageful negation of me and of my "distorted positive attitudes" toward him. As our intensity escalated, I felt us to be in a very familiar place together, one we had gone to many times before. Suddenly, I had a flash: "This is sexual!" I was aware my forearms were raised toward him and flushing, and that there was a definite charge of sexual energy and excitement running throughout my body. Momentarily flabbergasted, I let Charles carry on a bit until I gathered my wits about me and then interrupted.

Larry: This is sexual!

Charles: What?

Larry: This is sexual. What we are doing is sexual. And now that I think of it, whenever we get into this excited, agitated state fighting with each other, we are both in a highly stimulated state of arousal—but I had never thought of it before as sexual. This is our way of fucking, one we have developed over time and haven't ever seen as an erotic. I don't know why we haven't seen it before, but I just experienced this flush come over me, and I realized that we go to this place in order to express ourselves vividly to each other, and our interaction carries a strong sexual charge.

Charles: Like I get off to putting you in your place?

Larry: Maybe.

Charles: Like, by putting myself down so vigorously I can get you to build me up, to affirm me, to make me feel good about myself? Like this is a sexual dynamic that we get off to, me putting myself down and you building me up?

Larry: Actually, no—I'm thinking of something much worse. Paradoxically, the louder I insist that you are a good guy, in however many ways I may, and the more I confront you about how rotten your appraisals of yourself and your progress in relating are, the worse I end up putting you down.

Charles: Putting me down? No, you're building me up. I'm the one putting myself down.

Larry: No, I'm not talking so much about the specific content, but of our *process of relating* in this highly charged dance in which we collude in putting you into an essentially humiliating position.

Charles: Humiliation? How so? I don't feel like you are humiliating me.

Larry: *That* may be the problem, that you don't feel it. But implicitly, relationally I am diminishing you as a person. Why should *I* have to be the one to bolster your self-esteem, to shore up your nasty attitudes and behaviors about yourself? The more I do, the more I implicitly or tacitly agree that you are indeed a pathetic case, that you're so pathetic that you can't even do a passable job taking credit for yourself, allowing good feelings about yourself, or enjoying your hard-earned creative steps forward. You must be much worse off than I thought!

Charles: I gotcha. It's not that I put myself down and then I take heart in your building me up?

Larry: No, you take heart when I implicitly prove how little I really think of you by agreeing to trivialize you with support and faint praises!

Charles: There. You see, I've been telling you all along how much you hate me, how much contempt you have for me, and how you lie to me when you say that you respect me—when in fact you do see me as a pathetic case, a hopeless wretch! I knew it!

Larry: Not so fast! I'm not copping to any of that—at least not right away! What I am saying is that we have constructed a game, a dance between us that we often fall into—sometimes in quick steps, and other times (like tonight) in expansive ball-room ecstasy. The content per se of our banter is in some sense totally irrelevant; what is crucial is our interaction. This is our way of fucking. Look at us, how we both always get hyperaroused in all of this mutual misunderstanding, disrespect, and hatred! I'm saying this is relationally orgasmic and that we are both repeatedly drawn here to enjoy together this perverse level of erotic excitement—at your expense, and mine, too, because this is not a position I like to be in either.

Charles: I just thought of something. I don't think I've ever told you this. I must have been very little, probably 3 or 4, at home all day long with my mother, whom I now understand had not the slightest idea how to relate to me. It was like she was a withdrawn, unresponsive psychotic corpse. It must have been horrible for me. I can remember feeling lost and lonely wandering around the house waiting all day for the sound of the car in the drive when my father would come home. Not that in the long run he could relate to me any better than she could; but at least when he came into the house he would put on his slippers, put old Broadway musicals on the stereo, mix himself a couple of stiff martinis, and we would dance around the room acting silly, dancing and playing. It was the only sign of life there was for me during that time. Through it all he was always blaming and berating her for being such an inadequate and inept mother. Even then, I knew he felt sorry for me that I was stuck with her—a pathetic child stuck with a hopeless woman all day. So, even as we were playing together under the influence of music and martinis, *he was only doing it—building me up—because he saw me as a lost and pathetic child.* There it is: The only liveliness and excitement I knew was in the context of being seen as a poor, pathetic, essentially hopeless child who needed to be livened up. Like you just described how it often goes with us. I now know, of course, that this has always been his basic attitude toward everyone, that the only way he can bolster up his own devastatingly poor self-esteem and guard against his own psychotic fragmentations is to place himself on a pedestal as an omniscient and omnipotent being superior to me and to everyone else. That's why he married my mother: so he could look good compared to her. It *is* a supercharged erotic interaction. You're right, I see it all now. *This was my first love.*

Larry: Your first love and a way of keeping yourself from the black pit of loneliness, depression, and despair.

Charles: The homosexual parts of me suddenly seem clear for the first time ever. You know how I've often wondered if he didn't basically have homosexual dynamics of some kind. He never related to my mother or to any other women. Yes, female work colleagues would ogle over his genius and compete for his favor, but he treated them all like shit. He has only had a few long-term male friends, the kind you get together with occasionally to sip brandy, smoke cigars, and talk with about the woes of the world—and the dismal inferiority of women. He has basically never had any relationships in his life. Wow! I see it all so clearly now. And you say we replicate it here, the homosexual play and arousal?

Larry: Absolutely. What caused me to catch it tonight was a distinct flush and a charge of sexual energy I felt when we were mixing it up earlier.

Charles: Have you known this before?

Larry: No, not in the way I do now. But I think the emotional charge has been between us many times before when we have been at odds with each other. If there was a sexual charge I never consciously noticed it before. Or perhaps tonight—only after we have spent recent weeks engaging ourselves and you engaging

Jules and others in more complex and satisfying relational interactions—could I feel the perverse sexual charge of this old way of relating! You've set this same dynamic up with Jules, and he doesn't like it either, but you often snag him into the erotic fray, too.

Charles then recalled some experiences in adolescence in which he was aware of intense sexual yearnings toward boys whom he could idealize as much better looking than he was and much smoother than he was in relating to teachers and with girls. He was basically terrified of approaching these sexually idealized boys for friendship because he perceived them as so much superior to him and as looking down their noses at him as a weak, pathetic creature, certainly unworthy to be befriended. His sexual excitement toward them further left him feeling perverted and unworthy.

Larry: So explain to me now why I had that dream a while back in which I had to suck your balls to calm you down.

Charles: That's easy. Because, of course, my father would fly into rages all the time at her and her stupidities and at every tiny little thing I did that asserted even a small piece of me. In order to exist at all, to at least experience some semblance of being a living being I was always sucking up to him and his rages—just like *you* have to do to me to keep my rage assuaged and *I* have to suck up to you to keep you in the relating game.

Larry: But it isn't mutually satisfying this way because it's done out of desperation and fear. It may be stimulating, but it isn't satisfying. It's a way of controlling the other if you believe you are hopelessly inferior or if you are in need of getting off to being superior.

Charles: You got it! Shit! Well, *I* don't want to do this with you anymore!

Larry: But I'm sure we will. We're too addicted to this way of being with each other, so despite how perverse we now see it to be, no matter how much we want to change the quality of our play together right away, I'm sure it will take some time for us to learn what it's all about and for us both to give it up.

Charles: I can't help myself. I have to see myself as weak, inferior, and pathetic.
Larry: Then we have our work cut out for us.

A Not-So-Surprising Ending

You will not be surprised to learn that midway into writing up this case report it dawned on me that the name I had spontaneously chosen to disguise my client was, of course, my father's name, Charles. It also will not come as a surprise that my entire childhood was devoted to developing ways in which to assuage my father's violent temper and his constant abuse of me in the name of Our Lord Jesus Christ—an identification with an idealistically superior position, to say the least. For several days after I had discovered my naming slip, a recurring image haunted me of happily and excitedly playing in the bathtub with my father when I was less than 3 years old and his abruptly standing up to get out of the soapy bubbles, with water dripping down his fascinating body hair and his penis large, red, and partially erect.

In my psychoanalytic therapy some years ago, I remember crying bitterly over how I lost any semblance of warmth and play with my father by the time I was 4 or 5. I now believe that it was his dread of homosexual incestuous stimulation that took my father emotionally away from me forever. I mention these few personal associations without further comment simply to illustrate the depth to which unconscious relational enactments in the transference–countertransference matrix often go and to note the extent to which the personality dynamics of both participants have to be taken into account when considering psychotherapy from a relational standpoint. These private associations most likely belong to the asymmetrical sphere of the relationship—that is, barring some clear and compelling interpretive reason, sharing such personal associations with Charles would likely be gratuitous, distracting, or even boundary violating.

Conclusions

It is my belief that erotic dynamics, imagery, and experience are ubiquitous in all human relationships, including psychotherapeutic ones. With a relational lens, we are in a position to realize that the erotic dynamics, imagery, and experiences brought from the infantile pasts of both participants are necessarily replicated or enacted in some form or another in the therapeutic relationship for the limiting internalized object relations structures to become known and to work through them therapeutically.

We know that misunderstanding and miscommunication occur in all relationships and can be a special problem when communicating in the area of sexuality. However, the answer is not to avoid or back off from meaningful relating but rather to step up to relationships and work hard toward achieving rewarding interactions and good communication about whatever is important in the relationship. There is no need to confuse working on sexual images and dynamic enactments that arise in the transference–countertransference engagement with destructive sexualization of the relationship and the slippery slope of sexual acting out. The relational listening perspectives I have offered afford an opportunity to frame for analytic scrutiny distinctly different types of self- and other-relatedness possibilities along with whatever erotic dynamics may be present in the psychotherapeutic relationship.

We carefully protect ourselves, our clients, and the psychotherapy situation through clear communication, as well as through appropriate and timely consultation and documentation of all events that are puzzling, troubling, or subject to misinterpretation. By distinguishing sharply between countertransference disclosures that are simply gratuitous and distracting and countertransference interpretations that serve to give emotion and voice to the client's long-internalized child-self desperately struggling to be heard, we need no longer dread erotic feelings and images in countertransference experiencing and interpretation.

I have hoped in this book to demonstrate how sexuality, passion, love, and desire in the psychotherapeutic encounter are an infinitely complex interplay of the sex, gender, and identities of both participants. Human minds and sexuality are inextricably enmeshed in all of our relationships throughout our life spans. But the "just-so" stories we tell ourselves about our sexuality are necessarily highly simplified and condensed narrations that bear continuous investigation and expansion. Intimate relationships, including the psychotherapeutic one, provide us with an opportunity to experience ourselves and our sexual natures in ever new and rewarding contexts.

I began this book with a thumbnail history of human sexualities and then pointed toward our rapidly expanding knowledge of the brain and neurological functions that provide the basis for revised understandings of human sexuality. I then provided a series of listening perspectives from which to consider sex, sexuality, gender, and gender identity. I hope that the vignettes that have been gleaned from the therapeutic literature as well as the studies from my own practice have served to illustrate how the sexuality, passion, love, and desire of the psychotherapeutic encounter can be approached with developmental perspectives that can be used in a relational context.

References

Abraham, K. (1911). Notes in the psychoanalytical investigation and treatment of manic-depressive insanity and allied conditions. In *Selected papers of Karl Abraham* (D. Bryan & A. Strachey, Trans.). New York: Brunner/ Mazel.

Abraham, K. (1924). A short study of the development of the libido. In *Selected papers of Karl Abraham* (D. Bryan & A. Strachey, Trans.). New York: Brunner/Mazel.

Abraham, N., & Torok, M. (1994). *The shell and the kernel.* Chicago: The University of Chicago Press.

Aron, L. (1996). *A meeting of minds.* Hillsdale, NJ: Analytic Press.

Atwood, G. E., Stolorow, R., & Trop, J. (1989). Impasses in psychoanalytic therapy: A royal road. *Contemporary Psychoanalysis, 25,* 554–573.

Balint, A. (1943). On identification. *International Journal of Psycho-Analysis, 24,* 97–107.

Beebe, B., & Lachmann, F. (1994). Representation and internalization in infancy: Three principles of salience. *Psychoanalytic Psychology, 11,* 127–165.

Beebe, B., & Lachmann, F. (2003). *Infant research and adult treatment: Co-constructing interactions.* New York: Analytic Press.

Benjamin, J. (1988). *The bonds of love.* New York: Pantheon Books.

Benjamin, J. (1995). *Like subjects, love objects: Essays on recognition and sexual difference.* New Haven, CT: Yale University Press.

Benjamin, J. (1998). *Shadow of the other.* New York: Routledge.

Berger, P. L., & Luckmann, T. (1966). *The social construction of reality: A treatise in the sociology of knowledge.* New York: Anchor Books.

Bion, W. R. (1977). *Seven servants.* New York: Aronson.

Blackmore, S. (1999). *The meme machine.* New York: Oxford University Press.

Bollas, C. (1983). Expressive uses of the countertransference: Notes to the client from oneself. *Contemporary Psychoanalysis, 19,* 1–33.

Bollas, C. (1987). *The shadow of the object: Psychoanalysis of the unthought known.* New York: Columbia University Press.

Bromberg, P. M. (1993). Shadow and substance: A relational perspective on clinical process. In Mitchell & Aron. (1999). *Relational psychoanalysis: The emergence of a tradition.* Hillsdale, NJ: Analytic Press.

Butler, J. (1993). *Bodies that matter: On the discursive limits of "sex".* New York: Routledge.

Caghan, L. (2010, February). *Gender-near: Fitting theory to transgender realities.* Paper presented at the conference of the International Association of Relational Psychoanalysis and Psychotherapy, San Francisco.

Chodorow, N. (2002). Gender as a personal and cultural construction. In M. Dimen & V. Goldner (Eds.), *Gender in psychoanalytic space: Between clinic and culture* (pp. 237–261). New York: Other Press.

Collins, F. S. (2006). *The language of God: A scientist presents evidence for belief.* New York: Free Press.

Corbett, K. (2002). The mystery of homosexuality. In M. Dimen & V. Goldner (Eds.), *Gender in psychoanalytic space: Between clinic and culture* (pp. 21–37). New York: Other Press.

Cozolino, L. (2002). *The neuroscience of human relationships: Attachment and the developing social brain.* New York: Norton.

Damasio, A. (1994). *Descartes' error.* New York: Grosset/Putnam.

Damasio, A. (1999). *The feeling of what happens.* New York: Harcourt Brace.

Damasio, A. (2003). *Looking for Spinoza: Joy, sorrow, and the feeling brain.* New York: Harcourt.

Davies, J. M. (1994). Love in the afternoon: A relational reconsideration of desire and dread in the countertransference. *Psychoanalytic Dialogues, 4,* 153–170.

Davies, J. M., & Frawley, M. G. (1994). *Treating the survivor of childhood sexual abuse: A psychoanalytic perspective.* New York: Basic Books.

Davoine, F., & Gaudillière, J. M. (2004). *History beyond trauma: Whereof one cannot speak, thereof one cannot stay silent.* New York: Other Press.

de Beauvoir, Simone. (1949, 1952). *The second sex.* New York: Vintage Books.

Dimen, M. (2003). *Sexuality, intimacy, and power,* New York: The Analytic Press.

Downing, C. (1991). *Myths and mysteries of same sex love.* New York: Continuum.

Edelman, G. M. (1993). *Bright air, brilliant fire.* New York: Basic Books.

Edelman, G. M. (2006). *Second nature: Brain science and human knowledge.* New Haven, CT: Yale University Press.

Edelman, G., & Tononi, G. (2000). *A universe of consciousness: How matter becomes consciousness.* New York: Basic Books.

Ehrenberg, D. B. (1990). Playfulness in the psychoanalytic relationship. *Contemporary Psychoanalysis, 26,* 74–95.

Erikson, E. (1954). On the sense of inner identity. In R. P. Knight & C. R. Friedman (Eds.), *Psychoanalytic psychiatry and psychology* (pp. 351–364). New York: International Universities Press.

Erikson, E. (1959). Identity and the life cycle. *Psychological issues* (Monograph No. 1). New York: International Universities Press.

Fonagy, P. (2001). *Attachment theory and psychoanalysis.* New York: Other Press.

Foucault, M. (1978). *The history of sexuality: An introduction* (Vol. 1). New York. Random House.

Freud, S. (1912a). Papers on technique. The dynamics of transference. *Standard Edition of the Complete Psychological Works of Sigmund Freud, 12,* 97–108. London: Hogarth Press.

Freud, S. (1912b). Papers on technique. Recommendations to physicians practicing psychoanalysis. *Standard Edition of the Complete Psychological Works of Sigmund Freud, 12,* 109–120. London: Hogarth Press.

Freud, S. (1915). Observations on transference love. *Standard Edition of the Complete Psychological Works of Sigmund Freud, 12,* 159–171. London: Hogarth Press.

Freud, S. (1915). Instincts and their viscissitudes. *Standard Edition of The Complete Psychological Works of Sigmund Freud, 14,* 117–140. London: Hogarth Press.

Freud, S. (1924). Psychogenesis of a case of homosexuality in a woman. *Standard Edition of the Complete Psychological Works of Sigmund Freud, 18,* 145–174. London: Hogarth Press.

Freud, S. (1926). Negation. *Standard Edition of the Complete Psychological Works of Sigmund Freud, 19,* 235–242. London: Hogarth Press.

Freud, S. (1927). Fetishism. *Standard Edition of the Complete Psychological Works of Sigmund Freud, 21,* 152–157. London: Hogarth Press.

Freud, S. (1937). Analysis terminable and interminable. *The Standard Edition of the Complete Works of Sigmund Freud. 23*: 211–253. London: Hogarth Press.

Freud, S. (1938). A comment on anti-Semitism. *The Standard Edition of the Complete Psychological Works of Sigmund Freud, 23,* 287–294. London: Hogarth Press.

Freud, S. (1975). *Three essays on sexuality.* New York: Norton. (Original work published 1905)

Friedman, L. (1988). *The anatomy of psychotherapy.* Hillsdale, NJ: Analytic Press.

Frommer, M. S. (2006). On the subjectivity of lustful states of mind. *Psychoanalytic Dialogues, 16,* 639–664.

Gill, M. (1987). The analyst as participant. *Psychoanalytic Inquiry, 7,* 249–259.

Goldner, V. (1991). Toward a critical relational theory of gender. *Psychoanalytic Dialogues, 1,* 249–272.

Gorkin, M. (1985). Varieties of sexualized countertransference. *Psychoanalytic Review, 72,* 421–440.

Gorkin, M. (1987). *The uses of countertransference.* Northvale, NJ: Aronson.

Green, B. (1999). *The elegant universe: Superstrings, hidden dimensions, and the quest for the ultimate theory.* New York: Norton.

Green, B. (2004). *Fabric of the cosmos: Space, time, and the texture of reality.* New York: Knopf.

Greenspan, S. I., & Shanker, S. (2004). *The first idea: How symbols, language and intelligence evolved from our primate ancestors to modern humans.* New York: Da Capo Press.

Habermas, J. (1970). A theory of communicative competence. In H. P. Dreitzel (Ed.), *Recent sociology* (No. 2). New York: Macmillan.

Halberstam. J. (1998). *Female masculinity.* Durham, NC: Duke University Press.

Harris, A. (1991). Gender as contradiction. Reprinted in S. A. Mitchell & L. Aron (Eds.), *Relational psychoanalysis: The emergence of a tradition.* Hillsdale, NJ: Analytic Press.

Hedges, L. E. (1992). *Interpreting the countertransference.* Northvale, NJ: Aronson.

Hedges, L. E. (1994a). *Remembering, repeating, and working through childhood trauma: The psychodynamics of recovered memories, multiple personality, ritual abuse, incest, molest, and abduction.* Northvale, NJ: Aronson.

Hedges, L. E. (1994b). *In search of the lost mother of infancy.* Northvale, NJ: Aronson.

Hedges, L. E. (1994c). *Working the organizing experience: Transforming psychotic, schizoid, and autistic states.* Northvale, NJ: Aronson.

Hedges, L. E. (1996). *Strategic emotional involvement: Using countertransference experience in psychotherapy.* Northvale, NJ: Aronson.

Hedges, L. E. (2000a, revised edition 2007). *Facing the challenge of liability in psychotherapy: Practicing defensively.* Northvale, NJ: Aronson.

Hedges, L. E. (2000b). *Terrifying transferences: Aftershocks of childhood trauma.* Northvale, NJ: Aronson.

Hedges, L. E. (2003). *Listening perspectives in psychotherapy.* Northvale, NJ: Aronson. (Original work published 1983)

Hedges, L. E. (2005). Listening perspectives for emotional relatedness memories. *Psychoanalytic Inquiry, 25,* 455–483.

Hedges, L. E. (manuscript). *The third person in intimate relationships.*

Hedges, L., Hilton, R., Hilton, V., & Caudill, B. (1997). *Therapists at risk: Perils of the intimacy of the therapeutic relationship.* Northvale, NJ: Aronson.

Hegel, G. W. F. (1952). *Phänomenologie des geistes.* Hamburg: Felix Meiner Verlag.

Hilton, V. W. (1993). When we are accused. *Journal for Bioenergetic Analysis 5,* 45–51. Reprinted in Hedges, L., Hilton, R., Hilton, V., & Caudill, B. (Eds.), *Therapists at risk: Perils of the intimacy of the therapeutic relationship.* Northvale, NJ: Aronson.

Hirsch, I. (1994). Countertransference love and theoretical model. *Psychoanalytic Dialogues, 4,* 171–192.

hooks, bell. (1995). *killing rage: ending racism.* Bolton, Ontario, Canada: Fenn.

Isay, R. (1990). *Being homosexual: Gay men and their development.* New York: Avon.

Jacobson, E. (1954). The self and object world: Vicissitudes of their infantile cathexis and their influence on ideational and affective development. *The Psychoanalytic Study of the Child, 9,* 75–127.

Jacobson, E. (1964). *The self and object world.* New York: International Press.

Johnson, S. (1991). *The symbiotic character.* New York: Norton.

Karr-Morse, R., & Wiley, M. S. (1997). *Ghosts from the nursery: Tracing the roots of violence.* New York: The Atlantic Monthly Press.

Kernberg, O. (1976). *Borderline conditions and pathological narcissism.* New York: Jason Aronson.

Kernberg, O. F. (1984). *Object-relations theory and clinical psychoanalysis.* New York: Aronson.

Kernberg, O. F. (1994). Love in the analytic setting. *Journal of the American Psychoanalytic Association, 42,* 1137–1157.

Kinsey, A. C., Pomeroy, W. B., & Martin, C. E. (1948). *Sexual behavior in the human male.* Philadelphia: Saunders.

Kinsey, A. C., Pomeroy, W. B., Martin, C. E., & Gebhard, P. H. (1953). *Sexual behavior in the human female.* Philadelphia: Saunders.

Kohut, H. (1959). Introspection, empathy and psychoanalysis: An examination of the relationship between mode of observation and theory. *Journal of the American Psychoanalytic Association, 7,* 459–483.

Kohut, H. (1971). *The analysis of the self.* New York: International Universities Press.

Lacan, J. (1977). *Écrits: A selection.* New York: Norton. (Original work published 1938)

Laplanche, J. (1976). *Life and death in psychoanalysis.* Baltimore: Johns Hopkins University Press.

LeDoux, J. (1996). *The emotional brain.* New York: Simon & Schuster.

LeDoux, J. (2002). *The synaptic self.* New York: Viking.

Lewes, K. (2002). Homosexuality, homophobia, and gay-friendly psychoanalysis. In D. Moss (Ed.), *Hating in the first person plural* (pp. 175–179). New York: Other Press.

Lewis, T., Amini, F., & Lannon, R. (2000). *A general theory of love.* New York: Random House.

Loewald, H. (1979). On the therapeutic action of psycho-analysis. *International Journal of Psycho-Analysis, 41,* 16–33.

MacLean, P. (1997). The brain and subjective experience: Question of the multilevel role of resonance. *Journal of Mind and Behavior, 18,* 247–268.

Maher, F., & Tetreault, M. (1996). Women's ways of knowing in women's studies, feminist pedagogies, and feminist theory. In Goldberger, N., Tarule, J., Clinchy, B., and Belenky, M. (1996). *Knowledge, difference, and power: Essays inspired by women's ways of knowing* (pp 148–174). New York: Basic Books.

Mahler, M. (1968). *On human symbiosis and the vicissitudes of individuation,* Vol. 1, *Infantile psychosis.* New York: International Universities Press.

Marcus, S. (1975). *Introduction to Freud's Three essays on sexuality.* New York: Norton.

Maroda, K. (1994). *The power of countertransference.* Northvale, NJ: Aronson.

Maroda, K. (1999). *Seduction, surrender, and transformation.* Hillsdale, NJ: Analytic Press.

Masters, W. H., & Johnson, V. E. (1966). *Human sexual response.* Boston: Little Brown.

McDougall, J. (1995). *The many faces of Eros: A psychoanalytic exploration of human sexuality.* New York: Norton.

Mesulam, M. (2000). *Principles of behavioral and cognitive neurology.* New York: Oxford University Press.

Mitchell, S. (1988). *Relational concepts in psychoanalysis.* Cambridge, MA: Harvard University Press.

Mitchell, S. (1997). *Influence and autonomy in psychoanalysis.* Hillsdale, NJ: Analytic Press.

Mitchell, S. A., & Aron, L. (1999). *Relational psychoanalysis: The emergence of a tradition.* Hillsdale, NJ: Analytic Press.

Moss, D., & Zeavin, L. (1999). The female homosexual. In R. Lesser & E. Schoenberg (Eds.), *That obscure subject of desire: Freud's female homosexual revisited* (pp. 197–213). New York: Routledge.

Nagel, J. (2003). *Race, ethnicity, and sexuality: Intimate intersections, forbidden frontiers.* New York: Oxford University Press.

Norcross, J. (2002). *Psychotherapy relationships that work: Therapist contributions and responsiveness to patients.* New York: Oxford.

Ogden, T. (1997). *Reverie and interpretation.* Northvale, NJ: Aronson.

Orbach, S. (2004). The body in clinical practice. Part one: There is no such thing as a body. In K. White (Ed.), *TOUCH: Attachment and the body* (pp. 19–24). New York: Karnac Books.

Pearce, J. C. (2002). *The biology of transcendence: A blueprint of the human spirit.* Rochester, VT: Park Street Press.

Person, E., & Ovesey, L. (1983). Psychoanalytic theories of gender identity. *Journal of the American Academy of Psychoanalysis, 11,* 203–226.

Pert, C. (1997). *Molecules of emotion: The science behind mind-body medicine.* New York: Simon & Schuster.

Pope, K. S., Keith-Spiegel, P., & Tabachnick, B. G. (1986). Sexual attraction to clients; the human therapist and the (sometimes) inhuman training system. *American Psychologist, 41,* 147–157.

Pope, K. S., Sonne, J. L., & Holroyd, J. (1993). *Sexual feelings in psychotherapy.* Washington, DC: American Psychological Association Press.

Racker, H. (1968). *Transference and countertransference.* New York: International Universities Press.

Rorty, R. (1979). *Philosophy and the mirror of nature.* Princeton, NJ: Princeton University Press.

Rorty, R. (1989). *Contingency, irony, and solidarity.* Cambridge, MA: Cambridge University Press.

Rosiello, F. (2000). *Deepening intimacy in psychotherapy.* Northvale, NJ: Aronson.

Ryle, G. (1949). *The concept of mind.* New York: Barnes and Noble.

Sandler, J. (1976). Countertransference and role-responsiveness. *International Review of Psychoanalysis, 3,* 43–47, p.44 quoted by Wittkin-Sasso 1991. See Wittkin-Sasso 1991 in *Contemporary Psychoanalysis, 27,* 687–695 to get Sandler reference on PEP; same for Gill 1987 in this article.

Schafer, R. (1976). *A new language for psychoanalysis.* New Haven, CT: Yale University Press.

Schore, A. N. (1999). *Affect regulation and the origin of the self: The neurobiology of emotional development.* New York: Erlbaum.

Schore, A. N. (2003). *Affect regulation and disorders of the self.* New York: Norton.

Searle, J. R. (1992). *The rediscovery of the mind.* Cambridge, MA: MIT Press.

Searle, J. R. (2004). *Mind: A brief introduction.* New York: Oxford University Press.

Searles, H. F. (1959). Oedipal love in the counter-transference. *International Journal of Psycho-Analysis, 40,* 180–190.

Searles, H. F. (1979). *Countertransference and related subjects.* New York: International Universities Press.

Siegel, D. J. (1999). *The developing mind: How relationships and the brain interact to shape who we are.* New York: Guilford Press.

Siegel, D. J. (2007). *The mindful brain.* New York: Norton.

Stark, M. (1994). *Working with resistance.* New York: Aronson.

Stark, M. (1997). *Modes of therapeutic action.* New York: Aronson.

Stern, D. B. (1997). *Unformulated experience: From dissociation to imagination in psychoanalysis.* Hillsdale, NJ: Analytic Press.

Stern, D. B. (2010). *Partners in thought: Working with unformulated experience, dissociation, and enactment.* New York: Routledge.

Stern, D. N. (1985). *The interpersonal world of the infant.* New York: Basic Books.

Stern, D. N. (2004). *The present moment in psychotherapy and everyday life.* New York: Norton.

Stolorow, R., & Atwood, G. (1992). *Contexts of being: The intersubjective foundations of psychological life.* Hillsdale, NJ: Analytic Press.

Stolorow, R., Brandschaft, B., & Atwood, G. (1987). *Psychoanalytic treatment: An intersubjective approach.* Hillsdale, NJ: Analytic Press.

Sue, D. (2005, January 27). *About what we must do to survive and overcome racism.* Plenary address, the National Multicultural Conference and Summit, Hollywood, CA.

Tansey, M. J. (1994). Sexual attraction and phobic dread in the countertransference. *Psychoanalytic Dialogues, 4,* 139–152.

Trevarthen, C. (1980). The foundations of intersubjectivity: The development of interpersonal and cooperative understanding in infants. In D. R. Olson (Ed.). *The social foundations of language and thought.* New York: Norton.

Volkan, V. (2004). p. 47 [look in PEP for article on cross cultural]

Welles, J., & Wrye, H. (1991). The maternal erotic countertransference. *International Journal of Psycho-Analysis, 72,* 93–106.

Winnicott, D. W. (1947). Hate in the countertransference. In *Through paediatrics to psychoanalysis* (pp. 174–193). New York: Basic Books.

Winnicott, D. W. (1969). The use of an object. *International Journal of Psycho-Analysis, 50,* 711–716.

Winnicott, D. W. (1971). *Playing and reality.* New York: Basic Books.

Wittgenstein, L. (1953). *Philosophical investigations* (G. E. M. Anscombe, Trans.). New York: Macmillan.

Wittkin-Sasso, G. (1991). A female analyst's use of desire. *Contemporary Psychoanalysis, 27,* 687–695.

About the Author

 **Lawrence E. Hedges, PhD, PsyD, ABPP** is a psychologist-psychoanalyst in private practice in Orange, California, specializing in the training of psychotherapists and psychoanalysts. He is director of the Listening Perspectives Study Center and the founding director of the Newport Psychoanalytic Institute where he is a supervising and training psychoanalyst. He holds faculty appointments at The University of California–Irvine School of Medicine and the Newport Psychoanalytic Institute. Dr. Hedges holds diplomas from the American Board of Professional Psychology and the American Board of Forensic Examiners. He is author of numerous papers and books on the practice of psychoanalytic psychotherapy, including *Listening Perspectives in Psychotherapy, Terrifying Transferences: Aftershocks of Childhood Trauma, and Facing the Challenge of Liability in Psychotherapy: Practicing Defensively.*

About Lawrence Hedges' Other Books

Terrifying Transferences: Aftershocks of Childhood Trauma

There is a level of stark terror known to one degree or another by all human beings. It silently haunts our lives and occasionally surfaces in therapy. It is this deep-seated fear—often manifest in dreams or fantasies of dismemberment, mutilation, torture, abuse, insanity, rape, or death—that grips us with the terror of being lost forever in time and space or controlled by hostile forces stronger than ourselves. Whether the terror is felt by the client or by the therapist, it has a disorienting, fragmenting, crippling power. How we can look directly into the face of such terror, hold steady, and safely work it through is the subject of *Terrifying Transferences*. Contributing therapists: Linda Barnhurst, John Carter, Shirley Cox, Jolyn Davidson, Virginia Hunter, Michael Reyes, Audrey Seaton-Bacon, Sean Stewart, Gayle Trenberth, and Cynthia Wygal.

Listening Perspectives in Psychotherapy

In a fresh and innovative format, Hedges organizes an exhaustive overview of contemporary psychoanalytic and object relations theory and clinical practice. "In studying the Listening Perspectives of therapists, the author has identified himself with the idea that one must sometimes change the Listening Perspective and also the interpreting, responding perspective."—Rudolf Ekstein, PhD. Contributing therapists: Mary Cook, Susan Courtney, Charles Coverdale, Arlene Dorius, David Garland, Charles Margach, Jenna Riley, and Mary E. Walker. Now available in a 20th anniversary edition, the book has become a classic in the field.

Working the Organizing Experience

Hedges defines in a clear and impelling manner the most fundamental and treacherous transference phenomena: the emotional experiences retained from the first few months of life. Hedges describes the infant's attempts to reach out and form organizing connections to the interpersonal environment and how those attempts may have been ignored, thwarted, or rejected. He demonstrates how people live out these primitive transferences in everyday significant relationships and in the psychotherapy relationship. A critical history of psychotherapy with primitive transferences is contributed by James Grotstein and a case study is contributed by Frances Tustin.

Interpreting the Countertransference

Hedges boldly studies countertransference as a critical tool for therapeutic understanding. "Hedges clearly and beautifully delineates the components and forms of countertransference and explicates the technique of carefully proffered countertransference informed interventions. ... [He takes the view] that all countertransferences, no matter how much they belong to the analyst, are unconsciously evoked by the patient." —James Grotstein, MD. Contributing therapists: Anthony Brailow, Karen K. Redding, and Howard Rogers.

In Search of the Lost Mother of Infancy

"Organizing transferences" in psychotherapy constitute a living memory of a person's earliest relatedness experiences and failures. Infant research and psychotherapeutic studies from the past two decades now make it possible to define for therapeutic analysis the manifestations of early contact traumas. A history and summary of the Listening Perspective approach to psychotherapy introduces the book. Contributing therapists: Bill Cone, Cecile Dillon, Francie Marais, Sandra Russell, Sabrina Salayz, Jacki Singer, Sean Stewart, Ruth Wimsatt, and Marina Young.

Strategic Emotional Involvement

Following an overview of contemporary approaches to studying countertransference responsiveness, therapists tell moving stories of how their work came to involve them deeply, emotionally, and not always safely with clients. These comprehensive, intense, and honest reports are the first of their kind ever to be collected and published. Contributing therapists: Anthony Brailow, Suzanne Buchanan, Charles Coverdale, Carolyn Crawford, Jolyn Davidson, Jacqueline Gillespie, Ronald Hirz, Virginia Hunter, Gayle Trenberth, and Sally Turner-Miller.

Therapists at Risk: Perils of the Intimacy of the Therapeutic Relationship

Lawrence E. Hedges, Robert Hilton, and Virginia Wink Hilton, longtime trainers of psychotherapists, join hands with attorney O. Brandt Caudill in this tour de force that explores the multitude of personal, ethical, and legal risks involved in achieving rewarding transformative connections in psychotherapy today. Relational intimacy is explored through such issues as touching, dualities in relationship, interfacing boundaries, sexuality, countertransference, recovered memories, primitive transferences, false accusations against therapists, and the critical importance of peer support and consultation. The authors clarify the many dynamic issues involved, suggest useful ways of managing the inherent dangers, and work to restore our confidence in and natural enjoyment of the psychotherapeutic process.

Remembering, Repeating, and Working Through Childhood
Trauma: The Psychodynamics of Recovered Memories, Multiple
Personality, Ritual Abuse, Incest, Molest, and Abduction

Infantile focal as well as strain trauma leave deep psychological scars that show up as symptoms and memories later in life. In psychotherapy, people seek to process early experiences that lack ordinary pictoral and narrational representations through a variety of forms of transference and dissociative remembering, such as multiple personality, dual relating, archetypal adventures, and false accusations against therapists or other emotionally significant people. "Lawrence Hedges makes a powerful and compelling argument for why traumatic memories recovered during psychotherapy need to be taken seriously. He shows us how and why these memories must be dealt with in thoughtful and responsible ways and not simply uncritically believed and used as tools for destruction."—Elizabeth F. Loftus, PhD.

Facing the Challenge of Liability in Psychotherapy: Practicing Defensively

In this litigious age, all psychotherapists must protect themselves against the possibility of legal action; malpractice insurance is insufficient and does not begin to address the complexity and the enormity of this critical problem. In this book, Lawrence E. Hedges urges clinicians to practice defensively and provides a course of action that equips them to do so. After working with over a hundred psychotherapists and attorneys who have fought unwarranted legal and ethical complaints from clients, he has made the fruits of his work available to all therapists. In addition to identifying those patients prone to presenting legal problems, Dr. Hedges provides a series of consent forms (on the accompanying disk), a compelling rationale for using them, and a means of easily introducing them into clinical practice. This book is a wake-up call, a practical, clinically sound response to a frightening reality, and an absolute necessity for all therapists in practice today. Now available in a 2007 revised and updated edition.

Index

A

Abandonment, 92–94, 113–120
Abuse, child, 87–88, 113–117
Active versus passive positions
  sexuality and, 102–103
  vignettes, 98–105, 150–156,
    162–167
Actual interpersonal interaction, 34
Addiction, 29, 113–120
Affect; *see also* Emotion(s)
  independent experiences and, 123
  mirroring by parents, 7–8
  organizing experiences and, 56
  performance of, 88
  self-other experiences and, 98
  symbiotic experiences and, 83,
    134–135
  therapist expression of, 57–58
  vignette, 87–88
Affect mirroring, 7–8
Affection and sexuality, 134
Affective expressions of therapists,
  57–58

Aggression
  transgenerational internalization
    and, 29
  vignettes, 61–64, 87–88, 113–117,
    123–126
  violence and psychotherapy
    termination, 71
Agony, 150–156, 162–167
Agoraphobia, 126–130
Anal-retentive personality type,
  139–142, 147–150
Analysis, *see* Psychoanalytic
    psychotherapy
Anger
  Eros in countertransference,
    150–156, 162–167
  Eros in transference, 133–139
  self-other experiences, 98–101,
    113–117
Anxiety of patients
  independent experiences, 122,
    126–130
  self-other experiences, 98–101,
    103–105, 108–111

symbiotic experiences, 88–90, 94–95
Anxiety of therapists, 57–60
Aron, Lewis, 51–52
Arousal
  homosexuality and, 103
  of therapists, 66, 67–77, 150–156, 162–167 (*see also* Erotic countertransference)
Artists, 90–92
Asexuality, 108–111
Assault, 113–117; *see also* Aggression
Assertiveness, 90–92
Attachment
  communicative connection and, 64
  intimate adult interactions and, 7
  transgenerational phantoms and, 28, 31
  vignettes, 67–77, 98–101
Autonomy, 97–98

B

Betrayal, 90–92, 108–111, 117–120
Biological perspective, 3–6
Bisexuality, 4–5, 123–125, 126–130
Body countertransference, 88–90
Bondage and discipline fantasies, 139–142, 147–150
Bonding, 76, 77, 81–82; *see also* Symbiotic experiences
Borderline personality disorder, 98–101
Boundaries
  ethnosexual, 21–22
  mind-body, 134
  violations of, 159–161, 167
Boundary violations, 159–160, 167
Boy meets girl, xiii–xiv; *see also* Brain and neurology; Historical conceptions of sexuality

Brain and neurology
  cluster brain, xxv–xxvi
  interpersonal relationships and, xxiv–xxv, xxvii, 29–30
  overview of, xx–xxi
  reentrant brain, xxiii
  split brain and localization, xxii
  synaptic brain, xxiii–xxv
  transcendent brain, xxvi–xxx
  triune brain, xxii–xxiii
Bravado, 98–101
Breast implant surgery, 105–108
Brutalization, split-off homoerotic, 61–64
Buchanan, Suzanne, 66, 67–77

C

Call girls, 105–108
Case studies; *see also specific topics*
  Charles, Eros in countertransference, 150–156, 162–167
  Dora, Eros in transference, 133–139
  Ted, Eros in resistance, 139–142, 147–150
Castration anxiety, 122
Charles, Eros in countertransference, 150–156, 162–167
Chat-room fetishes, 144
Child abuse, 87–88, 113–117
Church attendance, 139–142, 147–150; *see also* Religion
Claustrophobia, 126–130
Cluster brain, xxv–xxvi
Cohesive self, 97–98
Complementary object relations, 157
Concordant object relations, 157
Confession by Catholics, xix–xx; *see also* Religion

Confrontation in psychotherapy,
150–156, 162–167
Connection/disconnection, 64,
66–67, 70
Consciousness, xxiii, 7–8
Constructionism, 17–19
Copulation, magical cure by, 92–94
Corbett, Ken, 101–103
Countertransference
errors in treatment and, 138–139
independent experiences and, 123
interpretation of, 134–138,
156–160, 168
organizing experiences and, 57,
60, 78
relatedness listening perspective
on, 46–47
relational approach on, 37, 46–47
resources on, 79
self-other experiences and, 98
symbiotic experiences and, 83
training of therapists and, 78
transference matrix (*see*
Transference/
countertransference matrix)
vignettes (*see* Countertransference
vignettes)
Countertransference disclosure,
see Disclosure
Countertransference readiness, 136
Countertransference vignettes
Charles, Eros in
countertransference,
150–156, 162–167
disclosure of sexual
responsiveness, 47–52
Dora, Eros in transference,
133–139
independent experiences,
123–125, 126–130
organizing experiences, 57–60,
61, 66, 67–77

self-other experiences, 101–103,
105–107, 108–110, 111–113
symbiotic experiences, 83–92,
93–96
Culture
ethnosexual frontiers, 19–22
gender identity and, 13–14, 18–19
memetic evolution and, 22–23
sexual development and, 12

D

Davies, Messler, 49–50
Denial, 123–126
Depression
Eros in transference, 133–139
independent experiences, 123–126
organizing experiences, 58
symbiotic experiences, 88–92
Desire; *see also* Eros
of boy for father, 102–103
I am what I am views and, 145–146
intersubjective space and, 8
mutual recognition and, 34–35
of therapists, 57–60, 72
vignettes, 57–60, 64–66,
101–103, 111–113
of women, 8, 64–66
Despair, 103–105
Development
of brain, xxii, xxv–xxvi,
xxvii–xxviii
differential listening and, 52–53,
130
of gender identity, 12–13
of intersubjective relationships,
33–34
organizing experiences and, 55–56
as relational possibilities
metaphor, 37–40, 39*f*, 56,
82–83, 98, 122, 123
sexual, xxviii, 4, 9–10, 12, 101–103

Developmental listening, 52–53,
    130; *see also* Relatedness
    listening perspective
Diagnoses
    independent experiences, 123
    organizing experiences, 55, 56
    self-other experiences, 98
    symbiotic experiences, 82, 83
Dialectics of personality formation,
    36–37
Discipline toys, 139–142, 147–150
Disclosure
    interpretation of
        countertransference versus,
        157–160, 168
    relatedness listening perspective
        on, 46–47
    restraint with neurotic layers of
        personality, 126
    of sexual responsiveness by
        therapists, 47–52
    vignettes, 47–52, 150–156,
        162–167
Disrespect, 150–156, 162–167
Dissimulation, 29
Dissociation
    interpersonal connection and
        (*see* Organization,
        personality in)
    as perspective on sexuality and
        gender, 14–17
    vignettes, 86–87, 113–117
Dominance
    heterosexuality and patriarchal, 3
    submission and, 51–52, 139–142,
        147–150
Dora, Eros in transference, 133–139
Dread, 92–94
Dreams of patients
    independent experiences,
        126–130

organizing experiences, 74–75,
    79–80
self-other experiences, 98–101,
    103–105
symbiotic experiences, 94–95
Dreams of therapists
    Eros in countertransference,
        150–156, 162–167
    independent experiences,
        126–130
    self-other experiences, 111–113
    symbiotic experiences, 84–85, 86
Dyadic responsiveness, 81

E

Earth, formation of, xiii
Edelman, Gerald, xxiii
Ego functions, 134
Electra/Oedipus triangulation
    experience, 121–122
Electromagnetism and heart-brain
    interaction, xxviii
Emergent self, *see* Self emerging
Emotion(s); *see also* Erotic feelings;
    specific emotions
    countertransference interpretation
        and, 157
    heart-brain interaction and,
        xxix–xxx
    performance of, 88
    triangulation and, 121–126
    vignettes, 113–117, 133–139,
        150–156, 162–167
Emotional triangulation
    independent experiences and,
        121–122
    vignettes, 123–126
Emotional unavailability, 113–120
Emotional-relatedness scenario, 157
Empathy
    for gay men, 101–103

self-other recognition and sexual
stimulation, 120
sensuality and, 111
symbiotic experiences and, 137
Enactments, 83, 167; *see also*
Organization, personality in;
Symbiosis and separation
Eros; *see also* Desire; Love by
therapists; *specific topics
beginning with erotic*
in countertransference, 150–156,
162–167
ensnared by, 66–80
in resistance, 139–142, 147–150
in transference, 133–139
Erotic countertransference
feelings of therapists and, 60
malpractice suits and, 92–94
as neglected topic, 47
training of therapists and, 78
vignettes (*see* Erotic
countertransference
vignettes)
Erotic countertransference vignettes
Charles, Eros in
countertransference,
150–156, 162–167
disclosure of sexual
responsiveness, 47–52
independent experiences, 123–126
organizing experiences, 66–80
self-other experiences, 111–113
symbiotic experiences, 83–87,
92–96
Erotic feelings; *see also* Desire;
Erotic countertransference;
Erotic transference
boundaries in psychotherapy and,
160–161
for mothers, 6–11, 126–130
mutual recognition and, 34–35
self and intersubjectivity, 9

of therapists, 47–49, 58–60,
123–126
Erotic transference
disclosure of sexual
responsiveness, 47–52
Eros in countertransference,
150–156, 162–167
Eros in transference, 133–139
mutual attunement and, 8–9
symbiotic experiences and,
83–87, 92–94
Ethnicity, 19–22, 26
Ethnosexual frontiers, 19–22
Evolution
brain development and, xxii
just-so stories and, xiii–xiv
memetic, 22–23
religion and, xxi
Exhibitionism, 98–101, 105–108

F

*Facing the Challenge of Liability in
Psychotherapy: Practicing
Defensively* (Hedges), 79
Fantasies of patients
countertransference and, 137
I am what I am views and,
145–146
meaning of satisfaction in
therapy, 146–147
vignettes (*see* Fantasies of patients
vignettes)
Fantasies of patients vignettes
bondage and discipline, 139–142,
147–150
independent experiences, 126–130
organizing experiences, 64–66
self-other experiences, 98–101,
103–108, 113–120
symbiotic experiences, 90–92,
94–95

Fantasies of therapists
  countertransference and, 88–90,
    137
  vignettes
  independent experiences, 126–130
  organizing experiences, 57–60,
    61, 62
  self-other experiences, 111–113
  symbiotic experiences, 92–96
Fathers
  infant-caregiver erotic
    interaction, 6–11
  transgenerational phantoms and,
    28–29, 31
  vignettes, 101–103, 150–156,
    162–167
  The Father Censure, 101–103
Fear of patients
  Eros in countertransference,
    150–156, 162–167
  Eros in resistance, 139–142,
    147–150
  Eros in transference, 133–139
  independent experiences,
    126–130
  self-other experiences, 98–101,
    108–111
Fear of therapists, 78, 88–90,
    101–103
Feelings, see Emotion(s); Erotic
    feelings
Femininity, 40, 103–105, 126–130
Fetishes
  Freud, Sigmund on, 143–145
  meaning of satisfaction in therapy
    and, 146–147
  vignettes, 139–142, 147–150
Flashing by patients, 105–108
Foucault, Michel, xv–xvi, xviii,
    xix–xx
Freud, Sigmund
  disclosure of therapists, 46–47

  fetishes, 143–145
  homosexuality, 3–5, 66, 90
  independent psychic life, 121, 122
  internal world, 24
  love between sexes, 6, 113
  negation and independence, 97
  neurosis and perversion, 142–143
  psychoanalytic interpretation, 156
  seduction and trauma, 80
  sexual development, 4, 9–10
  sexual feelings of therapists, 45
  sexuality, xv, 4–6, 67
Frigidity, partial, 126–130
Frustration, 113–117

G

Gay men; see also Homosexuality
  Eros in countertransference,
    150–156, 162–167
  self-other experiences, 98–105,
    108–111
Gender
  brain functioning and, xxii
  constructing, 18–19
  homosexuality and, 104
  identity and (see Gender identity)
  performance of, 88
  perspectives on (see Perspectives
    on sex, sexuality, gender,
    identity)
  vignettes, 87–88, 90–92
Gender identity; see also Sexual
    identity
  culture and, 13–14, 18–19
  development of, 12–13
  Freud, Sigmund on, 5–6
  homosexuality and, 101–103, 104
  in- and out-group identities and,
    21–22
  male, 90–92, 95–96, 101–103
  otherness and, 15

perspectives on (*see* Perspectives on sex, sexuality, gender, identity)

vignettes, 90–92, 95–96

Gender orientation, 101–103

Genital differences and gender identity, 13

Ghosts, transgenerational, 24–31

Giftedness, 117–120

Gorkin, Michael, 92–96

Graduate students, 98–101

Greek society, xvi, xvii, 3

Group identity, xviii–xx, 30–31

Guilt

    of patients and independent experiences, 123–126

    of therapists and erotic desires, 57–60, 72

H

Hatred, 150–156, 162–167

Heart-brain interaction, xxviii–xxix

Hedges, Lawrence E.

    on challenges of liability, 79

    Charles, Eros in countertransference, 150–156, 162–167

    Dora, Eros in transference, 133–139

    self-other experiences, 113–120

    Ted, Eros in resistance, 139–142, 147–150

Heterosexuality

    ethnosexual boundaries and, 21–22

    Freud, Sigmund on, 6

    historical conceptions of, xvi–xvii, xviii

    patriarchal dominance and, 3

vignettes, 64–66, 108–111, 126–130 (*see also specific topics*)

Historical conceptions of sexuality, xv–xx, 143–144

Homoerotic brutalization, 61–64

Homoerotic stimulation in countertransference, 126–130

Homophobia, 108–111

Homosexuality; *see also* Gay men; Lesbians

    erotic feelings for patients and, 58–60

    ethnosexual boundaries and, 21–22

    Freud, Sigmund on, 3–5, 66, 90

    historical conceptions of, xvi–xviii, xix

    phallic arousal and, 103

    vignettes (*see* Homosexuality vignettes)

Homosexuality vignettes

    Eros in countertransference, 150–156, 162–167

    independent experiences, 126–130

    organizing experiences, 64–66

    self-other experiences, 98–105, 108–111

    symbiotic experiences, 87–88

Horror of surrendering, 90–92

Hugging in psychotherapy, 66, 67–77, 87–88

Humiliation

    Eros in countertransference, 150–156, 162–167

    self-other experiences, 98–101, 103–107, 108–111, 113–120

    symbiotic experiences, 90–92, 94–95

I
I am what I am views, 145–146
Identity
    Freud, Sigmund on, 5–6
    gender (*see* Gender identity)
    group, xviii–xx, 30–31
    intergenerational transmission of
        trauma and, 26–27, 30–31
    perspectives on, 11–14, 41 (*see*
        also Perspectives on sex,
        sexuality, gender, identity)
    sexual (*see* Sexual identity)
    therapeutic relationships and,
        14–15
Imitation, *see* Mimetics perspective
Impasses
    erotic countertransference and,
        47–49, 150–156, 162–167
    horror of surrendering, 90–92
Incest, 94–95
Independence experiences
    overview of, 38–39, 39*f*
    psychotherapy and, 121–123
    vignettes, 123–130
Independent relatedness
    psychotherapy and, 121–123
    vignettes, 123–130
Individual internalization, 25–26
Infants
    caregiver erotic interaction with,
        6–11
    intersubjective development in,
        33–34
    mutual recognition and symbiosis
        of, 81
    organizing experiences of, 37–38,
        39*f*, 55, 56
    penetrative stimulation of, 150
    self and, 7–8, 40
Insomnia, 126–130
Intelligence of heart, xxix
Interactional patterns, 82

Internal worlds, 24–27
Internalizations, *see* Psychological
        internalizations
Internet pornography
    chat-room fetishes, 144
    vignettes, 113–120, 139–142,
        147–150
Interpersonal relationships; *see*
        also Intersubjective
        relationships; Intimate
        relationships
    actual interpersonal interaction
        and, 34
    brain functioning and, xxiv–xxv,
        xxvii, 29–30
    infant-caregiver/erotic
        interaction, 6–11
    organizing-level issues and, 79
    self-states and, 16–17
    symbiotic experiences and, 81–82
Interpretation of countertransference,
        134–138, 156–160, 168
Intersubjective field, 32
Intersubjective mutual recognition,
        34–35; *see also* Mutual
        recognition
Intersubjective relationships
    brain development and, xxv–xxvi,
        xxvii–xxviii
    as erotic life foundation, 9
    mentoring in ancient societies
        and, xvi
    mimicry and affect mirroring
        and, 8
    theories on, 31–36
Intimate relationships; *see also*
        Interpersonal relationships
    attachment and, 7
    expectations and, 14
    just-so stories and, 168
    mutual attunement and, 8–9
    symbiotic experiences and, 82

J

Jigsaw puzzles and sublimation, 72
Just-so stories
    on boy meets girl, xiii–xiv
    brain and, xxx–xxxi
    example of theoretical, 9–11
    intimate relationships and, 168
    psychotherapists and, xx, 6
    psychotherapy and, xiv, xx
    social-constructionist perspective
        and, 19

K

Kernberg, Otto, 123–126
Kohut, Heinz, 97–98

L

Left-brain functioning, xxii
Legal issues
    disclosure and slippery slope,
        158–159
    false accusations against
        therapists, 79
    malpractice suits and
        countertransference, 92–94
Lesbians; *see also* Homosexuality
    origins of term, xvi–xvii
    vignettes, 64–66, 87–88,
        126–130
Lewes, Kenneth, 98–101
Listening, *see* Psychotherapy;
        Relatedness listening
        perspective
Localization and split brain, xxii
Love by therapists, 57–60, 83–87,
        123–126; *see also* Eros
"Love in the Afternoon" (Davies),
        49–50

M

Magical cure by copulation, 92–94
Male bravado displays, 98–101
Male-gendered identity, 90–92,
        95–96, 101–105
Malpractice suits, 92–94
Man, having a, 64–66
Maroda, Karen, 47–49
Marriage and Internet pornography,
        113–120
Masculinity, 90–92, 95–96, 101–105
Masochism, 9–10, 123–126; *see also*
        Sadomasochism
Masturbation
    fantasies and, 146
    vignettes, 117–120, 139–142,
        147–150
McDougall, Joyce, 126–130
Mentoring relationships in
        Greece, xvi
Mimetics perspective, 22–24
Mimicry, 7–8, 22–24
Mind-body boundaries, 134
Mirroring, 7–8, 105–108
Mitchell, Stephen, 105–108
Mitchell, Steven A., 90–92
Modern versus postmodern
        attitudes, 17–19
Mommy-and-me dance, 81
Moss, Donald, 64–66
Mothers
    erotic feelings for, 6–11, 126–130
    Freud, Sigmund on, 143–145
    mutual relatedness and, 81
    transgenerational phantoms and,
        28–29, 31
    vignettes, 126–130, 133–139
Mouth-to-mouth resuscitation
        fantasy, 62
Multiple selves, 14–17

Mutual attunement, 8–9
Mutual recognition
　definition of, 34–35
　symbiosis of infant and, 81
　vignettes, 51–52
Mutual sexual regulations, 7–8
Mutually dependent relatedness,
　　　81–83; *see also* Symbiosis
　　　and separation

N

Narcissism
　erotic feelings of therapists
　　　and, 60
　self-other experiences and, 97–98
　vignettes
　　organizing experiences, 61
　　self-other experiences,
　　　105–108, 111–113, 117–120
　　symbiotic experiences, 83–87
Natural perspective, 3–6
Nature versus nuture, 24–25
Neurology, *see* Brain and neurology
Neuroses, 126–130, 142–143
Neurotransmitters, xxiii–xxiv
New versus old brain, xxii–xxiii

O

Object relations
　countertransference interpretation
　　　and, 157
　erotic interaction and, 161
　object usage and, 33
　relational configurations
　　　compared to, 36
　therapeutic relationships and,
　　　167–168
　transference usage and, 136
　vignettes, 88–90
Objectified social labels, xviii–xx

Obsessive-compulsive personality
　　　type, 139–142, 147–150
Oedipal conflict and desire,
　　　101–103, 121–122, 137
Ogden, Thomas H., 61–64
Old versus new brain, xxii–xxiii
Orbach, Susie, 88–90
Orbitofrontal loop, xxvi–xxviii
Organization, personality in
　listening to search for relatedness,
　　　55–57
　vignettes
　　commentary on, 66–67, 77–80
　　ensnared by Eros, 66–80
　　having a man, 64–66
　　love in countertransference,
　　　57–60
　　split-off homoerotic
　　　brutalization, 61–64
Organizing experiences
　countertransference and, 57–60,
　　　61, 66, 67–77, 78
　dreams of patients and, 74–75,
　　　79–80
　of infants, 37–38, 39*f*, 55, 56
　psychotherapy and, 55–57
　transference and, 58–59, 61, 66,
　　　67–77
　vignettes (*see* under Organization,
　　　personality in)
Organizing patterns, 55–57; *see also*
　　　Organization, personality in
Orgasm, 123–126, 146
Otherness, 14–17, 21
Outcomes of psychotherapy, xiv,
　　　57–58

P

Pain, 150–156, 162–167
Panic attacks, 126–130; *see also*
　　　Anxiety of patients

Parallel work, *see* Organization, personality in; Symbiosis and separation

Paranoid schizophrenia, 58–59

Paranoid-withdrawing pattern, 150–156, 162–167

Parents; *see also* Fathers; Mothers
infant-caregiver erotic interaction, 6–11
transgenerational phantoms and, 28–29, 31

Passion, *see* Desire; Eros; Love by therapists

Passive versus active positions
sexuality and, 102–103
vignettes, 98–105, 150–156, 162–167

Penis envy as explanation, 65–66

Personal identity, 11–14; *see also* Identity

Personality
anal-retentive/obsessive-compulsive type, 139–142, 147–150
borderline personality disorder, 98–101
disclosure with neurotic layers of, 126
in organization (*see* Organization, personality in)
relational approach on formation of, 36–37

Perspectives on sex, sexuality, gender, identity
dissociation, otherness, multiple selves, 14–17
infant-caregiver/erotic interaction, 6–11
intersubjective, 31–35
mimetics, 22–24
natural/religious/biological, 3–6
personal identity, 11–14

postmodern social-constructionism, 17–19
race/ethnicity/sexuality, 19–22
relatedness listening perspective, 37–41, 39*f*, 130, 167–169
(*see also* Relatedness listening perspective)
relational/thirdness, 35–37
trauma and transgenerational ghosts, 24–31

Perversion
historical conception of, xviii
overview of, 142–143
vignettes, 137–142, 147–156, 162–167

Phallic arousal and impulses, 98–101, 103; *see also* Arousal

Phantoms, transgenerational, 24–31

Phobias, 126–130; *see also* Anxiety of patients

Polysubstance abuse, 123–126

Pornography
chat-room fetishes, 144
vignettes, 113–120, 139–142, 147–150

Positional internalization, 26

Postmodern social-constructionism, 17–19

Prefrontal cortex, xxvi–xxviii

Primary recognition, 33

Prostitutes, 105–108

Psychiatric disorders, *see* Diagnoses; *specific disorders*

Psychoanalytic psychotherapy; *see also* Psychotherapy
countertransference interpretation and, 134–138, 156–160, 168
erotic function of boundaries in, 160–161
errors common in, 138–139

organizing experiences and, 55–57
(*see also* Organization,
personality in)
outcomes of, xiv, 57–58
vignettes, 108–111, 111–113,
123–126 (*see also specific
topics*)
Psychological internalizations
countertransference disclosure
and, 168
independent experiences and, 122
overview of, 24–31
role reversal and relational
dynamic, 157
symbiosis and, 81
Psychosis, 55, 56, 58–59; *see also*
Organization, personality in
Psychotherapeutic relationships
disclosure and slippery slope,
158–159
independent experiences, 123–126
living in the present and, 14–15,
17, 52, 75
object relations, 167–168
relatedness listening perspective
on, 39*f*
relational approach on, 36–37, 39*f*
sexually sensitive interactions in,
77–80
therapy outcomes and, xiv
Psychotherapists
arousal of, 66, 67–77, 150–156,
162–167 (*see also* Erotic
countertransference)
desire of, 57–60, 72
disclosure of sexual
responsiveness by, 47–52
(*see also* Disclosure)
dreams of (*see* Dreams of therapists)
erotic feelings of, 47–49, 58–60,
123–126
false accusations against, 79

fantasies of (*see* Fantasies of
therapists)
fear of, 78, 88–90, 101–103
just-so stories and, xx, 6
love by, 57–60, 83–87, 123–126
perspectives on sexuality and, 6,
24, 31, 40
training of, 78
voyeurism of, 105–108
vulnerability of, 134–135
Psychotherapy
affect replicated in, 134–135
boundaries in, 159–161, 167
confrontation in, 150–156, 162–167
countertransference interpretation
and, 134–138, 156–160, 168
errors common in, 138–139
history of sexuality and, xix–xx
hugging in, 66, 67–77, 87–88
I am what I am views and, 145–146
independent experiences and,
121–123 (*see also* Self and
other constancy)
just-so stories and, xiv, xx
organizing experiences and, 55–57,
77–80 (*see also* Organization,
personality in)
outcomes of, xiv, 57–58
perspectives on sexuality and
(*see* Psychotherapy and
perspectives on sexuality)
psychoanalytic (*see* Psychoanalytic
psychotherapy)
self-other experiences and, 97–98
(*see also* Self emerging)
sexualized therapeutic encounters
in (*see* Sexualized
therapeutic encounters)
symbiotic experiences and, 81–83,
94–95, 96, 121–123 (*see also*
Symbiosis and separation)
termination of, 71, 133–139

Psychotherapy and perspectives on
sexuality
ethnic and sexuality
dimensions, 22
intersubjective theory, 32
relatedness listening perspective,
37–41, 39f
relational approach, 36–37
transference as central concept, 25

Q

Queer sexual groups, xvii–xviii, 3–4;
see also Homosexuality

R

Race, 19–22, 26, 28–29
Rage, 150–156, 162–167; *see also*
Anger
Rape fantasy and
countertransference, 88–90
Rapprochement, 97–98
Recognition
mutual, 34–35, 51–52, 81
primary, 33
self-other, 120
Reentrant brain, xxiii
Rejection, 87–88, 150–156, 162–167
Relatedness
affective mode of, 134–135
independent (*see* Self and other
constancy)
listening perspective on (*see*
Relatedness listening
perspective)
mutually dependent (*see*
Symbiosis and separation)
organizing experiences and,
55–56
search for (*see* Organization,
personality in)

unilaterally dependent (*see* Self
emerging)
vignettes, 150–156, 162–167
Relatedness listening perspective
derivation of, 52–53
on identity, 41
overview of, 37–41, 39f, 130,
167–169
psychotherapy and, 55–57, 81–83,
94–95, 96, 97–98, 121–123
self-other tension and, 52–53,
97–98
on sexualized therapeutic
encounters, 45–47
Relational approach
intrapsychic psychological
perspective and, 32
relatedness listening perspective
(*see* Relatedness listening
perspective)
to sexuality and gender, 35–37
Relational enactments, 167
Relationships, *see* Interpersonal
relationships; Intersubjective
relationships; Intimate
relationships;
Psychotherapeutic
relationships
Religion
evolution and, xxi
history of sexuality and, xix–xx
on sexuality and gender, 3–6
vignettes, 139–142, 147–150
Repression, 122, 126–130
Reproduction and brain functioning,
xxv–xxvi
Resistance
countertransference entanglement
and, 138
independent experiences and, 123
organizing experiences and, 57
self-other experiences and, 98

symbiotic experiences and, 83
vignettes, 139–142, 147–150
Resources on transference and
        countertransference, 79
Restraining and discipline toys,
        139–142, 147–150
Revenants, *see* Phantoms,
        transgenerational
Revenge, 113–117
Right-brain functioning, xxii
Role reversal
    internalized relational dynamic
        and, 157
    vignettes
        Eros in countertransference,
            150–156, 162–167
        Eros in resistance, 139–142,
            147–150
        Love in the Afternoon, 49–50
        symbiotic experiences, 88–92
Roman society, xvi, xvii
Romantic desires and fantasies
        of therapists, *see* Desire;
        Fantasies of therapists
Rosiello, Frances, 83–88

S

Sadism
    Freud, Sigmund on, 9–10
    vignettes
        Eros in resistance, 139–142,
            147–150
        independent experiences,
            123–126
        organizing experiences, 61–64
        symbiotic experiences, 87–88,
            90–92, 94–95
Sadomasochism; *see also* Sadism
    Freud, Sigmund on, 9–10
    vignettes, 51–52, 61–64, 94–95,
        123–126

Scenarios, 81–83, 157; *see also*
        Symbiosis and separation
Schemas, 40–41
Schizophrenia, 58–59
Search for relatedness and
        psychotherapy, 55–57;
        see also Organization,
        personality in
Searles, Harold, 57–60
Seduction, 80
Self; *see also specific topics beginning
        with self-*
    brain functioning and, xxiv–xxv
    in erotic union, 9
    infant-caregiver interactions and,
        7–8, 40
    relatedness listening perspective
        on, 41
    self-states and, 15–17
    vignettes, 117–120
Self and other constancy
    listening to independent
        relatedness, 121–123
    vignettes, 123–130
Self emerging
    listening to unilaterally dependent
        experience, 97–98
    vignettes
        analytic use of desire, 111–113
        countertransference fear of
            passivity, 101–103
        countertransference reaction
            to budding exhibitionism,
            105–108
        expanding sexual identities,
            103–105
        maintaining open clinical
            position, 108–111
        male bravado displays, 98–101
        pornography and Internet,
            113–120

Self-betrayal, 90–92, 108–111
Self-definition, xviii–xx
Self-destructiveness, 123–126
Self-disclosure, *see* Disclosure
Self-esteem
  Eros in countertransference,
     150–156, 162–167
  self-other experiences, 103–105,
     117–120
Self-other experiences
  countertransference and, 98,
     101–103, 105–107, 108–110,
     111–113
  developmental listening and,
     52–53, 97–98
  overview of, 38, 39*f*
  psychotherapy and, 97–98
  transference and, 98–103,
     105–108, 111–113
  vignettes (*see under* Self
     emerging)
Self-states, 15–17
Sensuality, 111
Separation-individuation, 97–101
Sexual countertransference, *see*
     Erotic countertransference
Sexual development
  brain development and, xxviii
  Freud, Sigmund on, 4, 9–10
  masculinity and, 101–103
  spontaneous and creative
     expression and, 12
Sexual dysfunction, 108–111, 123–126
Sexual fantasies, *see* Fantasies of
     patients; Fantasies of
     therapists
Sexual feelings, *see* Erotic
     countertransference; Erotic
     feelings; Erotic transference
Sexual identity; *see also* Gender
     identity
  historical conceptions on, xix–xx

perspectives on, 11
  vignettes, 103–105, 108–111
Sexual intrusion, 133–139
Sexual inversion, xvii
Sexual transference, *see* Erotic
     transference
Sexuality
  active-passive mixtures of, 102–103
  affection and, 134
  experience with sexual variations
     and, 110–111
  Freud, Sigmund on, xv, 4–6, 67
  historical conceptualization of,
     xv–xx
  inhibition and excitation
     extremes in, 142–143
  otherness and, 16–17
  perspectives on (*see* Perspectives
     on sex, sexuality, gender,
     identity)
  race/ethnicity and, 19–22
  as relation not force, 40
Sexualized therapeutic encounters;
     see also Psychotherapy;
     specific topics beginning with
     erotic
  developmental listening and,
     52–53, 130
  organizing experiences and, 77–80
  relatedness listening perspective
     on, 45–47
  vignettes on relational
     countertransference, 47–52
Shame of patients, 113–120,
     139–142, 147–150
Shoe fetishes, 143–144
Slippery slope
  boundary violations and, 159–160
  disclosure and, 158–159
  transference-countertransference
     engagement and, 168

Sobriety commitment and sneaking,
    113–117
Social labels, objectified, xviii–xx
Social trauma, 27–28
Social-constructionism,
    postmodern, 17–19
Split brain and localization, xxii
Split-off homoerotic brutalization,
    61–64
Stress reduction, 66, 67–77
Subjectivity
    construction of internal worlds
        and, 25–27
    countertransference and, 136
    identity and, 11
    intersubjective theory on, 35
    mentoring in ancient societies
        and, xvi
    related complexity in, 39, 39f
    relational approach on, 36
    of sexual experience, 32
    sexuality and, xv, xix, xx
Sublimation, 72
Submission
    dominance and, 51–52, 139–142,
        147–150
    symbiotic experiences and, 90–92
Substance abuse, 123–126
Surrendering, 90–92
Symbiosis and separation
    I am what I am views and, 146
    listening to mutually dependent
        experience, 81–83
    vignettes
        countertransference rape
            fantasy, 88–90
        disavowed love as erotic
            countertransference, 83–87
        Eros in transference, 133–139
        erotic countertransference
            and gender identity issues,
            95–96

horror of surrendering, 90–92
magical cure by copulation,
    92–94
performance of affect and
    gender, 87–88
sadistic sexual
    countertransference
    fantasies, 94–95
Symbiotic experiences
    countertransference and, 137
    overview of, 38, 39f
    psychotherapy and, 81–83
    vignettes (*see under* Symbiosis and
        separation)
Synaptic brain, xxiii–xxv

T

Teasing titillation, 94–95
Ted, Eros in resistance, 139–142,
    147–150
Termination of psychotherapy, 71,
    133–139
Terrible twos, 97; *see also* Toddlers
Theories/approaches, *see* Brain and
    neurology; Perspectives
    on sex, sexuality, gender,
    identity; Relatedness
    listening perspective
Therapeutic modality
    independent experiences, 123
    organizing experiences, 57
    self-other experiences, 98
    symbiotic experiences, 83
Therapists, *see* Psychotherapists
Therapy, *see* Psychotherapy
The third, 35–37, 39, 39f; *see
    also* Psychotherapeutic
    relationships
Toddlers
    brain development in, xxvii
    self-other experiences and, 97–98

symbiotic experiences of, 82–83, 87

Touching in psychotherapy, 66, 67–77, 87–88

Toys, restraining and discipline, 139–142, 147–150

Transcendent brain, xxvi–xxx

Transference
  as central concept of psychotherapy, 25
  countertransference matrix (*see* Transference/ countertransference matrix)
  developmental listening and, 52
  independent experiences and, 123
  mutual attunement and, 8–9
  object relations and, 136
  organizing experiences and, 56, 60, 78, 79
  relational approach on, 37
  self-other experiences and, 98
  symbiotic experiences and, 82, 83–87, 92–94
  therapists and, 60, 78, 79
  vignettes (*see* Transference vignettes)

Transference vignettes
  disclosure of sexual responsiveness, 47–52
  Dora, Eros in transference, 133–139
  Eros in countertransference, 150–156, 162–167
  independent experiences, 123–130
  organizing experiences, 58–59, 61, 66, 67–77
  self-other experiences, 98–103, 105–108, 111–113
  symbiotic experiences, 87–92

Transference/countertransference matrix
  emotional-relatedness scenario and, 157
  relatedness listening perspective on, 39, 39*f*
  relational approach on, 37
  unconscious relational enactments and, 167

Transgendered MTF (male to female), 87–88

Transgenerational transmission of trauma, 24–31

Transgression, 28, 88–90

Trauma
  effects of social, 27–28
  Freud, Sigmund on, 80
  transgenerational transmission of, 24–31
  vignettes, 105–108

Treatment, *see* Psychotherapy

Triangulation, emotional
  independent experiences and, 121–122
  vignettes, 123–126

Triune brain, xxii–xxiii

Trust relationship and disclosure, 158–160; *see also* Psychotherapeutic relationships

U

Unconscious relational enactments, 167

Unformulated experience and interpersonal connection, *see* Organization, personality in

Unilaterally dependent relatedness, 97–98; *see also* Self emerging

Urinary frequency, 126–130

V

Vignettes, *see* Case studies; *specific topics*
Violence
    termination of psychotherapy and, 71
    transgenerational internalization and, 29
    vignettes, 87–88, 113–117, 123–126
Voyeurism of therapists, 105–108

Vulnerability
    of patients, 150–156, 162–167
    of therapists, 134–135

W

Withdrawal, 113–120, 150–156, 162–167
Wittgenstein, Ludwig, xv
Wittkin-Sasso, Gail, 111–113

Z

Zeavin, Lynne, 64–66